Abuse of Power

Also by Theodore Draper

Castroism: Theory and Practice
Castro's Revolution: Myths and Realities
American Communism and Soviet Russia
The Roots of American Communism
The 84th Infantry Division in the Battle of Germany
The Six Weeks' War

ABUSE
OF
POWER

THEODORE DRAPER

NEW YORK / THE VIKING PRESS

To the memory of
Joseph Freeman
(1897–1965)

•   •   •

Most melancholy at that time, O Friend!
Were my day-thoughts, my dreams were miserable;
Through months, through years, long after the last beat
Of those atrocities (I speak bare truth,
As if to thee alone in private talk)
I scarcely had one night of quiet sleep
Such ghastly visions had I of despair
And tyranny, and implements of death,
And long orations which in dreams I pleaded
Before unjust Tribunals, with a voice
Labouring, a brain confounded, and a sense
Of treachery and desertion in the place
The holiest that I knew of, my own soul.

William Wordsworth, *The Prelude*
Book X [397–415]

Preface

It has been said that we should concern ourselves primarily with the present state of the Vietnamese war and regard the question of how we got into it as of mainly historical interest.

Yet we are constantly told that the United States is fighting in Vietnam by virtue of "commitments" made as far back as 1954. We are admonished that the war in Vietnam is part of a larger struggle that started two decades ago or a half century ago and may go on for years. It seems hardly fair to justify the American intervention largely on historical grounds and then to disparage efforts to examine those grounds critically.

The immediate present is, of course, the most difficult and most treacherous of all times to write about because we are not taken into the confidence of those in power who ask us what we would do if we were in their place. The best we can do, from the outside, is to scrutinize the past, including the immediate past, for the light it may cast on the present and future. A few years, even a few months, may make a vast difference with respect to what we know about the past as compared with the present. Far from being of mainly historical interest, our past Vietnamese policy is of intensely present and future interest. In any case, there is no reason why historians should not concern themselves with matters of mainly historical interest.

Above all, it is my conviction that the larger and deeper aspects of the American role in the Vietnamese war can be understood only by viewing it as a whole and by relating it to similar actions elsewhere. However we may deal with the situation that exists, why it came to exist poses the most serious and lasting problems of policy and policymaking. As long as the war continues, how to end it must be a pressing and vexing question, but it is not the only one and, in historical perspective, it represents only the final phase of an already lengthy process. An end of the war brought about as a result of overwhelming American destructive power will not justify or extenuate the failure and folly that made the use of so much power necessary.

This is not a thought for which I can claim any originality. In a major speech at Johns Hopkins University in Baltimore on April 7, 1965, President Lyndon B. Johnson said, "The guns and the bombs, the rockets and the warships, are all symbols of human failure. They are necessary symbols. They protect what we cherish. But they are witness to human folly."

If inspiration were needed for a critical examination of the entire record of American policy in Vietnam, it might also be found in the words of one of our oldest, most powerful, most conservative, and best informed Senators, the Chairman of the Armed Services Committee, Senator Richard B. Russell of Georgia. On August 1, 1965, he voiced the opinion that "we have made every conceivable blunder" in Vietnam. Only a reckless extremist would hasten to agree wholeheartedly with this sweeping judgment, but a legislator of such experience and authority should not be lightly disregarded.

I have dedicated this book to my old friend and colleague, Joseph Freeman, the author of *An American Testament* (1936) and *Never Call Retreat* (1943), among other works. Some day I hope to tell something of his story, but I have mourned him too much to be able as yet to do it. I have chosen a passage from his favorite poem, *The Prelude,* by William Wordsworth, because it was very much on his mind, and he talked of it passionately in the last few of our many talks that used to go on for hours. Some of those who knew him will understand why I have chosen this passage; and some of those who thought they knew him will never understand.

I am indebted to The Hoover Institution on War, Revolution, and Peace, at Stanford University, and to its Director, Dr. W. Glenn Campbell, for making it possible for me to carry on my work, freely and independently. My editor, Aaron Asher, has contributed to this book far beyond the call of duty.

—THEODORE DRAPER

April 10, 1967

Contents

Preface vii

Abuse of Power

I

The Pattern of Intervention

In four short years, from April 1961 to April 1965, the United
States resorted to some form of military force in three major
crises—in Cuba, in the Dominican Republic, and in Vietnam.
This recurrence of military intervention was unprecedented;
so much use of armed force in so many countries in such a
short time had never occurred before in all American history. The three interventions were sufficiently different to
make it foolhardy to lump them together. Nevertheless, in
one respect, they resemble one another too closely and un-
comfortably to be regarded as totally unrelated or dissimilar.

What was there in each of these crises that made necessary
the use of military force, if only by proxy (as in the case of
Cuba), on the part of the United States? If we look at their
development, does a pattern emerge and suggest that they
have something fundamental in common? And if we can de-
tect a pattern, what does it tell us about where we are heading and what we may find on the way?

The more I have struggled with these questions, the more
I have come to believe that there is such a pattern, and that
it has brought us to the point of armed force as the key instrument of policy no less than three times in only four years.
If I am right, this pattern implies that we have been living
with an American crisis, or more exactly an ever more acute
and costly crisis in American foreign policy, of which the Cu-

ban, the Dominican, and the Vietnam cases have been distinctive incarnations. If countries so far apart and so different can bring forth essentially the same problem, that problem must be as much in us as in them.

One way of suggesting the nature of this American crisis is relatively simple, though its manifestations are far more difficult and complicated to trace. Roughly, the main instrumentalities of a country's foreign policy are political, economic, and military. It is, of course, not possible to seal them off from one another, as if they existed in isolation or alone. Nevertheless, they can surely be distinguished from one another; they may be used in different combinations and in different degrees.

At the present time, for example, the United States and France use all three instrumentalities. But the relatively modest economic and military means at President de Gaulle's disposal constrain French influence to be largely political. Our chief methods of persuasion, on the contrary, have increasingly become economic and military and, at crucial moments, almost exclusively military.

This pattern of American policy has come about as a result of one political failure and frustration after another. A weaker power might have suffered them in silence or in angry self-recrimination. But the United States is too rich and powerful to take a political setback without seeking some other way to impose its will. It is able, if it wishes, to transmute the political problem into an economic or, as a last resort, a military operation.

It is from this point of view that I wish to call attention to some aspects of the Cuban and Dominican crises as an introduction to a more extended consideration of how we got so deeply enmeshed in the Vietnam war.

The Cuban Precedent

The transmutation from the political to the military may be followed from beginning to end in the case of Cuba.

The political problem arose on March 10, 1952, the day Fulgencio Batista overthrew a duly elected, constitutional government in the midst of an election campaign he was sure to lose. The United States soon recognized Batista's regime, and the following year sent to Havana an Ambassador, Arthur Gardner, whose enthusiasm for the new order struck even Batista as somewhat excessive.* For almost four years the State Department, under John Foster Dulles, supported Batista unwaveringly and thereby dismayed all elements of the democratic opposition, which was seeking some peaceful way to return to constitutionalism.

In 1957 a change of ambassadors gave the State Department a second chance to deal with the political problem. The new Ambassador, Earl E. T. Smith, was instructed to make the United States position more nearly neutral in internal Cuban politics. But, after a brave start, he was more impressed by the growing threat of Fidel Castro's forces than by the dangers attendant on humoring Batista. As a result, no real change took place in American policy. It was still tied to Batista on the ground that any move which might weaken him would play into the hands of Castro and/or the Communists. Until 1958 there was plenty of non-Castro and anti-Castro opposition to Batista, but it was never able to make much headway against Batista's police and American discouragement.

As one democratic group after another met with disaster or disappointment, Castro picked up the pieces. His pre-eminence dated from 1958, or 1957 at the earliest. In effect, the United States had had at least five or six years to head him off, and could have done so easily, if it had not put all its eggs in Batista's political basket.

In the pinch, Batista left everyone, including the United

* The veteran *New York Times* correspondent in Cuba, R. Hart Phillips, wrote that Mr. Gardner gave the impression that at times he "even embarrassed President Batista with his support" (R. Hart Phillips, *Cuba: Island of Paradox* [New York: McDowell, Obolensky, 1960], p. 311).

States, in the lurch. When he fled at the end of 1958, he was still far superior to Castro in military force. His regime broke down for political and social far more than for military reasons; his own henchmen would no longer fight for him; not a few of them in high places sold out to Castro; and he betrayed most of them by taking flight without warning.

Until 1959, then, the Cuban problem was primarily political. It took the form of that crucial political question: *Which side are you on?* All the economic and military aid we gave Batista's regime counted as nothing compared with the answer we gave to this question.

When Castro took over Havana in January of that year, a new American policy had to be erected on a foundation of total political bankruptcy. Fear, failure, and guilt haunted the first confused, hesitant American overtures to the new Cuban regime. At this point, American policymakers could think of nothing better than to trade economics for politics. I am inclined to believe that the Eisenhower administration would have been glad to buy itself out of its embarrassment. But Castro refused to let it off so easily. Though Castroite circles spread the tale that Washington officials had rudely turned down Castro's requests for economic and financial aid, the truth was far more "revolutionary"—not only was Castro unwilling to accept anything which implied continued Cuban economic dependence on the United States, but he was also determined to break the economic ties which had bound Cuba to the United States.

When the Eisenhower administration failed to entice Castro into accepting an economic sop, it attempted to bring him down by economic means. The last and by far the ablest United States Ambassador in Havana, Philip W. Bonsal, has revealed that the final rupture between Cuba and the United States was precipitated in the summer of 1960 by a decision in Washington to reject a Cuban demand that the American- and British-owned oil refineries on the island should refine a quota of Soviet oil. The Cuban demand was a hard one for the oil companies to swallow; they had not been paid for over two years; they were committed to the use of Venezuelan crude oil; their refineries were not set up for the substitution of Soviet oil without considerable and perhaps expensive technical adjustments; and the Cuban demand might well have been merely the first of a series of pretexts to justify eventual expropriation.

Nevertheless, Bonsal relates, the companies "would probably have reluctantly gone along" with the Cuban government's request, if they had not been urged at a meeting in the office of the Secretary of the Treasury in Washington to refuse. Ambassador Bonsal counseled against forcing a showdown on this issue at this time. But, in retaliation for the Cuban move, President Eisenhower irately ordered a cut in the Cuban sugar quota. Within three months, Castro expropriated and nationalized the huge United States investment in Cuba, including the sugar mills, in a tit-for-tat of economic warfare. Bonsal is probably right in his estimation that "Castro and Guevara doubtless were highly pleased at our decision" to use economic sanctions to punish them. These sanctions doubtless were predicated on the assumption that American economic power could not be defied by the Cubans with impunity. But defied it was, and once that power was spent, the United States was left without either a political or an economic instrumentality for its future Cuban policy. The point is not that Castro was the aggrieved party; he was looking for trouble with the United States and would probably have provoked it one way or the other. From a practical viewpoint, however, the worst thing that can be said about American policy in Cuba in 1960 is that it played into his hands and made it easy for him to carry out his plans "in an atmosphere of heightened zeal and enthusiasm." [1] * It is difficult to believe that the Eisenhower administration would have rejected its own ambassador's advice if it had not recklessly overestimated the American economic prepotency even in Cuba.

Once the economic instrumentality had exhausted itself, both as carrot and as stick, the Eisenhower administration

* Reference notes begin on page 221.

went on fatally to the next and last option—military action. As early as April 1959, former Vice President Richard M. Nixon advocated training Cuban exile forces to overthrow Castro, and this step was actually taken by the Eisenhower administration in March 1960, though no concrete plan was made or adopted at that time. President John F. Kennedy inherited this exile force in 1961, and its very existence helped to tip the balance in the debate whether to use it or not. It is sometimes forgotten, however, that Kennedy's thinking on the Cuban problem before he took office was not very different from that of his predecessor or his Presidential opponent.

The Bay of Pigs adventure was a military failure. But even a military victory would not have changed the fundamental fact that it was made necessary by, and was intended to recoup, the losses sustained by ten years of political failure.

This was the real meaning of the Bay of Pigs, though it has been obscured by the fruitless debate over who or what was most responsible for the military fiasco. It would have been far more profitable if the debate had been less over why military victory evaded us than why we needed it at all. The United States had possessed such overwhelming political and economic influence in Cuba for so many years that a resort to force could only mean an admission of political insolvency.

The "missile crisis" in October 1962 did not change the Cuban problem in any essential. President Kennedy carefully staged the showdown with the Soviet Union as a military confrontation of a limited character. The removal of Soviet missiles from Cuba did not represent an advance by the United States so much as a retreat by the Soviet Union. All the United States demanded and succeeded in re-establishing was the *status quo ante*. This operation was far more military than political, though it was not without United States–Soviet political repercussions.

In terms of the Cuban problem, however, the missile crisis had an unexpected denouement. The prestige gained by Mr. Kennedy in October actually enabled him to execute a political retreat in Cuban policy in the spring of 1963. The existing instrument of United States policy, the Cuban Revolutionary Council, headed by Dr. José Miró Cardona, was abandoned, and a sizeable corps of Cuban exiles was unceremoniously removed from the CIA's payroll. Not a few of these victims came to me in that period with their tales of woe. They were bitter and humiliated for two reasons—that they had taken the checks, and that they were no longer getting them. The demobilization of the Council signified that four more years of political bankruptcy in our Cuban policy had come to an end.

Ironically, this was the best thing that could have happened. Our fortunes improved as soon as we permitted Castro to make mistakes without being able to blame them altogether on us.

The Dominican Variant

The same political-military pattern can easily be discerned in the Dominican Republic.

The Dominican instrument of United States policy, Donald Reid Cabral, was another beneficiary of a military coup. The constitutional government of Juan Bosch was overthrown in September 1963; Reid, more a businessman than a politician, assumed the leadership of the new regime that December and headed the provisional government for the sixteen months before the revolt of April 1965.

In these months, the United States did not stint on funds to shore up Reid Cabral's regime. But economic aid availed little because Reid was beset politically from two sides—the Right, which wanted to replace him, and the Left, which wanted to replace the Right. By January 1965, three months before the revolt, any reader of the Dominican press would or should have known that Reid was virtually finished. The reason was not so much what was taking place on the Left as what was happening on the Right. The traditional right-wing politicians saw no reason why he, a relatively late interloper in Dominican politics, without a party or a cause, should be the sole beneficiary of United States largesse and support. When Reid intimated in December 1964 that he did not intend to give up power by staying out of the elections scheduled for June 1965, as tradition demanded, the right wing unleashed a furious political offensive against him personally and against the United States embassy for backing him. The pro-Bosch military conspiracy was able to get rid of Reid so easily because he had previously been deserted by the Right and had been left suspended in a political vacuum.

Thus, in the months before the revolt, the same decisive political question was posed in the Dominican Republic: *Which side are you on?* The answer, given clearly and loftily by the United States Ambassador, W. Tapley Bennett, Jr., and his Washington superiors was: Donald Reid Cabral's. Not that they were unaware of the deteriorating situation. But Washington's remedy for the disease was even more tangible support for Reid Cabral. As usual, this took an economic form; the last half of another $10,000,000 loan from the Bank for International Development was announced in the Dominican press two days before the revolt.

The bankruptcy of this policy was revealed at 10 a.m. on April 25, 1965, the morning after the revolt. Reid Cabral appealed to the United States and to the Dominican military to support him—in vain. Neither wished the revolt to succeed, but neither was willing to fight for Reid Cabral. When Reid Cabral was tossed aside, the United States had no *political* alternative to take his place. All that remained was military action, by the Dominican armed forces or by the United States.

We now know that the Dominican Air Force decided to fight by 3 p.m. on April 25. The first air attack was carried out an hour and a half later. But before the Dominican military leaders made up their minds, they asked the United States embassy what they could expect from the United States. The United States chargé d'affaires, William B. Connett, Jr., who handled the exchange in the absence of Ambassador

Bennett, told the Dominican military to go ahead with their plans.* In effect, the United States first tried to stifle the revolt through the Dominican armed forces. But three days later the Dominican military had to admit failure because, as Colonel Pedro Bartolomé Benoit, head of the first military junta, later explained, planes were not enough to put down the revolt and "we did not have the troops." [2] Inasmuch as the Dominican armed forces and national police numbered about forty thousand, this was quite a confession to make about the real reason for United States military intervention on April 28. The Dominican and United States military actions were two sides of the same coin, two stages in the same process.

The point I am trying to make has little to do with the question that is still hotly debated—whether the Dominican Republic was actually threatened by a Communist takeover in the first week of the revolt. Even if the fifty-three to sev-

* A semi-official report, for which "restricted" sources were made available, has affirmed: "The [U.S.] embassy was asked by all three [Dominican] military services what support they could expect from the United States [before launching their attacks]." But it is typical of this source that it has concealed the main purport of the embassy's reply. According to this version, the embassy's cable to Washington at 5 p.m. on April 25, 1965, merely "referred to Communist influences in a confused situation, but indicated that in the embassy's view any military support at that time would be against the best interests of the United States" (*Dominican Action—1965*, [Washington, D.C.: The Center for Strategic Studies, Georgetown University, 1966], pp. 20-21). Fortunately, one reliable and honorable Washington correspondent, Philip L. Geyelin, was able to paraphrase this same cable in his paper, *The Wall Street Journal*, of June 25, 1965, and to quote textually from it in his book, *Lyndon B. Johnson and the World* (New York: Praeger, 1966), p. 246. The operative sentence in the cable by William B. Connett, Jr., was: "I have reluctantly agreed to the de los Santos-Wessin [Dominican military leaders] plan even though it could mean more bloodshed." As Geyelin comments in his book: "In other words, the United States was *promoting* the anti-rebel fight at this stage, so great was the embassy's interest in heading off a rebel success, even though no responsible United States official was then ready to identify a single key Communist in the rebel movement or to document the degree to which it might be subject to Communist influence." No one from reading the Georgetown Center's report could gather that the embassy had given the Dominican military the "green light" to attack. I have cited two other key sentences in the embassy's cable in *The New Leader*, May 9, 1966.

enty-seven Communists on the State Department's various lists could have "taken over and really seized" the country, as President Johnson claimed, the deeper problem is this: How could such a takeover have come about so quickly and easily after sixteen months of Reid Cabral's United States-backed regime? Why did this regime fall apart, with no one willing to defend it, even before the fighting had broken out? Why did the United States invest so heavily in a political house of cards?

John Bartlow Martin, the United States Ambassador to the Dominican Republic from 1962 to 1963 and President Johnson's special envoy during the 1965 crisis, has himself remarked on how "remarkably similar" were the American "frustrations" in the Dominican Republic and in Vietnam in 1963, the year of the downfall of those two very dissimilar figures, Juan Bosch and Ngo Dinh Diem. Two observations in Martin's story of his ordeals suggest the deeper roots of his "frustrations" in 1965.

He was sent to the Dominican Republic because he had earned credit with the pro-Bosch movement two years earlier; yet he personally handpicked as the United States instrumentality in the 1965 upheaval a man whom he himself described as a "political primitive" who "did not understand ideas," General Antonio Imbert Barrera. Imbert had been one of the ringleaders in the anti-Bosch coup of 1963; he was as much feared and distrusted on the Right as on the Left. That Martin should have identified himself with a totally unscrupulous adventurer such as Imbert after he had identified himself with—whatever else may be said of him—a man of humane principle such as Bosch shows how wildly the political gyroscope of the former American Ambassador could spin. The choice of Imbert was not even very expedient because the United States could not afford to keep him in power and soon had to disappoint him as well as Bosch. Martin's reflection on this dual deception is his own best review of his book and his work. After recounting Imbert's understandable wrath at the way the United States used him and then tossed him aside, Martin writes: "I thought: This is the second time I have betrayed my Dominican friends. First the rebels; now Imbert." A harsher verdict on Martin's role—he is candid enough not to put "betrayed" in quotation marks—would be hard to imagine.

Martin's other observation is even more revealing. As he rightly notes, a "political structure" collapsed in the Dominican Republic on April 24, 1965. It collapsed, he feels, for many different reasons—"Boschist idealism, revenge, plunder, Communist directive, anti-Reid, anti-corruption, sheer adventure and excitement, the highest ideals of liberalism and the meanest effort to pick a winner." Once the masses were swept into the struggle, however, he argues that only the Communists could benefit from it. "Men and women like this," he asserts, "have nowhere to go except to the Communists. All other doors are shut." And again, he theorizes: "It is not names of Communists, or numbers, that is important. It is the process itself—the fusion of the bloodbath." [3]

From this point of view, there is no need to find out who and how many the Dominican Communists were that took over the revolt in such short order.* The "process" was

* This is not the place to subject Martin's evidence of the alleged "Communist takeover" of the Dominican revolt to extended examination. It is enough to say that little of the evidence is his own, and that little is almost derisible in nature (e.g., because "a powerful hand" had jerked away a "Communist" who had yelled "Yankee go home" at Martin's car). It is clear from Martin's own story that most of his information came from CIA and other intelligence reports and from none other than General Imbert. One example of his methods may suffice: "I had the names of two Italians who had turned up at [Colonel Francisco] Caamaño's headquarters and whom the CIA suspected were Communists sent from Europe. I asked Caamaño who they were. He said, 'They are my bodyguards'" (p. 689). I happened to be in London in September 1966, with advance proofs of Martin's book, and read this passage to Colonel Caamaño, then stationed there. Colonel Caamaño laughed uproariously and told me as follows: About seven years ago the Trujillo regime had brought in two Italians to train the newly formed corps of "frogmen." These two Italian instructors had stayed on after Trujillo's assassination in 1961. When the April 1965 revolt broke out, one of them sided with the anti-Bosch military, one with the pro-Bosch military rebels. The first could not have been, and the second

enough to do the job for them. With such a theory of popular revolution, it is small wonder that Martin quickly lost his
bearings in the confused Dominican outburst. That this
should have happened to a liberal ambassador who obtained
his post as a result of his services, first to Adlai Stevenson
and then to John F. Kennedy, in the presidential campaign
of 1960, indicates that the far Right is not alone in identify-
ing every popular revolt with Communism.

Unfortunately, much or even most of the controversy about
the Cuban and Dominican crises has tended to be confined
to their terminal stages, when immediate, hasty, drastic decisions had to be made under stress of seemingly imminent
disaster. Such decisions belong to the closing-the-barn-door-
after-the-political-horse-has-been-stolen department. The problem that concerns us here antedates these decisions and,
therefore, requires a larger historical perspective. That is
why I have gone back to 1952 in Cuba and to 1963 in the
Dominican Republic in order to see how we made the tran-
sition from the political to the military. And I have recalled
these cases because they have a direct bearing on the present
war in Vietnam.

---

was never asked to be and would have considered it beneath his dignity
to be, Colonel Caamaño's bodyguard. Further inquiry from Dominican
sources has confirmed Colonel Caamaño's explanation. Yet most of
Martin's evidence of the "Communist takeover" consists of piling up
such unintelligent "intelligence." One wonders what John Bartlow
Martin the professional journalist would think if he had bothered to
check up on all the second- and third-hand stories passed on uncriti-
cally by John Bartlow Martin the amateur diplomat.

II

From Roosevelt to Eisenhower

From this point of view, the Vietnam war is only the Cuban and Dominican crises writ large.

On February 10, 1954, when the French faced defeat, President Eisenhower declared that "no one could be more bitterly opposed to ever getting the United States involved in a hot war in that region [Vietnam] than I am" and that he could not "conceive of a greater tragedy for America than to get heavily involved now in an all-out war in any of these regions, particularly with large units." How did we get so far that, toward the end of 1966, the same man could advocate "putting in the kind of military strength we need to win," not excluding the possibility of nuclear weapons? [1]

On September 2, 1963, two months before his assassination, President John F. Kennedy said: "In the final analysis, it is their war. They are the ones to win it or lose it. We can help them, we can give them equipment, we can send our men out there as advisers, but they have to win it—the people of Vietnam—against the Communists." How did it become, three years later, "our" war which we must win at all costs?

On March 26, 1964, Secretary of Defense Robert S. McNamara said that "the large indigenous support that the Vietcong receives means that solutions must be as political and economic as military. Indeed, there can be no such thing as

a purely 'military' solution to the war in South Vietnam."
Less than three years later, why were we heading in the direction of a "purely 'military' solution"?

On September 25, 1964, President Lyndon B. Johnson protested that we don't want to "get tied down in a land war in
Asia." And on October 21, 1964: "We are not about to send
American boys nine or ten thousand miles away from home
to do what Asian boys ought to be doing for themselves."
Only two years later we were getting tied down in a land
war in Asia, and we were sending American boys nine or ten
thousand miles away to do what Asian boys should have been
doing.

In 1965 two conservative American Senators spoke up
against an "open-ended commitment" in the Vietnam war.
Republican Senator Karl E. Mundt of South Dakota said:
"To do whatever is needed to win that war would involve
an open-ended commitment which could result in another
situation like we had in Korea—and I certainly am not prepared to say that I want to go that far." Democratic Senator
George A. Smathers of Florida said: "To the idea of committing the United States to whatever effort is needed to win that
war, I say: No. I don't believe we should get ourselves in a
major land conflict over there." [2] A year later, what both
these Senators—and they were not the only ones—had feared
and rejected was coming true—without any perceptible protests on their part.

How? And why?

When the course of our increasing absorption into the
Vietnam struggle from 1950 to the present is studied, the central fact that emerges is this: political failure paved the way
for every step on the road to full-scale, open-ended military
engagement. An examination of seven turning points makes
this clear. They were June 1950, October 1954, December
1961, November 1963, February 1965, Fall 1966, and February 1967.

In the Beginning

World War II enabled the Vietnamese Communists to make
their first important bid for power. The founder of Vietnamese Communism, known as Nguyen Ai Quoc (Nguyen
the Patriot) before he assumed the name Ho Chi Minh, was
a typical product of the cross-fertilization of Vietnamese
nationalism and European Communism. He had left his
native province of Nghe An in North Annam, the traditional seedbed of Vietnamese revolts, in his early twenties
before World War I, and his formative political years had
been spent in France just when French Communism was
going through its own birth pangs. In 1920, as a delegate
to the Tours congress of the French Socialist Party, he had
voted with those who had split away to form the French
Communist Party. He had worked and studied in France,
the Soviet Union, China, and elsewhere during the next
decade, preparing himself for his historic role as the outstanding Communist leader in his own country. It was not
until January 1930 that he was able to bring together three
incipient Communist groups to form the Vietnamese Communist Party, the name of which was changed to the Indochinese Communist Party in October of that year. A combination of official persecution, competition by non-Communist nationalists, and a Stalinist-Trotskyist split made the
party's progress slow, painful, and fitful until the outbreak
of World War II at the end of the decade.

The Allies first gave the Vietnamese Communists, who
had taken refuge in South China, new and more lucrative
opportunities. By themselves, the Communists were too few
and too weak to threaten the French or, later, the Japanese,
who moved into Indochina in 1940 and ruled it in collusion
with the Vichy French administration. But the Communists
could make themselves useful to the Allies by sending agents
across the Chinese border into North Vietnam to gather

intelligence information as they went about strengthening
their own clandestine party cells. In May 1941, a month
before the German invasion of Russia, Nguyen Ai Quoc was
instrumental in setting up a "united front," called the Viet
Nam Doc Lap Dong Minh (League for the Independence of
Vietnam) or Viet Minh in short. It was dedicated to fight
for an "independent" and "democratic" Vietnam against
"French and Japanese fascism." Its program invoked the
"immortal principles" of Rousseau, Voltaire, and the French
Revolution; Communists in united fronts did not then consider it good form to bring up the names of Marx, Engels,
Lenin, and Stalin.

The Viet Minh was designed to give the Communists
access to the large, amorphous reservoir of Vietnamese nationalism on condition that the nationalists were willing to
accept Communist leadership. Since the nationalists lacked
strong leadership of their own—and many did not have any-
where else to go—the tactic was not unsuccessful. It was,
however, not successful enough with the Chiang Kai-shek
regime in China, embroiled with its own Communists;
Chinese authorities at the end of 1941 or the beginning of
1942 caught up with the General Secretary of the Viet
Minh, Nguyen Ai Quoc, and cast him into prison. According
to a colorful and perhaps apocryphal story told by the French
historian Philippe Devillers, this experience led Nguyen
Ai Quoc to change his name to Ho Chi Minh. Dissatisfied
with the intelligence information he was getting from another group of Vietnamese exiles, the military governor of
Kwangsi province in southeast China, bordering on North
Vietnam, General Chiang Fa-k'uei, offered the Viet Minh's
leader his freedom in return for a reliable espionage network in North Vietnam. Nguyen Ai Quoc was willing, but
General Chiang Fa-k'uei was not sure that his superior,
Chiang Kai-shek, then ensconced in faraway Chungking,
would take kindly to a deal with the most notorious Vietnamese Communist. To get around this difficulty, Nguyen

Ai Quoc changed his name in 1943 to Ho Chi Minh,* whom General Fa-k'uei could describe as a capable Vietnamese "revolutionary militant" of obscure origin. For the trouble of exchanging one false name for another, the newly yclept Ho Chi Minh also fell heir to a subvention of $100,000 (Chinese) a month, which had previously been given to a Vietnamese nationalist rival who had failed to give the Chinese their money's worth.[3]

As the war dragged on, the Viet Minh's services were also sought by the American intelligence agency. The decline in the fortunes of the Rome-Berlin-Tokyo axis began to encourage increasing restlessness among the French in Vietnam. In March 1945, the Japanese decided to get rid of the French façade altogether and to set up a nominally "independent" Vietnam, headed by the always available Emperor Bao Dai, who had faithfully served the French as long as they had been able to keep him in his accustomed style, mainly on the French Riviera. But this Japanese protectorate, for such it was, tended to dry up French sources of information, with the result that the United States Office of Strategic Services (OSS)—predecessor of the Central Intelligence Agency (CIA) —is said to have turned to Ho Chi Minh's Viet Minh to provide it with additional intelligence and to carry out other

* This name has been interpreted to mean *"Celui qui éclaire"* (He Who Enlightens) by Philippe Devillers; as "Ho the Enlightened" by Ellen J. Hammer; as "Ho who-aspires-to-enlightenment" by Hoang Van Chi; and as "He Who Is Enlightened, or Has Wisdom" by I. Milton Sacks. His real name is said by Hoang Van Chi to be either Nguyen Van Coong or Nguyen Tat Thanh, born in 1890. The best short biography of Ho Chi Minh is contained in Bernard B. Fall's *The Two Viet-Nams* (New York: Praeger, revised edition 1964) pp. 81-103. Fall cites Wilfred Burchett as authority that Ho's original name was Nguyen Van Thanh; states that Ho was arrested by the Chinese on August 28, 1942, and released on September 16, 1943; gives 1944 as the date Nguyen Ai Quoc adopted the name Ho Chi Minh; does not repeat Devillers' charming story of the reason for the change of name; and, among several available versions, Fall mentions that General Chiang Fa-k'uei claims that Ho Chi Minh was sent to Kunming, China, for special training at the request of the American military.

underground missions. OSS agents allegedly furnished the Viet Minh with funds, small arms, communication equipment, and other appurtenances of the trade.[4] These visible signs of American favor did not hurt the Viet Minh's prestige in Vietnam. As long as the United States and Nationalist China were primarily interested in defeating Japan, they used the Viet Minh and thus enabled the Viet Minh to use them.

For this and other reasons, the Viet Minh was able to fill the vacuum produced by the Japanese collapse in August 1945. In effect, the Japanese had ruined the French, the Americans had ruined the Japanese, and no one else was immediately able to take their place. In the north of Vietnam, where the Japanese military presence was almost nonexistent, a Viet Minh regime, headed by Ho Chi Minh, quickly established itself. In the south, the Viet Minh also came to power temporarily because the Japanese were less averse to it than to the French.* "The Viet Minh," an American historian has written, "could never have come to power so easily without the benevolent neutrality of the Japanese." [5] Thus, on September 2, 1945, Ho Chi Minh proclaimed the independence of Vietnam and formed a government with its capital in Hanoi. The French rule of almost a century seemed to have receded for good into the past. The ever cooperative Bao Dai abdicated and agreed to serve the regime with the title of Supreme Political Advisor.

Meanwhile, however, the fate of Vietnam was being decided elsewhere. At the Potsdam conference, in July 1945,

---

* It should be noted that, in 1945, the Viet Minh was regarded by objective foreign observers as a genuine "united front" movement, and the Communists gradually eliminated all non-Communist elements to dominate it completely only later (Ellen J. Hammer, "Nationalism vs. Colonialism and Communism," in *Viet-Nam: The First Five Years,* ed. by Richard W. Lindholm [East Lansing: Michigan State University Press, 1959], p. 4 note). Devillers notes that the nationalist leaders decided to join the Viet Minh front at this time (Philippe Devillers, *Histoire du Viet-Nam* [Paris: Editions du Seuil, 1952], p. 141).

the American, British, and Soviet leaders decided to divide Vietnam at the sixteenth parallel, with the British in charge in the south and the Chinese in the north, for the purpose of disarming the Japanese and evacuating prisoners. On September 12, ten days after Ho Chi Minh's proclamation of Vietnamese independence, General Douglas D. Gracey arrived in Saigon at the head of an Indian division. Chinese troops soon began to pour into the north. Ostensibly the Potsdam decision did not prejudge the larger question of who was to hold power in Vietnam. But the influx of new forces could not fail to impinge on the highly unstable and inflammable political situation.

Again, a succession of ironies helped to determine the fate of the Vietnamese Communists. In the southern British sector, there were plenty of French soldiers without arms and French officials without authority. All they needed was support and encouragement from the Allied commander to recover their physical force and political nerve. General Gracey cracked down on the Viet Minh and rearmed the French.* All this he did in violation of orders which had limited him to disarming the Japanese. "At a time when the British Labor Government was already committed to freeing India and Burma," writes Ellen J. Hammer, "General Gracey took it upon himself to restore Indochina south of the sixteenth parallel to the French and thereby engaged the British Government in a responsibility for the war which followed." 6

In the north, the Chinese were less amenable to the restoration of French rule. Indeed, the French strongly suspected the Chinese of conniving to take their place. As a result, the Chinese threatened both the French and the Viet Minh regime in Hanoi. To make his government less vulner-

* "I was welcomed on arrival by Viet Minh, who said 'welcome' and all that sort of thing," General Gracey later wrote. "It was a very unpleasant situation and I promptly kicked them out" (*Journal of the Royal Central Asian Society,* July-October 1953, p. 213). His instructions had read: "Sole mission: disarm the Japanese. Do not get involved in keeping order."

able to attack as Communist, Ho Chi Minh formally dissolved the Indochinese Communist Party in November 1945, though, as a sympathetic American journalist later learned, this merely meant that the party went underground, to reappear openly six years later as the Dang Lao Dong Viet Nam (Vietnamese Workers' Party or Lao Dong in short).[7] To get the Chinese out, the French were forced to renounce their extraterritorial rights and other concessions in China. To make peace with the Viet Minh, the French agreed on March 6, 1946, to recognize Ho's "Democratic Republic of Vietnam" as a "free state with its own government, parliament, army and finances," but forming part of the Indochinese Federation and the French Union. In return, Ho Chi Minh agreed to permit French troops to return to the North, the only part of the country from which they were still excluded. He apparently counted heavily on a provision that called for the withdrawal of all French soldiers from the entire country in a five-year period.

According to Philippe Devillers the French made this agreement in order not to throw the Communist-controlled Hanoi regime into the arms of the Chinese.[8] Forced, in effect, to choose between Chiang Kai-shek and Ho Chi Minh, the French preferred the latter, at least for the moment. If the agreement of March 6, 1946, had been honored, Vietnam and the world would have been spared the bloodshed and anguish of the next quarter century.

Unfortunately, the agreement was not honored. Reequipped with shining and powerful American arms and headed by traditionalist generals bent on restoring France's old authority in Vietnam, the French armed forces and the colonial-minded officialdom sabotaged the existing agreements. A clash between Viet Minh and French units in Haiphong on November 20 was followed by a series of French provocations which resulted in a full-scale Vietnamese attack on the French in Hanoi on December 19. The American historian Ellen J. Hammer has summed up the responsibilities as follows: "The Vietnamese chose the date on which it broke out, but the policy followed by members of the French administration in Saigon made the war almost inevitable. They had systematically obstructed the carrying out of the March 6 Agreement." [9] Philippe Devillers called the Vietnamese war the "Dreyfus case of the Fourth Republic." [10] To an eminent American historian and economist who has been particularly influential in both the White House and the State Department in the past few years, however, the conflict which broke out in Indochina in 1946 was merely the result of Stalin's decision to launch an offensive in the East.[11]

The dominant French military faction, headed by Admiral Georges Thierry d'Argenlieu, refused to make concessions to Vietnamese nationalism on the ground that anti-Communism was the main issue. But as General Philippe de Hautecloque Leclerc observed, "Anti-Communism will be a useless instrument as long as the national problem will not have been resolved." In 1949, the French brought back Bao Dai to head another French puppet regime. The French could never gain the confidence of the non-Communist Vietnamese nationalists without giving up more power than they were willing to surrender. As a result, the Communists used nationalism more effectively against the French than the French were able to use anti-Communism against the nationalists. If the entire French military effort was frustrated by a crucial political flaw, this was it.

In the annals of Vietnamese Communism, the first betrayal of a compromise agreement with a Western power occurred in 1946. Ho Chi Minh knew that he was taking an enormous risk permitting the French armed forces to return unopposed to North Vietnam. When Jean Sainteny, the French official who signed the March 6, 1946, agreement, expressed his satisfaction, the Communist leader replied, "As for me, I am troubled because basically you have won; you very well know that I wanted more than that." And he added, "Anyway, I also understand that one cannot have everything in a day." [12] Anti-Communist Vietnamese nationalists vio-

lently attacked Ho Chi Minh for having sold out their cause.
Philippe Devillers says that the half-a-loaf agreement was
so unpopular and misunderstood—because it did not give
Vietnam full independence immediately—especially in the
middle and lower ranks of the Viet Minh itself, that only
Ho Chi Minh's personal prestige enabled him to overcome
the resistance to it.[13] From the other side, the French Communist Party, which had traditionally acted as the Vietnamese
Communists' mentor, counseled the Vietnamese not to go
too far. A French Communist leader warned that "every
attempt to leave the French Union can only lead to an
illusory and momentary pseudo-independence, and the
strengthening of imperialism." [14] In effect, the French Communists were then trying to prove how nationalistic they
were, and even the Communist caricature of French nationalism could not be made to dovetail with the Communist
version of Vietnamese nationalism.

In 1940, then, Vietnamese Communism had been a small,
hunted, fragmented movement, its leadership forced to operate outside the country, without any discernible future.
In 1946, Vietnamese Communism stood on the threshold of
power, having successfully manipulated national and international forces much larger than itself. The ultimate success of the 1946 agreement would have entrenched a Communist state in Vietnam three years before Mao Tse-tung's
party was able to seize power in China. Without the self-
destruction which the Western powers—and their enemies—
had brought on themselves, this extraordinary transformation
could never have taken place.

Turning Point Number 1 (June 1950)

As long as Indochina* was simply another French colonial

* French Indochina was made up of the kingdoms of Laos and Cambodia,
which were formally "protectorates," and of the former empire of
Vietnam. The latter was divided into Tonkin in the north, Annam in
the center, and Cochin China in the south. The first two were formally

possession, the United States merely accepted it as such. There was no need to have an American policy for a single French colony. The beginnings of a specifically Indochinese component of American foreign policy came with the defeat of France in 1940. Since France could no longer defend her Indochinese colony, the question arose in Washington what, if anything, to substitute for French rule. But the Roosevelt administration was not prepared to do anything itself, and it was not able to prevent the Japanese from obtaining *de facto* control of Indochina in 1940.

President Franklin D. Roosevelt was no admirer of French colonial rule. He seems to have had a particularly intense interest in the independence of Indochina and was determined to prevent France from reasserting her previous position there in the event of an Allied victory. From 1943 on, he tried to ensure that a somewhat vaguely thought-out "trusteeship" would take the place of France in postwar Indochina. But Prime Minister Winston Churchill blocked this proposal and nothing ever came of repeated American attempts to oust the French.

The Truman administration inherited what was then known as the Indochina war. By 1950, the French knew that they were in trouble. On May 8 of that year the United States took the first step that led, seventeen years later, to the employment of about 500,000 American combat troops in Vietnam. Secretary of State Dean Acheson announced that the United States had decided to send "economic aid and military equipment" to the French in Indochina "in order to assist them in restoring stability" and to encourage a "peaceful and democratic development." On June 27 of that same year President Truman made known "the dispatch of a [United States] military mission to provide close working relations" with the French forces. In August 1950 a thirty-five-man American military assistance group was sent to Indo-

---

one protectorate and the latter an outright French colony. The independence of Laos, Cambodia, and Vietnam was formally recognized by the Geneva Conference in 1954.

china as "advisers" on the use of American equipment.

For Truman and Acheson, however, aid to the French in Indochina was mainly linked to the Korean war, which broke out in June 1950. Mr. Truman then viewed Communist China as a "satellite" of Soviet Russia, and he saw the Communist moves in both Korea and Indochina, as well as elsewhere, as "part of a pattern." By the end of the Truman administration, the United States was providing between one-third and one-half of the cost of the Indochinese war. The United States tried without success to work out a military agreement embracing five powers—the United States, Great Britain, France, Australia, and New Zealand—to resist overt Chinese intervention in Indochina. Toward the end of the Truman administration, the French sought to reach a political as well as a military understanding with the United States, but this task was left for the incoming Eisenhower administration.[15]

The new Secretary of State, John Foster Dulles, recognized that as long as Indochina was nothing but a French colony, in fact if not in name, the United States did not have the political basis for all-out support of the Indochinese war. Under pressure from Dulles and French internal politics, the French government promised on July 3, 1953, "to perfect the independence and sovereignty" of the Associated States of Indochina, made up of Vietnam, Laos, and Cambodia. This declaration, which was never made good, gave Dulles the political basis to, as he put it, "underwrite the costs" of a new French military plan to defeat the Communists.[16]

From June 1950 to May 1954, when the French were defeated at Dien Bien Phu, the United States provided $2.6 billion worth of military and economic aid to the French in Vietnam, no less than 80 per cent of the total cost of the French war effort.[17]

After the American investment in a French victory was made, American military and diplomatic leaders came to believe—or at least said publicly that they believed—in the likelihood of a French victory. Senator John F. Kennedy once made an inventory of these optimistic predictions. In June 1952 Secretary of State Acheson declared: "The military situation appears to be developing favorably. . . . Aggression has now been checked and recent indications warrant the view that the tide is now turning in our favor. . . . We can anticipate continued favorable developments." In May 1953 President Eisenhower and Secretary Dulles told Congress that United States aid would help "reduce this Communist pressure to manageable proportions." On December 2, 1953, Assistant Secretary of State for Far Eastern Affairs Walter S. Robertson assured an audience in New York that "the tide is now turning" in Indochina. In February 1954 Secretary of Defense Charles E. Wilson said that a French victory was "both possible and probable." In that same month Under Secretary of State Walter Bedell Smith reported: "The military situation in Indochina is favorable. . . . Tactically the French position is solid and the officers in the field seem confident of their ability to deal with the situation." In March 1954 Admiral Arthur W. Radford stated flatly, "The French are going to win." That same month, about six weeks before the French surrender at Dien Bien Phu, Secretary of State Dulles declared that he did "not expect that there is going to be a Communist victory in Indochina" and praised the French forces at Dien Bien Phu for "writing, in my opinion, a notable chapter in military history." [18] When the American press reported French setbacks, Mr. Dulles accused American journalists of exaggeration and blamed them for attributing too much "importance" to the current Communist offensive. Asked about Communist "peace feelers," he brushed them off as lacking in "sincerity."

Thus, for the first time in American history, two Presidents, Truman and Eisenhower, and their respective Secretaries of State, Acheson and Dulles, enlisted the United States actively on the side of a colonial power—a total about-face from the Roosevelt position. From their point of view, of course, colonialism was preferable to communism. At best, then, the United States was faced with a choice of evils and could not win either way. The first step was, in many ways, typical of all the other steps. Dulles tried to get around the dilemma by arguing, as his successors proceeded to argue later in very different circumstances, that Ho Chi Minh's forces fraudulently purported to represent the cause of nationalism and independence but actually amounted to nothing more than an "arm of Communist aggression," directed, supplied, and equipped by the "Red masters of China." [19] In this period, the American theory seemed to be that China was a satellite of Soviet Russia, and the North Vietnamese Communists were puppets of China. By making the Chinese the wire-pullers in Vietnam, Dulles sought to sidestep the issue of anti-colonialism and made the war against France a type of "foreign aggression," the foreigners in this case being the Chinese. It has been hard for later State Department officials to think of anything new or original after John Foster Dulles.

Despite Secretary of State Dulles' tortuous efforts to avoid the stigma of colonialism, one of the most severe judgments of American policy from 1946 to 1954 was made by Professor Frank N. Trager, an ardent supporter of post-1954 American intervention: "Throughout the long devastating years from the post-war return of the French in Indochina to Dien Bien Phu in 1954, the United States supported with incredible consistency the imperialist aims of France in Indochina." * Even if Professor Trager may be doing some injustice to Secretary Dulles' attempts to get the French to make some commitment to Vietnamese independence, the fact remains that he was satisfied with words rather than with deeds, and even the words were too slippery for anyone to grasp.

* Frank N. Trager, "American Foreign Policy in Southeast Asia," *Studies on Asia, 1965* (Lincoln: University of Nebraska Press, 1965), p. 28. Joseph Buttinger's verdict is not very different: "Of American policy in Indochina up to Bao Dai's reinvestiture by the French in 1949, the best one could say was that it did not exist. . . . Thus, when Washington finally became active in the affairs of Indochina after 1949, the policy it adopted was not American but French" ("The Miracle of Viet-Nam," in *Viet-Nam: The First Five Years*, op. cit., p. 27).

In this respect, the situation in Vietnam after 1950 discouragingly resembled the situation in Cuba after Batista's coup in 1952. The opposition to Batista for several years was so varied, and the Communists made up such a small part of it, if any, that there was no reason why American policy should have been reduced to the option of being for or against Batista. In the same way, Vietnamese nationalism before 1954 was so heterogeneous that the Communists, though they were better organized and disciplined than any other group, were hardly the only alternative to French "imperialism." The Communists maneuvered themselves into increasingly advantageous positions precisely because the French administration was hostile to Vietnamese nationalism, not merely to the variety represented by the Communists. If the French, backed by the Americans, had wished to isolate the Communists from the other nationalist tendencies, the task would not have been beyond their joint resources and ingenuity. The American decision to support the French was all the more incongruous in view of the fact that, at this very time, the United States was urging, if not pressing, the British to get out of India and Burma and the Dutch to give up Indonesia.

Once France was defeated, however, American leaders professed not to be surprised and even to know the reason for the outcome. In his memoirs, President Dwight D. Eisenhower explained the French fiasco this way: "I am convinced that the French could not win the war because the internal political situation in Vietnam, weak and confused, badly weakened their military position." [20] General Walter Bedell Smith, head of the American delegation to the Geneva Conference in 1954, which ended the Indochina war, told French Foreign Minister Georges Bidault that "any second-rate general should be able to win in Indochina if there were a proper political atmosphere." [21] In 1965 Henry Cabot Lodge, then between his ambassadorships in Vietnam, cited General Smith's remarks as "one of the best things that any American has ever said about Indochina." [22]

From all this it is clear that the United States would have been far better off in the late 1960s if its leaders had been as clairvoyant about their own problems in Vietnam as they had been about the French. For the American criticism of the French implicitly contained the indispensable ingredient for victory. That ingredient was essentially political in nature. If we may trust Generals Eisenhower and Smith, the formula for victory was a strong, clear internal Vietnamese political situation, a "proper political atmosphere." With that, even a second-rate general could win; without it, no first-rate general could win. If there was one lesson which the Americans should have learned from the French, and which they themselves said they had learned, it was that sound politics in Vietnam was the precondition of military victory, not that military victory was the precondition of sound politics.

Turning Point Number 2 (October 1954)

The French defeat at Dien Bien Phu confronted the Eisenhower administration with a difficult and painful decision: Should the United States take the place of France in the Indochinese war?

Abstractly, Eisenhower and Dulles did not give themselves much choice. They were the first to apply the "domino theory" to Southeast Asia and even beyond. On April 7, 1954, President Eisenhower gave official status to what he then called the " 'falling domino' principle." It implied that the loss of Indochina would inevitably cause the fall of the rest of Southeast Asia like a "row of dominoes." * Secretary Dulles tried to convince British Foreign Secretary Anthony Eden that the loss of Indochina would lead to the eventual loss of Thailand, Malaya, Burma, and Indonesia.[23] This prospect

* Apropos of Indochina and Southeast Asia, Mr. Eisenhower said: "Finally, you have broader considerations that might follow what you would call the 'falling domino' principle. You have a row of dominoes set up, you knock over the first one, and what will happen to the last one is a certainty that it will go over very quickly."

seemed so alarming that leading figures in the Eisenhower administration advocated American military intervention in Vietnam to prevent it.

The outstanding "hawks" in 1953 and 1954 were Vice President Nixon, Secretary of State Dulles, and Admiral Radford. Nixon told the American Society of Newspaper Editors on April 16, 1954, that it was necessary to "take the risk now by putting our boys in" to avoid further Communist expansion in Asia and Indochina. Dulles also spoke publicly in favor of taking "serious risks." In March, Dulles told Eden, the United States Chiefs of Staff had suggested intervening in Vietnam with American naval and air forces.[24] Even the possible use of atomic weapons, it is said, was raised in some fashion.* According to General Matthew B. Ridgway, then the Army's Chief of Staff, "we very nearly found ourselves involved in a bloody jungle war in which our nuclear capability would have been almost useless." General Ridgway also recorded that "individuals of great influence, both in and out of government," raised the cry for United States intervention "to come to the aid of France with arms." [25]

But the hawkish wing of the administration met with determined opposition from at least three directions. Despite —or perhaps because of—his military background, President Eisenhower was most sensitive to Congressional approval of so serious a step as getting into an Asian war. In Congress the Nixon-Dulles-Radford line of military intervention encountered an extremely cold reception. Two of the most powerful

* According to Senator Fulbright's biographer, the Senator was told by Senators Lyndon B. Johnson and Richard B. Russell, who attended the secret meeting on April 3, 1954, that "Secretary Dulles and Vice President Nixon favored a plan by Admiral Arthur W. Radford, chairman of the Joint Chiefs of Staff, to attack a major supply area close to the Chinese frontier with atomic weapons" (Tristram Coffin, *Senator Fulbright* [New York: Dutton, 1966], p. 232). Other evidence that some kind of atomic attack was brought up in some connection is discussed by Bernard B. Fall, *Hell in a Very Small Place* (Philadelphia: Lippincott, 1967, pp. 299, 306-307, 475 note 12). But an atomic attack does not seem to have been taken very seriously and the evidence is very unsatisfactory; Admiral Radford apparently had in mind a conventional bombing attack to relieve the French garrison at Dien Bien Phu.

and most conservative Senators came out strongly against an interventionist policy. One of them was Democratic Senator Richard B. Russell of Georgia, chairman of the key Armed Services Committee, a Southern patrician who was able to make or break both legislation and careers in the upper house. Later, Senator Russell recalled that he had been visited by Assistant Secretary of State Thruston B. Morton, who informed him of President Eisenhower's decision to assist the South Vietnamese. Senator Russell told Morton that he "feared this course would be costly in blood and treasure," though, once it was decided on, he "had no alternative but to support the flag." [26] Another conservative Southern Senator who strongly opposed the Eisenhower decision on the Senate floor in 1954 was Democratic Senator John Stennis of Mississippi. According to Stennis, the first two hundred American Air Force mechanics, sent to South Vietnam early in 1954, were temporarily withdrawn as a result of Congressional objections.[27] In his memoirs Eisenhower recalls that these two Senators were "uneasy about any American participation whatever," and he informed Secretary of State Dulles: "They fear that this may be opening the door to increased and unwise introduction of American troops into that area." [28]

At a secret meeting on April 3, 1954, five senior Senators and three Representatives made known their apprehensions to Secretary Dulles and Admiral Radford. One of those who asked the most searching and embarrassing questions was the then Democratic Minority Leader, Senator Lyndon B. Johnson. He appeared to take the position that the United States could not intervene in Vietnam without allies and forced the Secretary of State to admit that he had not as yet even consulted them. Thus Lyndon Johnson's first important contribution to American policy in Vietnam tended to encourage restraint.* Yet, with the fall of Dien Bien Phu the following month, Senator Johnson spoke publicly in

* The most circumstantial account of the April 3, 1954, meeting is in Chalmers M. Roberts, "The Day We Didn't Go to War," *The Reporter,* September 14, 1954, pp. 31-35.

quite another vein. He made the French defeat into the most "stunning reversal" ever suffered by American foreign policy "in all its history." He mourned that "we have been caught bluffing by our enemies" and had made our friends and Allies "frightened and wondering, as we do, where we are heading." The United States, he said, stood "in clear danger of being left naked and alone in a hostile world." Then, unaccountably, instead of advising his listeners to meet the danger in the world, he said that the prospect was so terribly painful "that we should turn our eyes from abroad and look homeward." * It was, of course, a strictly partisan, rhetorical performance at a fund-raising dinner for his party in Washington, and only the fact that it was made by the future President in another Vietnamese crisis has invested it with any significance. Still, if this is what Senator Johnson thought of the responsibility that President Eisenhower bore for a *French* defeat, one wonders what Senator Johnson would have said of all the *American* setbacks and frustrations suffered by President Johnson.

After the April 3 meeting with the congressional leaders, however, Mr. Dulles did not give up so easily. He hit on the idea that he could sell his plan to Congress if he could make American intervention part of a larger "collective effort." For this purpose he needed the agreement and cooperation of Great Britain. On April 11, 1954, almost a month before the fall of Dien Bien Phu, Dulles went to London to convince Prime Minister Churchill and Foreign Secretary Eden. He tried out all the arguments which have become so familiar— the "domino theory" and historical analogies from the 1930s. The situation in Indochina, Dulles told Eden, "was analogous to the Japanese invasion of Manchuria in 1931 and to Hitler's reoccupation of the Rhineland." But Churchill and Eden refused to be persuaded. Churchill even saw through Dulles' game and confided to Eden that what the British "were being asked to do was to assist in misleading Congress into approv-

* At the Jefferson-Jackson Day dinner sponsored by the Democratic Party in Washington, D.C., May 6, 1954.

ing a military operation, which would in itself be ineffective, and might well bring the world to the verge of a major war." [29]

Finally, opposition came from an unexpected quarter—the United States Army's high command. General Ridgway and General James M. Gavin, Chief of Plans and Development, took the position that the United States could hold on to Indochina, but that it was not worth the price that would have to be paid. An Army team of experts in every field was sent to Indochina to study the ramifications of a major intervention. The Army leaders, General Gavin related, projected the need for eight infantry divisions, plus about thirty-five engineer battalions.[30] General Ridgway told Republican Senator George D. Aiken of Vermont that even if 2 million men were sent to Vietnam, they would be "swallowed up." [31]

Thus the interventionist pressure from Vice President Nixon, Secretary of State Dulles, Admiral Radford, and others was more than offset by the reluctance of influential Senators, the disapproval of the British, and the misgivings of the Army command. This formidable opposition was too much for the innately prudent Eisenhower, whose most popular move was to get us out of one Asian war and who was now confronted with the demand to get us into another one. The line-up of forces was not lost on his Secretary of State.

Dulles was an extraordinarily artful diplomatist. He habitually reversed Theodore Roosevelt's advice about speaking softly and carrying a big stick. The Dulles method consisted of using strong words to hide inner weakness.* He was a progenitor of the "domino theory," according to which a French defeat in Indochina would be fatal in the whole of Southeast Asia and beyond. Yet, when attempts were made to pin him down, he refused to subscribe to the full implications of his own theory. In order to make the "domino theory" inopera-

* As Georges Bidault, the hapless French Foreign Minister in 1954, later observed in his memoirs, Dulles was always talking of "calculated risks," which in practice most often meant that he calculated a great deal and risked nothing (*D'une résistance à l'autre* [Paris: Les Presses du Siècle, 1965], p. 200).

tive, he expounded, it was only necessary to form a "collective-security arrangement" in Southeast Asia. Moreover, he added, "I do not want to give the impression either that if events that we could not control and which we do not anticipate should lead to their [the states of Indochina] being lost, that we would consider the whole situation hopeless, and we would give up in despair." 32 On another occasion, on May 11, 1954, Dulles was specifically asked whether he thought the Southeast Asia area could be held without Indochina. He answered: "I do." This was not exactly orthodox "domino theory," but it served to give Dulles a safe line of retreat. Dulles succeeded in patching together a Southeast Asia Treaty Organization (SEATO)—composed of France, Britain, Australia, New Zealand, Thailand, the Philippines, Pakistan, and the United States—in September 1954, too late to prevent the French domino from falling in Indochina.

Once United States military intervention was doomed, Dulles hedged it about with so many conditions that he was in no danger of ever seeing it brought about. He propounded no fewer than five conditions as the necessary justification for intervention: (1) an invitation from the French; (2) clear assurance of complete independence to Laos, Cambodia, and Vietnam; (3) evidence of concern by the United Nations; (4) a collective effort on the part of other nations in the area; and (5) assurance that France would not itself withdraw from the battle until it was won.33 None of these conditions were in the circumstances of 1954, likely to be completely satisfied, and Dulles would probably have added a few others if he had thought that these might be accepted.

The last American stand at the Geneva Conference was exquisitely Dullesian. First, Dulles professed to regard with holy horror any agreement which handed over more people and territory to a Communist regime. As a result, the United States refused to sign the Geneva Agreements. But then Under Secretary of State Bedell Smith was authorized to declare that the United States would "refrain from any threat or use of force to disturb" the agreements and "would view any renewal of the aggression in violation of the aforesaid agreements with grave concern and as seriously threatening international peace and security." After it was all over, though over eighteen million people of North Vietnam had been "handed over" to the Communists, President Eisenhower opined that the Geneva settlement had not been so bad after all; it was, he wrote in his memoirs, "the best" the French "could get under the circumstances" and he even "saw the beginning of development of better understanding between the Western powers and the nations of Southeast Asia." [34] And Secretary Dulles later confided his thoughts about the agreements to a favorite American magazine; one of these was that handing over half of Vietnam to the Communists had actually "eliminated the possibility of a domino effect in Southeast Asia" by "saving" the other half, Laos and Cambodia.[35] Finally, the United States looked on with favor, if nothing else, as Ngo Dinh Diem deliberately upset the Geneva applecart and defiantly repudiated the Geneva Agreements in 1955.

One of the most ardent proponents of the "domino theory" in Southeast Asia was at that time Senator John F. Kennedy. He rose in the Senate on March 9, 1954, two months before the fall of Dien Bien Phu, to argue that "the security of French Indochina is vital to the security of all South Asia." When Senator Stennis criticized the sending of American technicians to Vietnam to assist the French, he defended the gesture. Kennedy sought to stave off the future division of Vietnam by taking the view that a partition "would be the first step toward the seizure of complete control in that area by Communist forces." He strongly urged the United States to adopt a position at the coming Geneva Conference that "the war should be continued and brought to a successful conclusion." [36]

Only a month later, however, a somewhat different Kennedy spoke in the Senate in a far-ranging discussion of Indochinese policy. The then junior Senator from Massachusetts still maintained that partition or a coalition government would result in "eventual domination" of the entire country by the Communists. But his main emphasis now was on the French failure to grant the Vietnamese people real independence, which he considered the precondition for persuading the Vietnamese people to fight for themselves and for inducing other Asian nations to join the United States in the struggle. He ridiculed a 1951 assertion by the then Assistant Secretary of State Dean Rusk that the French had made the Indochinese responsible for their own affairs. "I am frankly of the belief," he said, "that no amount of American military assistance in Indochina can conquer an enemy which is everywhere and at the same time nowhere, 'an enemy of the people' which has the sympathy and covert support of the people." Without the participation "by the armed forces of the other nations of Asia, without the support of the great masses of the [Vietnamese] peoples," and with the increasing reluctance of the French to fight, he considered United States intervention to be "virtually impossible in the type of military situation which prevails in Indochina." Much as he wanted the French to stand firm, Mr. Kennedy indicated that he had lost faith in them, and, if the French withdrew, he saw the same difficulties even if American troops were sent in, as long as both Vietnamese and other Asian support was not forthcoming.[37]

Senator Kennedy's remarks were favorably received on both sides of the house. The Republican Majority Leader, Senator William Knowland of California, volunteered that he fully agreed with "much, and probably the predominance," of the new Kennedy position. Republican Senator Everett M. Dirksen of Illinois declared that he did not want to see the United States do in Indochina what it had done in Korea, where it had provided 90 per cent of both the troops and the funds. "Would there be a similar result in Indochina?" Mr. Dirksen asked apprehensively. "I hope not, because I would be the last to go along with a program of that sort."[38]

In fact, the proponents of the 1954 "domino theory" were

not prepared to think through and live up to their own doctrine. If, as President Eisenhower asserted, the French loss of Indochina would cause the fall of Southeast Asia "like a set of dominoes," and, as others did not fail to add, the fall of Southeast Asia would cause the loss of huge areas as far away as India, the stakes were so high that the advocates of this theory were obliged to take the most "serious risks," without the impossible conditions posed by Secretary Dulles. Not only did Eisenhower back away from the implications of his own theory but also the immediate consequences of the French defeat did not bear out his dire foreboding.

It is still important to keep in mind how the Indochinese war ended in 1954 because the story helps to explain the bitterness and doggedness of the Communists today. Ho Chi Minh made far-reaching concessions in the Geneva Agreements of July 1954, possibly under both Soviet and Communist Chinese pressure, as most authorities believe.* Ho's victory over the French was decisive, but he agreed to take over only the northern half of the country, undoubtedly in the expectation that the South, then in seeming chaos, would soon fall of its own accord into his hands. The Final Declara-

* Professor P. J. Honey attributes the Communist willingness to take far less "than even their most pessimistic supporters could have expected" to "strong Soviet pressure" (*Communism in North Vietnam* [Cambridge, Mass.: The M.I.T. Press, 1963], p. 5). Ellen J. Hammer credits both the Russians and Chinese with influencing the Vietnamese Communists to make concessions (*The Struggle for Indochina 1940-1955* [Stanford: Stanford University Press, rev. ed., 1966], p. 331). Douglas Pike goes farthest in his estimate of how much the Vietnamese Communists gave up in the Geneva Agreements: "Only the Viet Minh, the winners, lost. Or were sold out. Ho Chi Minh somehow was persuaded—apparently by a joint Sino-Soviet effort—to settle for half the country . . ." (*Viet Cong* [Cambridge, Mass.: The M.I.T. Press, 1966], p. 52). Melvin Gurtov, whose book, *The First Vietnam Crisis* (New York: Columbia University Press, 1967), is the most detailed study of United States policy during the Indochina war, thinks that the Chinese Communists favored a compromise because "active pursuance of the peace line could gain more friends for China than interminable prolongation of talks amid continued fighting," and the Soviets were even more concerned than the Chinese "about the potential explosiveness of the Indochina situation in the event talks failed to produce results" (pp. 152-53).

tion of the Geneva Conference, a unique diplomatic instrument agreed to by all but signed by none, provided for general
elections to unify the country in July 1956.* Though there
is reason to believe that no one, including the Communists,
took this commitment very seriously, it gave the new regime
in South Vietnam a breathing spell of two years. In short, the
Communists have been fighting since 1954 to win back what
they and everyone else thought they had already won. They
had hardly intended to have Diem, who had contributed
nothing to the victory over the French, reap its fruits. In
1954 Ho Chi Minh snatched compromise out of the jaws
of victory; today the United States is afraid that he will
snatch victory out of the jaws of compromise. In any case,
this odd background makes Vietnam idiosyncratic in Communist bids for power. It is hard to imagine the same chain
of events elsewhere.

President Eisenhower's "solution" in 1954 was a compromise between extremes—one demanding full military intervention, the other complete abstention. To the question
which side it was on, the Eisenhower administration answered
unequivocally—it was for Ngo Dinh Diem. He took office as
Prime Minister under Emperor Bao Dai—who had worked
for the French, the Japanese, the Communists, and again
the French—just before the Geneva Agreements of July 1954
brought to an end the war waged by the Vietnamese Communists against French colonial rule. Diem, a long-time exile,
had not taken part in this struggle but had stayed in the
United States for a period before the French collapse, making
friends in high places and impressing a variety of Americans,
official and unofficial, that he was a man of nationalist con-

* It has been generally overlooked, however, that the future general
elections and unification of Vietnam were also mentioned in the "Agreement on the Cessation of Hostilities in Vietnam, July 20, 1954," which
was signed by Ta-Quang Buu, Vice-Minister of National Defense of the
Democratic Republic of Vietnam (North Vietnam), and by Brig. Gen.
Delteil, for the Commander-in-Chief of the French Union Forces in Indochina. Article 14 of this signed agreement referred to political and administrative measures "pending the general elections which will bring
about the unification of Vietnam."

victions and progressive ideas. While Ngo Dinh Diem became
the first Vietnamese instrument of American policy, he was
far from being the first choice of the Vietnamese themselves.
Of all the things Mr. Eisenhower has regretted putting down
on paper, the list may well be topped by the admission in
his memoirs that all knowledgeable persons at the time agreed
that "had elections been held as of the time of the fighting,
possibly 80 per cent of the population would have voted for
the Communist Ho Chi Minh as their leader rather than
Chief of State Bao Dai." [39] He might also have said rather
than Ngo Dinh Diem, who at first merely seemed to represent the Bao Dai regime. As late as 1965, Senator Russell
said that Ho could have won again. [40]

I do not cite these statements as evidence of how democratic Ho Chi Minh would have been. He might have taken
power democratically, but he would not have kept power
democratically, which is far more important. In 1960 the
"elections" in North Vietnam resulted in a 99.8-per-cent
majority for the ruling Communist Party and its two small
satellite groups, with no one permitted to run on an opposition platform. For this reason it is fatuous to imagine that
Vietnam would have been more "democratic" if Ho Chi
Minh had been permitted to get an 80-per-cent majority in
a national election, as provided for by the Geneva Agreements. The only reason for citing Eisenhower's statement is
that it underlines the unique character of the Vietnam problem. In what other country could a Communist leader have
been assured of anything close to an 80-per-cent sweep in a
free election?

But the Eisenhower administration made far more a political and economic than a military commitment. The American gamble was held down by the understanding that the
United States was willing to help Diem's regime only if it
proved capable of helping itself. On October 23, 1954, President Eisenhower sent Prime Minister Diem a letter in which
he explicitly stated the conditional nature of this support.
The American aid program was contemplated, the letter said,

"provided that your Government is prepared to give assurances as to the standards of performance it would be able to maintain in the event such aid were supplied." The American offer, it went on, was intended to make the government of Vietnam "a strong viable state, capable of resisting attempted subversion or aggression through military means. The Government of the United States expects that this aid will be met by performance on the part of the Government of Vietnam in undertaking needed reforms." Yet this letter has been cited as if it were an unconditional "commitment" on the part of the United States "to resist Communist aggression" from then to the present and seemingly for all time. It should also be noted that the letter put the burden of resistance on the government of Vietnam, not on the United States. On June 2, 1964, President Johnson said that "our commitment today is just the same as the commitment made by President Eisenhower to President Diem in 1954—a commitment to help these people help themselves." * If so, it is still nothing more than an offer of aid conditional on "the standards of performance" of, and "needed reforms" by, the government of South Vietnam. The Eisenhower policy was one of limited liability and, in principle, it set the pattern until 1965.

For our purposes, the main thing to note is that, in the end, the main reason given by the Americans, from President Eisenhower to Senator John F. Kennedy, for the French defeat was political. The French could not win, as President Eisenhower put it, as long as the internal political situation in Vietnam was "weak and confused." This is no less true of the United States, with the addition of something else, for which the French were not strong enough: our military position has been strengthened every time the internal political situation in Vietnam has weakened.

* One word can sometimes make a big difference. It would have been more exact if President Johnson had said that the commitment was made to help these people *if* they helped themselves.

III

From Eisenhower to Kennedy

This general rule can best be seen in operation during the
seven years that separated the second and third turning points
in American policy.

When Ngo Dinh Diem took over the shell of an administration and an economy left by the French in 1954, he was
not expected to be able to fulfill the conditions posed by
President Eisenhower's offer of aid. In fact, Diem was not
expected to stay in power very long—perhaps a few months.
He seemed to have little or nothing to work with on the Vietnamese side, and the French, still there, were soon out to get
rid of him. But with American economic and political support, Diem surprised everyone. He cracked down successfully
on the politically minded sects and their private armies in the
spring of 1955; he eliminated the French puppet chief of
state, Bao Dai, and made himself an all-powerful President
in October of that year; the French command pulled out
completely by April 1956. In two years Diem seemed to have
performed a minor miracle by consolidating his power around
himself, his family, and his Catholic coreligionists.

In these two years, when he was weakest, Diem had least
trouble with the Communists. Two reasons appear to account
for this trucelike atmosphere. Ho Chi Minh had no more
faith than anyone else in Diem's chances of survival, and,

despite their own cynicism about it, the promised general election in July 1956 may have sufficiently intrigued the Communist leaders to give them a reason for adopting a "wait and see" attitude in the South. In 1955, at any rate, North Vietnam went through the motions of inviting South Vietnam to discuss the promised elections; the bid was summarily rejected on the ground that no free election could be held in the North.* Secondly, Ho Chi Minh was just then consolidating his own rule in the North. His methods from 1954 to 1956 were every bit as ruthless and brutal as any used in China or Soviet Russia at their worst. At least fifty thousand and possibly one hundred thousand peasants were physically exter-

* On this point, some State Department officials have—to be charitable —not done their homework. Deputy Under Secretary for Political Affairs U. Alexis Johnson, for example, declared: "Thus it is a travesty on the truth to allege that the present situation was brought about by the failure of the South to carry out the 1954 accords. In fact, it was the North that was not willing to submit itself to the test of free elections under international control" (*Department of State Bulletin,* April 4, 1966, p. 530). The fullest account of the election maneuvers in 1955 appears in B. S. N. Murti, *Vietnam Divided* (New York: Asia Publishing House, 1964), pp. 182-93. Mr. Murti, while apparently more favorable to the case of North Vietnam than to that of South Vietnam, provides abundant information about the efforts and concessions made by the North Vietnamese to test the Ngo Dinh Diem regime's willingness to abide by the electoral agreement. On July 29, 1955, Ho Chi Minh himself publicly proposed an election campaign in which, among other things, "All Vietnamese citizens, *whether from the North or the South,* have the right to canvass freely throughout the country through conference, leaflets, press, etc. The Government of the North and the authorities of the South should ensure the liberty and the security for all citizens during their activities for elections" (my italics, T.D.). This may have been a ruse or deceit, but the South Vietnamese regime never tested it. Mr. Murti was Deputy Secretary-General of the International Control Commission from 1954 to 1957, during this very period. In fact, the State Department's White Paper of 1961 refutes Alexis Johnson's allegation: "It was the Communists' calculation that nationwide elections scheduled in the Accords for 1956 would turn all of South Vietnam over to them," it declared. Therefore, it went on: "The authorities in South Vietnam refused to fall into this well-laid trap" (*A Threat to the Peace,* p. 3). If this is true, it hardly bears out Alexis Johnson's version. The North Vietnamese overtures to the South in 1955-1960 are also touched on by Philippe Devillers, "The Struggle for the Unification of Vietnam," *The China Quarterly,* January-March 1962, pp. 6 and 10.

minated in the North Vietnamese "land reform" of those years. A virtual peasant rebellion broke out in one Northern province in November 1956.[1] This upheaval gave Ho Chi Minh more than enough to do in the North, but it indicates what would have happened in the South if Ho had been given the opportunity to get his 80-per-cent majority there.

Diem and the Communists

Diem, then, treated the Communists just as roughly as they would have treated everyone else. From the outset he made clear that he did not intend to honor the Geneva Agreements, especially the one providing for general elections. By July 1955, he initiated a Campaign for Denunciation of Communist Subversion. In 1958 he created a Committee for the Liberation of North Vietnam. In effect, Diem beat the Communists to the punch; he caught them off balance and forced them on the defensive. Opinions differ as to whether he provoked them first or vice versa, but all agree that he hurt them at first far more than they could hurt him.

Even the State Department's White Paper of February 1965, a highly tendentious document, tends to confirm this view. After the Geneva Agreements of 1954, it relates, the Communists adopted a strategy of "all means short of open violence" to weaken Diem's regime. Diem's anti-Communist campaign in the South was so successful that "morale in the Communist organization in the South dropped sharply" and "defections were numerous." For this reason, the Communist cadres in the South had to be "rebuilt, reorganized, and expanded" after 1956. The appreciable increase of Communist terror in the South is dated from 1958.*

* Only Professor Frank N. Trager seems to insist that the Communists constituted a "genuine threat to security" in South Vietnam in 1955 and 1956 (*Why Viet Nam?* [New York: Praeger, 1966], pp. 119-21). This was a somewhat more moderate statement than one by Professor Trager the year before—that North Vietnam had been inflicting "*military* punishment*" (my italics, T.D.) on South Vietnam since 1955 (*Studies on Asia, 1965*, p. 53). In those years, and for two or three more years,

The Communist version agrees that Diem had the Communists at bay from 1955 to 1959. Wilfred G. Burchett, an Australian Communist journalist, was told that the Communist line in the South until the end of 1959 was exclusively for "a legal, political, non-violent form of struggle." It allegedly changed at that time to permit "the use of arms in self-defense only" because the Communists were "faced with the wholesale wiping out of all former resistance cadres." The local Communists interpreted "self-defense" rather freely as an authorization to launch small-scale attacks for the purpose of seizing arms, and the first such attack was carried out by about 260 men with only 170 weapons early in 1960.[2] This version neglects to mention the epidemic of Communist terrorism before 1959, which cost several hundred lives. But isolated terrorist attacks were symptomatic of Communist desperation rather than of any massive threat. An apparently well-informed pro-Communist source gives the autumn of 1957 as the beginning of the campaign of terrorism, mainly against village chiefs, and 1960 for the first "really military assaults." [3] Other, non-Communist sources essentially agree that the violent Communist threat started in 1959 and 1960.*

however, pro-Diem supporters used to deride the seriousness of the Communist threat and boast of South Vietnam's peacefulness and stability. Even George A. Carver, Jr., later revealed as a CIA official, states that the "incipient insurgency" did not become a "serious threat" until the end of 1958 and that the Vietcong was still unable "to win a really significant political following" by the following year (*Foreign Affairs,* April 1966, p. 359). Of the 1955-1960 period, Douglas Pike writes: "In terms of overt activity such as armed incidents or distribution of propaganda leaflets the period was quiet and the Communists within the remnant Viet Minh organization relatively inactive. In addition, much of the activity that did take place apparently was the work of impatient cadres operating in the South independently of Hanoi's orders" (*Viet Cong,* op. cit., p. 75). One of those whom Professor Trager has failed to convince is Secretary of State Rusk, who is on record with: "There was no serious threat until 1959-60, when North Vietnam set in motion a systematic effort to seize control of South Vietnam by force" (*Department of State Bulletin,* December 5, 1966, p. 842).

* "Insurgency efforts in the 1958-1960 period involved violence such as assassinations but few actual armed attacks. This was so partly be-

But Diem was too successful for his own good. If he had cracked down only on the Communists, he would not have had too much to worry about. The Communists, however, made up only a small part of those caught in Diem's dragnet. By 1956, Diem was well on his way to creating a police state which silenced, exiled, imprisoned, or put to death all rivals and critics indiscriminately. His repression atomized and pulverized the Vietnamese society to which he had just succeeded in giving some semblance of unity. The Communists picked up allies as quickly as he made enemies. An able and sensitive observer, Robert Shaplen, says that the popularity of Diem's regime "began to wane seriously" as early as 1957.[4] By November 1960, a sizable segment of his own army made a first, almost successful attempt to overthrow him. Since the Communists also went over to organized guerrilla warfare in 1960, Diem's regime was beset on all sides at once. At this time, however, the Communists were still far from being his main concern. Secretary of State Dean Rusk himself estimated the guerrillas' strength in late 1959 at only 3000.[5] Diem inflated the Communist strength by making no distinction between Communists and anyone else who opposed him. Burchett's account also makes clear that the Communists had hardly succeeded in getting their military actions started in 1960.

The "initial organizational phase," as Douglas Pike calls it, of the Communist effort to overthrow Diem extended from mid-1959 to the end of 1960.[6] Belligerent statements started to come out of North Vietnam in May 1959, though it was not at first clear what they imported. Publicly, the Northern

---

cause the cadres had little military capability but chiefly because doctrine counseled against violence" (Douglas Pike, op. cit., p. 78). Robert Scigliano, who was from 1957 to 1959 in South Vietnam as a member of the Michigan State University Vietnam Advisory Group, says that the "serious threats" to the Diem regime from 1954 to 1956 came from nationalist, not Communist or foreign, quarters, and that "propaganda activities" constituted the main thrust of the Communist program until early 1959 (*South Vietnam: Nation Under Stress* [Boston: Houghton Mifflin, 1963], pp. 18 and 137).

Communists first served notice in September 1960 that they were out to "liberate" the South.

This preparatory phase was completed on December 20, 1960, with the formation of the National Liberation Front of South Vietnam (NLF), a typical Communist-organized and Communist-controlled "united front," which was the anti-Diem successor of the anti-French Viet Minh. Diem's repression, however, had driven various non-Communist elements into identification with or support of the Communists in the NLF. In addition, the Lao Dong, or official Communist Party, which had been formed in 1951, operated in the South as well as in the North. As with most such "united fronts," it is just as much a mistake to ignore its Communist leadership and control as to neglect the existence in it of fellow-traveling and non-Communist elements without which it would not be a "united front."

Strictly speaking, the "Vietcong" is not Communist usage. It is merely a contraction for Vietnamese Communists and has become the non-Communist term for the Communist movement in South Vietnam. The name is used here because it is now so common, though it tends to obscure the fact that the Communists in the South operate within a "united front" containing an indeterminate number of non-Communist elements.

Two main reasons have been given·for the emergence of organized Communist insurgency in 1959 and 1960. The official United States explanation, given by Secretary of State Rusk, is that the North Vietnamese Communists decided to resort to force in 1959 because they had given up hope of taking over South Vietnam any other way and because the South was "far outstripping" the North socially and economically.[7] Another high State Department official has asserted that the North resorted to guerrilla warfare "only when the success of the South Vietnam Government persuaded them that they could not achieve their designs by subversion alone." This theory, therefore, asks us to believe that the Communists decided to overthrow Ngo Dinh Diem because his regime by 1959 or

1960 was an outstanding success rather than a hollow failure.*
If so, it would be the first time that Communists decided to
risk an all-out military offensive on the basis of political failure. This theory, incidentally, cuts the ground from under
the view that the Communists represented a "genuine threat"
to the security of South Vietnam before 1959.

The other theory is that the South Vietnamese Communists, having suffered Diem's persecution for years, took up
arms to prevent themselves from being wiped out and to take
advantage of his precipitous decline. Whatever economic
gains may have been registered in the first five years of Diem's
regime, his undifferentiated repression made him weaker
and weaker politically. It is not even certain that the original signal for armed Communist resistance in the South
came from the North. Philippe Devillers believes that the
Southern guerrillas were so hard-pressed that "they had to
act, whether Hanoi wanted them to or not." 8 According to
Jean Lacouture, another outstanding French student of Vietnamese politics, the National Liberation Front was actually
set up in the South in March 1960; a group of "old resistance
fighters" held a meeting in a southeastern forest and issued
a proclamation which he considers the "signal" that forced
the Northern government "to assume its responsibility." †

* State Department officials have never coordinated their stories about
the North Vietnamese decision to begin military operations in the
South. It was in 1956, said Deputy Under Secretary of State U. Alexis
Johnson (*Department of State Bulletin*, April 4, 1966, p. 530). Two dates,
1957 and 1959, were given by Assistant Secretary of State William P.
Bundy within a three-month period (ibid., March 1, 1965, p. 292, and
June 7, 1965, p. 891). Legal Adviser Leonard C. Meeker was partial to
1957 (ibid., January 9, 1967, p. 56). Secretary of State Rusk has been
the most consistent; for him it was in 1959 or 1959-1960 (ibid., December 27, 1965, p. 1007, and December 5, 1966, p. 842).
† Lacouture writes: "It must be pointed out that the Hanoi leaders—
still careful—did not make this turn except at the specific demand and
under the moral pressure of the militants in the South, who criticized
their Northern comrades' relative passivity in the face of the repression
exercised against them by the Saigon authorities; they expressed their
disappointment in the softness with which the Hanoi leaders and their
allies in the socialist camp had reacted to the non-observance of the

In September the third Congress of the Lao Dong (Communist) Party in the North decided to back the "liberation of the South"; the NLF then made its public appearance two months later.[9] By this time, the first attempt to overthrow Ngo Dinh Diem, in November 1960, had narrowly failed, and the Communists had reason to believe that the time was ripe for a violent push to topple him from power. Inasmuch as, even by Secretary of State Rusk's count, the Vietcong's armed strength had grown only from about 3000 in late 1959 to over 12,000 in May 1961, this push was initially far from a massively mounted affair, and no North Vietnamese forces took part in it.

Turning Point Number 3 (December 1961)

And yet, no sooner had John F. Kennedy been sworn into office than the highest Washington officials were spreading the word among themselves that Diem's regime was on the point of collapse. Kennedy's first appointment as Ambassador to South Vietnam, Frederick E. Nolting, Jr., was sent off to Saigon in April 1961 with this news ringing in his ears. According to John Mecklin, the American Public Affairs Officer in Saigon from 1962 to 1964, Nolting was told in Washington before he left for his post that "it would be a miracle if South Vietnam lasted three months longer." [10] On March 26, 1964, Secretary of Defense McNamara gave a more restrained version of the situation which had forced President Kennedy's hand three years earlier: "When President Diem appealed to President Kennedy at the end of 1961, the South Vietnamese were quite plainly losing their fight against the Communists, and we promptly agreed to increase our assistance."

That Diem, who had had the Communists on the run from at least 1955 to almost the end of the decade, should

---

1956 general elections that had been stipulated by the negotiators in Geneva with a view to reunifying the country" (*Vietnam: Between Two Truces* [New York: Random House, 1966], p. 54).

have faced defeat at their hands by early 1961 is inexplicable in terms of the Communists' own strength. It is understandable only in terms of the inner degeneration of Diem's regime and its suicidal estrangement from other non-Communist forces in South Vietnam. The fatal disease was political, not military.

The problem before John F. Kennedy in 1961 was, in essence, the problem that had faced Dwight D. Eisenhower in 1954. What should the United States do to stave off a complete collapse in Vietnam? The most detailed and candid account of Mr. Kennedy's decision appears in Arthur M. Schlesinger, Jr.'s chronicle *A Thousand Days*. It is a veritable case history of how the military submerged the political in action, if not always in intention and thinking.

Kennedy came to the Vietnam problem, as he did to other problems, without a consistent position behind him. Professor Schlesinger cites the speech Kennedy made in the Senate on April 6, 1954, against unilateral United States intervention to bolster an essentially colonial regime which the "great masses" of Vietnamese did not support.[11] Another biographer, Theodore C. Sorensen, even cites the same passage as the "key" to the late President's decision in 1961.[12] (Neither of them recalls the more bellicose, pro-French Kennedy of March 9, 1954.) Professor Frank N. Trager has dug up another speech on June 1, 1956, which was delivered by still another John F. Kennedy. By this time, Diem seemed to have consolidated his rule, and Senator Kennedy hailed it as our "offspring" which we could not afford to permit to fail.[13] Schlesinger and Sorensen do not mention the June 1956 speech, and Trager does not mention the April 1954 speech. The difference in emphasis may be defended on the ground that the situation in South Vietnam had changed markedly in two years, but even so, the conclusion is inescapable that Kennedy was too pessimistic in 1954 and too optimistic in 1956. The ease with which Kennedy can be quoted against Kennedy suggests the dangers and difficulties of evaluating a statesman whose style is considered more important than his substance.

In his first months in office, Kennedy had to make up his mind whether Diem had failed and, if so, what to do about it. As Schlesinger tells the story, his advisers lined up in two camps, the "political" and the "military." Those who put a political effort in Vietnam as the first consideration saw no hope short of a "change of leadership" in Saigon, which meant dropping Diem in favor of some other South Vietnamese leader. Among those explicitly or implicitly urging this course were John Kenneth Galbraith, then Ambassador to India, W. Averell Harriman, appointed Assistant Secretary of State for the Far East in 1961, and the writer Theodore H. White. Schlesinger refers to a "Harriman group" in the State Department which questioned subordinating the political to the military. Vice President Johnson went to Saigon in May 1961 and was so impressed by Ngo Dinh Diem that he compared him to George Washington, Andrew Jackson, Woodrow Wilson, Franklin D. Roosevelt, and Winston Churchill.[14] Mr. Johnson apparently advocated a substantial increase in all kinds of American aid, short of military manpower, which, he said, was not needed.

This seems to have been Mr. Johnson's second important contribution to America's Vietnamese policy. In 1954, his reluctance to have the United States go it alone without allies had served to restrain Secretary of State Dulles; in 1961, his recommendation for increased aid and all-out support of Ngo Dinh Diem, with no more Allied support than in 1954, served to discourage restraint on the part of President Kennedy.

But the main pressure on Kennedy inside the government came from the military side. A special mission to South Vietnam headed by General Maxwell D. Taylor and Walt W. Rostow of the State Department recommended sending a relatively small American military task force with combat capabilities. Except for the so-called Harriman group, Professor

Schlesinger says, the State Department in the person of Secretary Dean Rusk "was well satisfied with military predominance in the formation of United States policy toward Vietnam." [15] General Taylor has revealed that both the introduction of American ground forces and American bombing of Northern military targets were under consideration at least since November 1961, when he presented his report.* [16] Sorensen goes so far as to say that "all" of Kennedy's principal advisers on Vietnam favored the commitment of American combat troops.[17]

Finally, Kennedy did more or less at the end of 1961 what Eisenhower had done at the end of 1954. He decided, as General Taylor later put it at the Vietnam hearings of the Senate Foreign Relations Committee, to change the number but not the "quality" of our military advisers. He ruled out combat missions but gradually increased the number of "advisers" from about 800 to about 17,000.† Schlesinger quotes Kennedy in one of his most appealing, astute, and antic moods, turning down the advice of those who wanted an American com-

* In order to cope with what he called "para-wars of guerrilla aggression," General Taylor wrote in his report of November 3, 1961, "it is clear to me that the time may come in our relations to Southeast Asia when we must declare our intention to attack the source of guerrilla aggression in North Vietnam and impose on the Hanoi government a price for participating in the current war which is commensurate with the damage being inflicted on its neighbors in the south" (letter of President Johnson to Senator Henry M. Jackson, *The New York Times,* March 3, 1967). It should be noted that at the very time of this Taylor report, the State Department's White Paper of December 1961 estimated the full-time regular Vietcong fighting force at less than 10,000 men (pp. 9-10); that it boasted "something close to an economic miracle" had taken place in South Vietnam (p. 5); that, as other sources later admitted, the Vietcong's weapons came almost wholly from the United States via captured South Vietnamese weapons; and the first regular North Vietnamese troops did not allegedly arrive in the south for another three years. Yet General Taylor already projected widening the war to take in North Vietnam, and President Johnson cited his more-than-five-year-old report as justification for turning the full force of American might on North Vietnam.

† The exact figures are 773 at the end of 1960 and 16,500 at the end of 1963 (*Congressional Record,* Senate, October 10, 1966, p. 24855).

bat commitment: "It's like taking a drink. The effect wears off, and you have to take another." [18]

Yet Schlesinger admits that Kennedy's decision at the end of 1961 "was to place the main emphasis on the military effort." This emphasis required renewed and intensified political support of the Diem regime. The new American Ambassador, Frederick E. Nolting, Jr., and the new American military commander in Saigon, General Paul D. Harkins, made Diem's cause their own. Nolting established a relationship with Ngo Dinh Diem similar to that of Ambassador Arthur Gardner with Fulgencio Batista in Cuba from 1953 to 1957 or of Ambassador W. Tapley Bennett, Jr., with Donald Reid Cabral in the Dominican Republic in 1964 and part of 1965. Thus there was an unmistakable political side to the military decision.

For some reason, Kennedy's military decision, which was halfhearted, has come in for far more attention than its political counterpart, which was not. Ambassador Nolting represented a do-or-die, wholehearted political gamble on the durability and reformability of Diem's regime.

Why did Kennedy do it? Why did Kennedy, as John Mecklin put it, act the way Eisenhower had acted, only "more so"? [19] The answer given by President Kennedy's intimates and biographers is most revealing. Both Schlesinger and Sorensen plead in his defense that past American policy had virtually given Kennedy no other alternative. Kennedy, writes Schlesinger, "had no choice now but to work within the situation he had inherited," and Dulles's policy in South Vietnam had "left us in 1961 no alternative but to continue the effort of 1954." [20] Sorensen strikes the same note.[21] In exculpation, they emphasize that Kennedy's military contribution was still limited. But the principle they accept would make it difficult for a President to refuse to go from a low-level to a high-level limit and, if necessary, to an unlimited effort. Moreover, they neglect to pay enough attention to the fact that, while his military investment in the Diem regime was then limited, he threw in a practically unlimited political bonus in the persons of Ambassador Nolting and General Harkins, and the latter may have been by far the more important of the two.

It is, of course, a truism that no policy is made *in vacuo* and that the past weighs heavily on every important Presidential decision. But if Professor Schlesinger is right that President Kennedy's options were so limited, even in 1961, when we had fewer than eight hundred noncombat military personnel on the scene, the implications are truly frightening. One gets the impression from these memoirs and memorials of Kennedy's associates that they are writing of a man who did what he did not want to do, what he knew or felt he should not do, and what he had little faith would come out right in the end. There is nothing so devastating about our entire Vietnam policy as the sense of fatality, and this is the best argument that Kennedy's friends have been able to muster in his behalf. I rather think that President Kennedy would not have given himself such an easy way out, any more than he did in the Bay of Pigs case.[22] Inasmuch as some of his former aides experienced a partial change of heart in 1966, it is hard to see how, if President Kennedy's options were so limited in 1961 without American combat troops in South Vietnam, they could think President Johnson would have any options with about 400,000 combat troops there. The Vietnam war will go down in history as another "war of lost opportunities," and some of the best opportunities to re-examine and reshape the war were lost in 1961.

Turning Point Number 4 (November 1963)

The fourth turning point came about primarily because John F. Kennedy lost his political gamble on Ngo Dinh Diem.

Diem's regime benefited at first from the increased American military and political support. The military approach seemed to be paying off. Our policy in 1962, writes Professor Schlesinger, was "dominated by those who saw Vietnam as primarily a military problem and who believed that its solution required unconditional support of Diem." When Diem's durability proved to be an illusion, there was nothing to fall back on. Diem's power was based on the demoralization of South Vietnamese political life, and he succeeded so well that we are still living with the political wasteland that he left, not without our cooperation.

What supporting Ngo Dinh Diem unconditionally after 1961 meant has been most intimately described by John Mecklin, whose official duties brought him into contact with the highest officials on both sides. He and other observers agree that we were not even supporting a government; we were supporting a slightly pixilated family's fief. The awesome or awful threesome of this family—Ngo Dinh Diem; his brother, Ngo Dinh Nhu; and the latter's wife, Madame Ngo Dinh Nhu—are most often described in psychiatric terms. Mecklin's bizarre account of their habitual behavior belongs in a textbook of mental pathology. He gently diagnoses the three of them as victims of "blank-wall irrationality." Mecklin relates whimsically that he once had a dream "about an American diplomatic mission that gradually discovered it had been dealing for years with a government of madmen." But when he awoke, he asked himself whether he had been dreaming after all.[23] Shaplen refers to the condition of Nhu, generally considered the power behind the throne, as "seemingly paranoid." [24] Even Professor Trager, always inclined to give the Diem regime the benefit of a doubt, finds it necessary to acknowledge that Ngo Dinh Nhu was "at the end, perhaps crazed." [25]

If the present Premier of South Vietnam, Air Vice Marshal Nguyen Cao Ky, can be trusted, "the collapse of the Ngo Dinh Diem regime was the inevitable consequence of the long treason of a regime deeply engaged in the path of dictatorship, corruption, and brutality. The armed forces could not tolerate the Diem regime, the more so because this regime was deliberately using, while already on the decline, the armed forces as a tool not to protect national freedom and independence against foreign invasion but only to suppress the people's just aspirations." [26] The Communists never denounced Diem in stronger terms than those used by Diem's successor. Either Diem or Ky must have been unfit for the job.

The fall of Diem was not the work of the Communists. It was not the result of an imminent military collapse. Secretary McNamara went to South Vietnam in late September 1963 and on his return reported that the military situation was so favorable a thousand American troops could be withdrawn by the end of the year and "the major part of the United States military task can be completed by the end of 1965." General Harkins was quoted on November 1 as saying that "victory" was just "months away" and the reduction of American "advisers" could begin at any time. On that same day Diem's own generals carried out the coup which resulted in his and his brother's assassination. Whether the United States directly connived in the coup is a matter of dispute; but that the United States prepared the way for the coup, knew of it in advance, and did nothing to discourage it, is not.

That Ngo Dinh Diem could not have fallen without American approval is beyond doubt, though the exact measure of the approval is still arguable. At one extreme is Arthur Schlesinger's assurance: "It is important to state clearly that the coup of November 1, 1963, was entirely planned and carried out by the Vietnamese. Neither the American Embassy nor the CIA were involved in instigation or execution." [27] Schlesinger is probably right about the "execution," but "instigation" is a broad word which, in this case, may cover too much ground. The other extreme view is represented by former Ambassador Frederick E. Nolting, Jr., who has publicly charged that the anti-Diem generals were "encouraged by the United States Government." [28] Shaplen, who learned a great deal about the inside story of the coup, says that the coup was executed with the "full knowledge" and "consent" of the Americans.[29] Mecklin reviews the available evidence and clearly believes that United States policy from early October 1963 encouraged and even "led to" the coup. He sums up bitingly: "But to assert that the United States was 'not involved' in the coup was a bit like claiming innocence for a night watchman at a bank who tells a known safecracker that he is going out for a beer." [30] Sorensen states that President Kennedy sent a cable in late August 1963 "indicating that the United States would not block any spontaneous military revolt against Diem" but he denies that the plotters received any "assistance" from the United States, as if the hands-off attitude were not assistance enough.[31] The *coup de grâce* was probably given to Diem on September 2, 1963, when President Kennedy publicly affirmed that the Diem regime had, for the past two months, "gotten out of touch with the people." All that Ambassador Lodge would admit was that the United States wanted Ngo Dinh Nhu out of the government and to see "the behavior of the Government" changed. Lodge also agreed that the Communists had no part in the *coup* and did not even want to see Ngo Dinh Diem ousted because they thought there might be "total disintegration" if he remained in power another month or six weeks—and Lodge thought they were probably right.[32] The upshot seems to be that Shaplen is right in his judgment that the coup "succeeded in the end primarily because it was a genuine homegrown plot that expressed real grievances against a regime that had become totally corrupt and oppressive." But the homegrown plotters needed, if not encouragement, then at least a lack of discouragement from the United States. In the circumstances the latter was almost as positive as the former.

Former Vice President Nixon's view of the complicity of the United States in Diem's overthrow is particularly interesting because he tied it up with the problem of political and military instrumentalities. "Our greatest mistake was in putting political reform before military victory in dealing with the Diem regime," Mr. Nixon averred. "Diem, and more particularly some members of his family, were without question at times hard crosses for America to bear in Vietnam. But when the United States supported a *coup d'état* which led to his murder we set in motion a violent chain reaction not only in Vietnam but throughout southeast Asia." [33]

Factually, Mr. Nixon's analysis left something to be desired. If President Kennedy had put political reform before military victory, he would not—with the encouragement of Vice President Johnson—have given Diem a political blank check in 1961. It is also hard to see how Diem could have obtained any military victory, since Diem had completely alienated his own army leadership, and not a single South Vietnamese general backed him in the showdown.* Diem was so much the creation of American policy that the Kennedy administration moved against him with the greatest reluctance, long after it might have made the change with less risk and bloodshed. And the chief wire-puller in bringing about Diem's downfall was a member of Mr. Nixon's own party and a recent candidate for the Republican Presidential nomination, Ambassador Henry Cabot Lodge. But Nixon's strictures, even if they may be wanting in verisimilitude, point to the political-military issue which has bedeviled American policy at every stage. The irony is that there was still time to put political reform before military victory in South Vietnam in 1961, but President Kennedy did not do it and, therefore, paid heavily in 1963. After Diem's debacle, political reform became increasingly more difficult, and Mr. Nixon's predilection for "military victory" as against "political reform" was later satisfied because of the earlier failure.

In any event, Ngo Dinh Diem fell the way Fulgencio Batista had fallen and Donald Reid Cabral would fall. No one cared; no one moved; no one grieved—except possibly

* In the Army newspaper, *Stars and Stripes,* of November 1, 1963, the United States deputy commander was quoted as follows: "The Vietnamese armed forces are as professional as you can get. Sure, they worry about political and religious disputes, but, just like the American soldier, they're loyal to their Government" (cited by Bernard B. Fall, *U.S. News & World Report,* September 28, 1964, p. 59). The South Vietnamese generals showed how "loyal" they were to the government that very day, but at least the *coup* was, if nothing else, "as professional as you can get."

those American officials who had staked their reputations
and careers on him. When he heard of the deaths of Diem
and Nhu, Schlesinger tells us, President Kennedy no doubt
"realized that Vietnam was his great failure in foreign policy." [34] Mecklin remarks that the Diem-Nhu raids on the Bud-
dhist pagodas in August 1963, which precipitated the *coup,*
"were an act of political bankruptcy, confession of a catastrophic failure of leadership." [35]

It does not really matter what one thinks of the Diem
regime, whether it was worth overthrowing or preserving. If
Diem deserved his fate, American policy in South Vietnam
for at least eight years under two Presidents could not have
been more misbegotten and misdirected. If the United States
should have opposed the anti-Diem coup, the implicit encouragement given to the plotters was no less wrongheaded. Either
way, Diem's downfall represented the political bankruptcy
and catastrophic failure of not only his own policy but that of
the United States. Kennedy's decision in 1963 not to block
Diem's overthrow was the most deadly criticism of Kennedy's
decision in 1961 to back Diem to the hilt. The most persuasive argument against Diem's downfall has been that there
was nothing better to put in his place. If this is true, it merely
indicates how well Diem and his family had done their work
of political devastation. In the last few months of Diem's regime it was hard to tell whether he was more anti-American
than the Americans were anti-Diem. The ghastly tragedy was
not without the overtones of a macabre farce.

No one could blame the Communists for this contretemps.
Even Secretary McNamara explained Diem's collapse in political terms: "But this progress [in 1962] was interrupted in
1963 by the political crises arising from troubles between the
government and the Buddhists, students, and other *non-Communist* oppositionists. President Diem lost the confidence and
loyalty of his people; there were accusations of maladmin-
istration and injustice" (my italics).[36] The same admission
is made in the State Department's White Paper of February
1965: "The military and insurgency situation was complicated

by a *quite separate internal political struggle* in South Vietnam, which led in November, 1963, to the removal of the Diem government and its replacement with a new one" (my italics).[37]

In the last stage of the Diem regime, the threat of Communist despotism mattered far less than the reality of Diem's despotism. The most scathing indictment of the political failure was probably pronounced by the responsible and experienced Australian correspondent Denis Warner, who wrote that "the tyranny the West allied with in Saigon was in many ways worse than the tyranny it was fighting against." [38]

The eight lost years of Ngo Dinh Diem were, then, the Vietnamese equivalent of Batista's seven years in Cuba and Reid Cabral's sixteen months in the Dominican Republic.

IV

From Kennedy to Johnson

Once more, a deceptive temporary improvement seemed to take place after the November 1963 *coup*. First a government dominated by General Duong Van Minh, better known as "Big Minh," came in, and then, in January 1964, it was overthrown by a military junta headed by General Nguyen Khanh. By this time, the agony of making the final American decisions had been handed on to Lyndon B. Johnson.

The leading American officials had especially "high hopes" for General Khanh, as Secretary McNamara expressed it in one of his most illuminating and ill-fated speeches, on March 26 of that year. General Khanh, said Secretary McNamara, was just the man to defeat the Communists. McNamara credited Khanh with a demonstrated grasp of the basic political, economic, and psychological elements needed to assure victory.

Five months later, in August, the State and Defense Departments issued a pamphlet which discounted the use of American combat units in a guerrilla war of the Vietnamese type "in which knowledge of terrain, language, and local customs is especially important." The pamphlet also warned that American combat units would provide "ammunition for Communist propaganda which falsely proclaims that the

United States is conducting a 'white man's war' against Asians." [1]

At this late date, then, American policy was still ostensibly anchored to the Eisenhower-Kennedy principle of limited commitment and limited liability. All the right things were said on the eve of doing just the opposite.

What caused this abrupt and seemingly unanticipated change of policy at the beginning of 1965 in favor of sending massive American combat units to wage an increasingly "white man's war"?

A Sense of Timing

The official American explanation is that a "foreign aggression" on the part of North Vietnam took place at the end of 1964. The foreign aggressor was North Vietnam. Its victim was South Vietnam. This did not mean that North Vietnam had previously watched the struggle in the south with folded arms; Southern cadres were undoubtedly trained and equipped in the North before the end of 1964.

But at that time, according to the official American thesis, a qualitative change occurred in the war. It came about because North Vietnam had allegedly exhausted its reserves of Southerners, who had moved to the North in the exchange of populations arranged ten years earlier, and had been forced to resort to its own regular troops to prosecute the war in the South. After the United States began to bomb North Vietnam regularly at the beginning of 1965, the appearance of a North Vietnamese regular division in the South was given as the crucial reason.

Of all the turning points in the war, this one was the most fateful because it increasingly changed the character of the conflict. Under Presidents Eisenhower and Kennedy, the main antagonists were still South Vietnamese, even if one side owed its training and equipment to the United States and the other side to North Vietnam. But the bombing of the North introduced a new factor—the direct confrontation between the United States and North Vietnam. The introduction of almost 200,000 American troops in 1965 was justified on the ground that the North Vietnamese were feeding their own regular army into the southern theater of the war.

This new stage of the war was additionally significant because it made an early compromise settlement infinitely more difficult. Later, the United States seemed to take the position that the war could be ended with ease and without delay if only the North Vietnamese agreed to withdraw their forces from the South. On the other hand, the North Vietnamese demanded the unconditional cessation of the bombing of their territory as a prior condition for any peace negotiations.

As a result, if there is one phase of the war that bears the closest and most critical examination, it is that which led to the American decision to bomb North Vietnam. The American change of course in this period is seemingly infected with contradictions and confusions because of the peculiar circumstances in which it took place.

The Vietnam issue occupied a prominent, if not the foremost place, in the 1964 Presidential campaign. To the average American voter, the choice seemed to be between a Democratic candidate, Lyndon B. Johnson, who opposed bombing North Vietnam or sending American troops to South Vietnam, and a Republican candidate, Barry Goldwater, who spoke as if he might conceivably decide to use nuclear weapons or permit the military to make such a decision. Throughout the campaign, Mr. Johnson pushed this issue to the utmost, and the peculiar convolutions of his Vietnamese policy after the election can be understood only in terms of the "commitments" he made in the course of winning the Presidency.

The first American bombing of North Vietnam came in August 1964 in the midst of the presidential campaign. On August 2, according to the United States, three North Vietnamese torpedo boats fired torpedoes and machine guns at the United States destroyer *Maddox*, one of the most heavily armored and armed in the fleet, about 30 miles from the mainland of North Vietnam in the Gulf of Tonkin. In the exchange, two enemy boats were damaged at no cost to the American side. On August 4, enemy torpedo boats again allegedly fired at the *Maddox* and another destroyer, *C. Turner Joy,* this time 65 miles from the North Vietnamese shore. The score this time was reported to be two North Vietnamese boats sunk, no American losses.

Despite the one-sidedness of the engagement, Mr. Johnson chose to interpret the incidents as evidence of "open aggression on the high seas against the United States of America." On August 4 he ordered retaliatory air attacks on the North Vietnamese torpedo-boat bases and their oil-storage depots. This action constituted the first American air attacks on North Vietnamese soil.* The President also called for a Congressional resolution to give him authority to use whatever armed force he deemed necessary in Vietnam. On August 7, by a vote of 88 to 2, with only Democratic Senators Wayne Morse of Oregon and Ernest Gruening of Alaska opposed, the Senate authorized the President "to take all necessary measures to repel any armed attack against the forces of the United States and to prevent further aggression." The House of Representatives passed the resolution 416 to 0. The resolution was so loosely worded that it later enabled the President to claim, despite Senatorial protests to the contrary, that the Congress had given him a "blank check" in Vietnam.†

* Two well-informed correspondents have gone so far as to write: "President Johnson, after the Gulf of Tonkin incidents, felt he had to prove his mettle even though, in retrospect, it now seems doubtful whether the second Gulf of Tonkin incident, on the basis of which the first retaliatory bombing of North Vietnam had been ordered, was actually caused by enemy action" (Edward Weintal and Charles Bartlett, *Facing the Brink* [New York: Scribner's, 1967], p. 207).

† Ironically, Senator Fulbright served as floor leader in support of this resolution. The following exchange took place between Democratic Senator Daniel B. Brewster of Maryland and Senator Fulbright:

MR. BREWSTER: I would look with great dismay on a situation involving the landing of large land armies on the continent of Asia. So my question is whether there is anything in the resolution which

Later information on the Gulf of Tonkin incident seemed to present it in a somewhat different light. The Senate Foreign Relations Committee held hearings on the resolution on August 6, 1964, but the text of these hearings was not released until November 24, 1966, and then in a highly truncated form, especially in those sections devoted to the Tonkin Gulf incident itself. However, some members of the Senate Committee who participated in the debate on the resolution on August 5 and 6, 1964, had listened to the full testimony, and one of them, Senator Morse, referred to some of the secret testimony.

But first it should be noted that a Saigon newspaper had already reported a sharp stepping-up of *South* Vietnamese commando raids on Northern territory, beginning on July 10, 1964, more than three weeks before the first torpedo-boat attack.[2] On July 31, 1964, *South* Vietnamese torpedo boats, obtained from the United States through the aid program, had bombarded two North Vietnamese islands, approximately 3 and 5 miles from the North Vietnamese coast. Senator Morse asserted that American authorities "knew that the bombing was going to take place." American destroyers, which had been patrolling the waters of the Gulf of Tonkin for about a year and a half, moved within the 12-mile "limit" (claimed by North Vietnam but not recognized by the United States) of the North Vietnamese shore on July 31. Then, evidently as a result of some intelligence information which Senator Morse did not feel privileged to reveal in detail, the *Maddox* hastened away from the scene of the South

would authorize or recommend or approve the landing of large American armies in Vietnam or in China.

MR. FULBRIGHT: There is nothing in the resolution, as I read it, that contemplates it. I agree with the Senator that that is the last thing we would want to do. However, the language of the resolution would not prevent it. It would authorize whatever the Commander in Chief feels is necessary. It does not restrain the Executive from doing it. . . . Speaking for my own committee, everyone I have heard has said that the last thing we want to do is to become involved in a land war in Asia . . .

(*Congressional Record,* Senate, August 5, 1964, p. 18403).

Vietnamese attacks, and the alleged engagement with the pursuing North Vietnamese torpedo boats took place approximately 65 miles from the North Vietnamese shore.[3]

In any event, the North Vietnamese "aggression," which the torpedo boats' audacity supposedly heralded, failed to materialize. Despite the severe American reaction, North Vietnam licked its wounds and at that time made no effort to hit back. Senator Morse took the position that the American ships were entirely justified in returning the North Vietnamese torpedo boats' fire but that President Johnson's subsequent order to bomb North Vietnamese naval facilities in retaliation constituted a serious violation of international law and "a major escalation of this war." As Morse predicted about the resolution, "Senators who vote for it will live to regret it." One of those Senators who voted for it and lived to regret it most was J. William Fulbright.

President Johnson's "sense of timing" in obtaining this wide-open authorization from the Senate, which was filled with doubters about the wisdom of our Vietnam policy, struck journalistic observers as little less than "awe-inspiring." Tom Wicker, head of *The New York Times* Washington bureau, later wrote: "Usually the timing is precisely his own —as when he presented his Vietnam resolution to Congress the day after the Gulf of Tonkin crisis. He had been carrying it around in his pocket for weeks waiting for the moment." [4]

Nevertheless, the Gulf of Tonkin incident did not seem to portend any American enlargement or intensification of the war. In fact, Presidential candidate Johnson accused his opponents of harboring just such designs, and his campaign speeches were pervaded with protestations of innocence and remonstration.

On August 12, 1964, Mr. Johnson said in New York:

Some others are eager to enlarge the conflict. They call upon us to supply American boys to do the job that Asian boys should do. They ask us to take reckless action which might risk the lives of millions and engulf much of Asia and certainly threaten the peace of the entire world. Moreover, such action would offer no solution at all to the real problem of Vietnam.

As the campaign warmed up, he spoke up directly on the subject of bombing North Vietnam. On August 29, 1964, he declared in Texas:

I have had advice to load our planes with bombs and to drop them on certain areas that I think would enlarge the war and escalate the war, and result in our committing a good many American boys to fighting a war that I think ought to be fought by the boys of Asia to help protect their own land. And for that reason, I haven't chosen to enlarge the war.

His most extended statement in this vein was made on September 28, 1964, in Manchester, New Hampshire:

Some of our people—Mr. Nixon, Mr. Rockefeller, Mr. Scranton, and Mr. Goldwater—have all, at some time or other, suggested the possible wisdom of going north in Vietnam. Well, now, before you start attacking someone and you launch a big offensive, you better give some consideration to how you are going to protect what you have. And when a brigadier general can walk down the streets of Saigon as they did the other day, and take over the police station, the radio station, and the government without firing a shot, I don't know how much offensive we are prepared to launch. As far as I am concerned, I want to be very cautious and careful, and use it only as a last resort, when I start dropping bombs around that are likely to involve American boys in a war in Asia with 700 million Chinese.

So just for the moment I have not thought that we were ready for American boys to do the fighting for Asian boys. What I have been trying to do, with the situation that I found, was to get the boys in Vietnam to do their own fighting with our advice and with our equipment. That is the course we are following. So we are not going north and drop bombs at this stage of the game, and we are not going south and run out and leave it for the Communists to take over. Now we have lost 190 American lives, and to each one

of those 190 families this is a major war. We lost that many
in Texas on the Fourth of July in wrecks. But I often wake
up in the night and think about how many I could lose if
I made a misstep. When we retaliated in the Tonkin Gulf,
we dropped bombs on their nests where they had their PT
boats housed, and we dropped them within 35 miles of the
Chinese border. I don't know what you would think if they
started dropping them 35 miles from your border, but I
think that that is something you have to take into consideration.

So we are not going north and we are not going south;
we are going to continue to try to get them to save their
own freedom with their own men, with our leadership and
our officer direction, and such equipment as we can furnish
them. We think that losing 190 lives in the period that we
have been out there is bad. But it is not like 190,000 that
we might lose the first month if we escalated that war. So
we are trying somehow to evolve a way, as we have in
some other places, where the North Vietnamese and the
Chinese Communists finally, after getting worn down, conclude that they will leave their neighbors alone. And if
they do, we will come home tomorrow.

Thus Mr. Johnson succeeded in demonstrating that he
could be as tough as anyone else in the Gulf of Tonkin; he
extorted a seemingly indeterminate, all-inclusive war resolution from Congress on the basis of a local, limited incident
for which the responsibility was far from clear; and he successfully presented himself as the candidate who could be
trusted to prevent the enlargement of the war.

Turning Point Number 5 (February 1965)

But other things were happening at the same time. In
retrospect, they suggest that the bombing of North Vietnam
was not as far away as President Johnson's campaign speeches
seemed to imply.

In Saigon, the South Vietnamese regime headed by General Nguyen Khanh began to show familiar signs of disintegration in the summer of 1964. To bolster his regime, it

was reported in early August, he called for an extension of the war to the North. This was not, from the American point of view, the right thing to say at that time, and the American Ambassador, General Taylor, was reported to have told him so.[5] Almost two years later, however, an editorial in *The New York Times* stated flatly: "In the summer of 1964 Premier Khanh was promised a bombing offensive against the North, presumably on Presidential authority, to extract pledges from Saigon of governmental stability and efficacity."[6] Inasmuch as the editorial gave no source or further details, the entire incident is still obscure, except that it seems clear that Premier Khanh, if not Mr. Johnson's Republican opponents, was just then demanding "going north in Vietnam." That pressure for such a move was coming from the South Vietnamese was also intimated later by one of the reasons given for the bombing—that it was intended to bolster their morale.

At least two hints of what was to come or what was tentatively being considered in the State Department came from Assistant Secretary for Far Eastern Affairs William P. Bundy in August and September 1964, before any incidents took place to provide possible justification for American bombing of North Vietnam or large-scale American troop movements to South Vietnam.*

---

* Edward Weintal and Charles Bartlett have provided background which, if verified, goes far to explain Mr. Bundy's intimations. "It was not publicly known at the time that, since March of 1964, the government had a plan for 'measured pressure' against North Vietnam. The plan had been thrashed out by an inter-agency task force and was to become the blueprint for escalation. This was planning of a bold and thorough variety—the assumptions and anticipations which were an integral part of the thick loose-leaf volume prepared for the President have been proved by time to be valid. The planners recognized that little short of direct U.S. intervention would be likely to deter the Viet Cong more than momentarily and that the Viet Cong threat could not be dissipated even by subversion of the support coming from North Vietnam. They accepted the likelihood that Hanoi would respond to an American escalation by escalating its own role in the war, and warned that a major Communist escalation would be successfully met only by the introduction of 'several U.S. divisions.'" (*Facing the Brink,* op. cit., p. 73.)

On August 15, 1964, Mr. Bundy was asked whether the United States might decide to interdict supply routes in North Vietnam. First he replied that "we want no wider war." Then he added, still sticking close to the old line but not excluding a new one: "We have made it clear that we cannot exclude the possibility that wider action against the North might become necessary, and we have carefully studied what might be involved, and all the rest, but I think it is clear enough that anything in the nature of attacks on North Vietnam of a systematic character by the South Vietnamese or by ourselves would involve very grave issues and we would, therefore, prefer to pursue the policy we are now pursuing of maximum assistance in South Vietnam." [7]

On September 29, 1964, he delivered a major address in Tokyo in which he again obliquely referred to the possible expansion of the war:

> Expansion of the war outside South Vietnam, while not a course we want to seek, could be forced upon us by the increased pressures of the Communists, including a rising scale of infiltration. [8]

This and similar official views, privately expressed, apparently aroused the suspicions of James Reston, the noted Washington commentator of *The New York Times*. On October 2, 1964, he reported that

> it is difficult to understand why prominent officials, a few weeks before a national election, should be talking so openly about expanding the war, and not only advocating it but almost lobbying for such a course of action.
>
> It is even possible now to hear officials of this Government talking casually about how easy it would be to "provoke an incident" in the Gulf of Tonkin that would justify an attack on North Vietnam, and thus, according to this thesis, enable the United States to bring strong military pressure on the Communists there to let up on their pressure on South Vietnam.

Another well-known Washington correspondent, Charles

Roberts of *Newsweek,* made October 1964 even more significant. "As a matter of fact," Roberts later wrote, "he [Johnson] had made the momentous *decision* to bomb North Vietnam nearly four months earlier. That decision was made, it can now be revealed, in October, 1964, at the height of the Presidential election campaign." According to Roberts, the President had personally told him "he had made the decision to bomb four months before Pleiku." [9]

Whether or not the President made a personal decision in October, before the election, the official decision was reported to have been made in December, after the election. The last half of 1964 was an especially exasperating period for the American ambassador in Saigon, General Taylor, whose travails with one South Vietnamese government after another forced him to return to Washington for consultation with unusual frequency. These visits seemed to coincide with important American decisions. On December 1, 1964, during one of the ambassador's sojourns in Washington, the attendance at a top-level meeting in the White House indicated that it was rather less routine than usual. Those present were President Johnson, Ambassador Taylor, Secretary of State Rusk, Secretary of Defense McNamara, Director of Central Intelligence John A. McCone, and the Chairman of the Joint Chiefs of Staff, General Earle G. Wheeler.[10] Later, John W. Finney of *The New York Times* reported that the Johnson Administration had adopted a new strategy for the war during Ambassador Taylor's visit to Washington in December 1964. This strategy, according to Mr. Finney, called for, among other things, "air strikes against the north to persuade the Hanoi regime to stop its support of the insurgents and to seek a negotiated settlement." [11]

Richard N. Goodwin, then an Assistant to President Johnson, has given a somewhat later date for the crucial decision. According to Goodwin,

early in 1965, the President was advised that morale in South Vietnam could be revived only if we bombed military targets in North Vietnam. This would assure Saigon of our determination to stay the course, and perhaps, if we were lucky, would so weaken Hanoi's will to fight that we could avoid the unpleasant, looming need to send in large numbers of combat troops. Thus the most fateful decision of all was made. The war went North.[12]

Mr. Goodwin's version raises some questions that only a complete disclosure of the record may answer. Pressure on the President to bomb North Vietnam to buck up South Vietnamese morale undoubtedly antedated 1965. Indeed, news of such demands began to appear in the American press by the summer of 1964. The advice the President received early in 1965 may have been particularly urgent or persuasive, but it did not start that train of thought. It is also hard to understand how anyone could have believed that the bombing might somehow save us from sending in troops, though Goodwin may be perfectly right about the existence of such an official delusion. Unless Hanoi's will was expected to weaken almost immediately, the decision to send in troops followed the decision to bomb with so little delay that the bombing was given very little time to work its wonders. Whatever the time sequence may be, however, Goodwin's main point further suggests that there was a predisposition to bomb North Vietnam before there occurred any "incident" on which to pin it.

Finally, on February 2, 1965, a high State Department official told Philip L. Geyelin of the *Wall Street Journal:* "We could hang on there for ten years. But as a practical matter, patience is wearing thin, in Congress, in the Administration, in the country, and a decision to change the rules of the game, one way or another, seems probable before very long." [13] General Taylor has also offered some evidence for the view that the bombing of North Vietnamese military targets was no sudden impulse brought about by the incident at Pleiku. "I do not know," he has written, "of any element in the Vietnamese situation which caused longer debate, longer discussions," dating at least as far back as 1961.[14]

Yet Mr. Johnson's campaign oratory had made it awkward
for him to change "the rules of the game." Only a month
after he was inaugurated, and four days after the tip to
Geyelin, another "incident" came providentially to the President's rescue.

On February 7, 1965 (Saigon time), Vietcong guerrillas carried out three attacks, including one against an
American installation at Pleiku, about 250 miles north of
Saigon. Seven American soldiers were killed and 109 were
wounded, 76 of them seriously. When the news reached the
White House, President Johnson reacted explosively. In retaliation, he ordered the United States Air Force to attack
barrack areas and staging areas in the southern portion of
North Vietnam. At first, the bombing of the North was made
to seem a perhaps over-forceful reaction to the Pleiku incident, which implied that the bombing might be short-lived
if the Vietcong did not manage to catch an American camp
off guard again. But on February 28, President Johnson announced a policy of continuous air strikes against Northern
military targets to force the enemy into a "negotiated settlement." And this step was soon followed by another, even
more far-reaching decision—to send thousands of American
combat troops to South Vietnam.

These measures were so extreme that they could not possibly be accounted for as mere reprisals for the Pleiku incident, though they were psychologically related to it in the
public mind. The entire sequence of events was apparently
another "awe-inspiring" example of Mr. Johnson's "sense of
timing."

The Mysterious 325th

The decision to commit American combat troops on a
large scale was also made early in 1965, though the exact
time has not yet been established.

In any event, we have been told by General Taylor that
the introduction of American ground forces was a "very

difficult, long-debated decision." [15] It had, in fact, been debated for at least eleven years, the first time in 1954, ever since Generals Ridgway and Gavin had successfully argued against it. The reluctance of Presidents Eisenhower and Kennedy was not based on what the North Vietnam Communists were doing; both presidents were rather motivated by what they thought the United States should not be doing —fighting another land war against Asians on Asian soil.

Once President Johnson decided to rid himself of this inhibition, however, a different kind of justification was needed. It was expressed no less than three times by Secretary of State Rusk at the Senate Foreign Relations Committee's hearings in January and February 1966.

The first time came on January 28, 1966, in an exchange with Democratic Senator Albert Gore of Tennessee:

> SECRETARY RUSK: From November of 1964 until January of 1965 they moved the 325th Division of the North Vietnamese Army down to South Vietnam. There was no bombing going on at that time. Now, this is an aggression by means of an armed attack.
>
> SENATOR GORE: Was that before or after we moved forces into South Vietnam?
>
> SECRETARY RUSK: Well, the division moved after we had put—had reinforced our own forces there.

The second time came on February 18, 1966, again in a reply to Senator Gore:

> At no stage have we ourselves wanted to escalate this war, as the expression goes. At no stage have we wanted a larger war. But it was in November, December, January, over the turn of the year 1964-65, that North Vietnam moved the 325th Division of the regular North Vietnamese Army from North Vietnam to South Vietnam to up the ante. That was before the bombing started. That wasn't in response to an escalation by the United States. It seemed to be the result of a decision on their part that, well, "the United States says it doesn't want a big war, maybe we can have a big one without undue risk."

The third time occurred the same day in a discussion with Democratic Senator Claiborne Pell of Rhode Island. At this point, Secretary Rusk merely reiterated that the North Vietnamese infiltration had "included a division of the regular North Vietnamese Army, before there was any bombing." The 325th was obviously Secretary Rusk's trump card, and he played it for all it was worth without arousing any suspicion on the part of his senatorial questioners that he might have overplayed his hand.

From all this, one might gather that North Vietnam, with a total population of about 18,500,000, had deliberately decided to pit its military manpower against the United States, with a population of almost 195,000,000. The usually cautious Ho Chi Minh, according to Secretary Rusk, had tried to get away with a one-sided "big war," and the United States had merely called his bluff. In terms of the main consideration which had weighed on Presidents Eisenhower and Kennedy, even the presence of an entire North Vietnamese division in the South might not have swayed them from the principle of avoiding an American land war in Asia against Asians, even Asian Communists. In any event, the role played by the 325th North Vietnamese Division in Secretary Rusk's rationale for the new line made it the crucial causative factor in the massive increase of American military manpower which took place in 1965 and 1966.

What we know of this division comes wholly from American sources. The least that might be expected from these sources is that they should tell the same story. Peculiarly, the Secretary of State did not seem to be speaking of the same war as the Secretary of Defense.

According to the former, the 325th, *as a division,* had moved from North to South Vietnam by January 1965.*

* That the 325th moved in "as a division" was emphasized by Secretary Rusk on a later occasion (*Department of State Bulletin,* September 19, 1966, p. 423). Assistant Secretary William P. Bundy said that the first "organized units" of the North Vietnamese army, presumably from the same 325th Division, first entered the South in December 1964 (ibid., June 20, 1966, p. 967).

At the end of the following month, however, the State Department issued its second White Paper entitled *Aggression from the North: The Record of North Viet-Nam's Campaign to Conquer South Viet-Nam.* This publication, one imagines, would have emphasized or at least mentioned the momentous 325th. But, no, it never appears in its pages at all. In one section, this White Paper states that one captured Private First Class of the 2nd Battalion of the North Vietnamese 9th Regiment said that his entire battalion had infiltrated into the South between February and May 1964; another captured Private First Class of the North Vietnamese 324th Division told of 90 North Vietnamese draftees who had infiltrated in May 1964; and a third prisoner gave information that one Vietcong battalion had received 80 North Vietnamese replacements in February 1964. One incident referred to in the document took place as late as February 16, 1965, only eleven days before it was issued. That the entire 325th Division should have been in the South by January 1965 without getting some publicity in this White Paper would seem to require some kind of explanation.

Other information in this White Paper, however, gives some idea of the order of magnitude of the alleged North Vietnamese infiltration. At least 4400 and possibly as many as 7400 "men" were said to have come in from the North in the entire year of 1964. In the six years from 1959 to 1964, "nearly 20,000 VC [Vietcong] officers, soldiers, and technicians" were ordered to enter the South from Hanoi, and an "estimated 17,000 infiltrators" were also dispatched southward in the same period. At this rate, even if these figures can be trusted, the North sent annually only about 6000 men southward, many if not most of them native Southerners. If we exclude the "estimated 17,000 infiltrators" as too vague a classification to merit being included in what is supposed to have been a full-fledged military "invasion," the annual rate must be reduced to less than 3500.[16] One suspects that the United States would not have needed to send hundreds of thousands of its own troops to South Vietnam if the rate of Northern infiltration could have been kept down to some such figure in 1965 and 1966.

But we are not finished with the memorable 325th.

The first official mention of it seems to have been made on April 27, 1965, three months after its alleged appearance, by Secretary of Defense McNamara. He said that "evidence accumulated within the last month," that is, since late March 1965, had confirmed the presence in the northwest sector of South Vietnam "of the 2nd Battalion of the 325th Division of the regular North Vietnamese Army." Then Secretary McNamara went on to estimate the size of the battalion "on the order of 400 to 500 men." [17]

In June 1965, a special subcommittee of the House Committee on Armed Services, headed by Democratic Representative Otis G. Pike of New York, visited South Vietnam, six months after the 325th had allegedly transformed the character of the war. Its report did not even mention North Vietnamese units or their military action in the South; it was written wholly in terms of what was still referred to as a "guerrilla war." [18] By August 1965, however, the 325th's battalion had allegedly grown to a regiment. In that month, General Earle G. Wheeler, Chairman of the Joint Chiefs of Staff, claimed evidence of the infiltration of "at least one regiment of about 1200 to 1400 men, I would think, of the 325th North Vietnamese Division." [19] Since the 325th's movement south was supposed to have started in November 1964, according to Secretary Rusk, it must have, even on this account, taken the North Vietnamese nine months to get only about a single regiment into the fighting zone. But the late Bernard B. Fall, that indefatigable student who refused to be hoodwinked by either side, happened to visit South Vietnam in late 1965. "As of the time I left a few days ago," he wrote in an article published in October, "no Intelligence officer was ready to swear that the 325th as a unit had joined the battle in South Vietnam." [20] A bipartisan group of the Senate Committee on Foreign Relations, headed by Senator Mike Mansfield, visited South Vietnam at the end of 1965. It reported that North Vietnamese regular soldiers made up only 14,000 of the estimated 230,000-man enemy force in December 1965, a year after the celebrated incursion of the Northern 325th Division. This report accepted the official version that North Vietnam regular army troops had begun to enter the South about the end of 1964, but it did not mention this division at all and, in any case, the numbers cited put the whole matter in a different perspective.[21]

But Secretary Rusk would not be satisfied with anything less than a division. At a press conference on November 5, 1965, he again called attention to the 325th Division which, he said, had been "brought down" late last year and early this year.[22] At the Senate Foreign Relations Committee hearings in January-February, 1966, as we have seen, he referred to the division at least three times. On April 27, 1966, in a television interview, he tried to prove that "Hanoi, encouraged and backed by Peiping," had escalated the war by giving as an example "the 325th Division of the North Vietnamese Regular Army" which had been moved "from North Vietnam into South Vietnam, before we started bombing North Vietnam." [23] Again on May 17, 1966, Secretary Rusk told a press conference: "The 325th North Vietnamese Division came from North Vietnam into South Vietnam before we started the bombing of North Vietnam." [24]

This was apparently too much for Senator Mike Mansfield, the Democratic Majority Leader. On June 16, 1966, he delivered an address at Yeshiva University in which he saw fit to make the following observation: "When the sharp increase in the American military effort began in early 1965, it was estimated that only about 400 North Vietnamese soldiers were among the enemy forces in the South which totaled 140,000 at that time." [25] Since the same estimate had previously been made by Secretary of Defense McNamara, Senator Mansfield was not revealing anything new or risking an official denial from the Pentagon, which was presumably in a better position than the Department of State to determine enemy forces. By this time, however, Secretary Mc-

Namara's original reference to the size of the 325th's battalion almost fourteen months earlier had been forgotten, and Ted Knap, a Scripps-Howard staff writer, went to the Department of Defense to inquire about Senator Mansfield's startlingly low figure. "Mansfield's office said the 400 figure came from the Pentagon and was for March 1965," Knap reported. "An official in the office of Defense Secretary Robert McNamara confirmed giving it to Mansfield's office and said it is 'essentially correct.'" The Defense Department spokesman also said: "The figures attributed to Senator Mansfield are accurate and reflect the confirmed North Vietnamese force presence in the South at that time." The spokesman added that "he is aware of the wide difference between the Pentagon's 'confirmed' figures and others' estimates." [26] The "others" were, of course, the military experts of the State Department. Unfortunately, Senator Mansfield's figure was not widely reported in the press, and he himself delicately refrained from suggesting that there might be any incongruity between his figure and the State Department's thesis.[27]

Still, this was not the end of the 325th's strange career as recorded by American officialdom. On May 30, 1966, less than three weeks before Senator Mansfield's address at Yeshiva University, President Johnson delivered a Memorial Day speech in which he tried to explain how confusing the war was:

The conflict in South Vietnam is confusing for many of our people.
    The aggression there does not take the form of organized divisions marching brazenly and openly across frontiers.

On July 12, 1966, Secretary Rusk also discouraged the idea that any significant change had taken place in the character of the war:

Well, we have not seen organized forces on a large scale who have tried to maintain themselves in sustained combat. . . . The primary problem still is to find the other fellow, to locate these units. . . . So the general technique is still basically that of the guerrilla tactic, the hit-and-run, the hide-and-seek, and not that of a sustained fixed engagement.

This seemed to put the war back where it had always been, despite the alleged presence of an entire North Vietnamese division or more in the South.* The previous emphasis on the divisional nature of the northern "invasion" had strongly implied that the North Vietnamese command had gone over to the so-called "third stage" of Mao Tsetung's famous formula, which called for a large-scale counteroffensive by the main armed forces. But Secretary Rusk explicitly denied that the Vietcong or the North Vietnamese regular troops had ever tried to move into this stage.

At this point, it might have seemed more important to stress the numbers rather than the organized units of the North Vietnamese incursion. But, no, Secretary Rusk soon went back to his favorite division. This occasion, on August 25, 1966, was all the more curious inasmuch as it took the form of a joint interview with Secretary McNamara, who was still talking in terms of the gradual infiltration of northern regiments while the Secretary of State was still determined to put an entire North Vietnam division into the south as early as the beginning of 1965.

Q. From what point do you date "on the basis of intelligence" we have the decision to send a full division across?

* A constant reader of the State Department's official publication might also wonder whether its highest officials bother to read each other's speeches and statements. On March 14, 1966, Deputy Under Secretary for Political Affairs U. Alexis Johnson assured an audience in Montreal: "Today we have every reason to believe that *nine* regiments of regular North Vietnamese forces are *fighting in organized units* in South Vietnam" (*Department of State Bulletin,* April 4, 1966, p. 531. My italics, T.D.). On July 7, 1966, Secretary of State Rusk assured a news conference in Tokyo: "There are more than *four* regiments of the official North Vietnamese army now present in South Vietnam" (ibid., August 1, 1966, p. 182. My italics, T.D.). Nine is, of course, more than four, but it does seem odd that Secretary Rusk might not have gone up at least to five or more almost four months after Alexis Johnson had escalated the North Vietnamese regiments to as many as nine.

SECRETARY McNAMARA: They began by sending regiments. So you should talk about formal military units across. I would think that decision was probably made sometime in 1964.

SECRETARY RUSK: It was the end of 1964, the beginning of 1965, one of their divisions as a division moved from North Vietnam to South Vietnam. That was the end of' 1964, the beginning of 1965, before the bombing started, by the way, if you are thinking about escalation.[28]

Unfortunately, no one reminded Secretary McNamara that on April 27, 1965, almost sixteen months earlier, he had "confirmed" the presence in South Vietnam only of a battalion of the 325th Division numbering 400 to 500 men, and that this figure had been repeated by Senator Mansfield on June 16, 1966, and again confirmed by the Pentagon. Since it is safe to assume that the State Department received its military information from the Department of Defense, the vicissitudes of the 325th North Vietnamese Regular Division, as far as we know them from American sources, probably tell us less about the division than about the sources.

Clearly we cannot be sure whether a battalion or a regiment or all of the 325th Division crossed into South Vietnam by January 1965 or at any other time. We could not be sure even if Secretaries Rusk and McNamara agreed, and their disagreement adds a dash of farce to what was otherwise one of the most grievous moments of the war. The most we can conclude from the available evidence is that it was extraordinarily necessary for the Secretary of State to have an "invasion" of South Vietnam by a North Vietnamese organized military unit at least as large as a division before the United States began its systematic bombing of the North in February 1965. The point is not that the North Vietnamese were incapable of making such a move; it may simply not have suited their interests to give the United States the pretext which American officials had been unmistakably hinting would bring on large-scale intervention. If Secretary McNamara is right and they sent in 400 to 500 regular troops, the number is too small for one to imagine that this was Ho Chi Minh's way of signifying that he was willing to take the risk of a "big war" against overwhelming odds.

We may still not know much about the elusive 325th, but we can know a great deal about how it was bandied to and fro by high American officials who could not even convince each other. The overwhelming impression one gets from studying the record is that this was an incredibly bumbling diplomatic operation. One almost yearns for the days of John Foster Dulles and his elegant casuistries. Perhaps the most perplexing problem raised by this and other episodes of the Vietnamese war is not whether the United States is right or wrong but rather whether it has the traditions, the ideology, and the bureaucracy to carry off such operations in Asia with the necessary finesse and dispatch. Those who fear the encroachments of "American imperialism" might take some comfort in the thought that it has come too late into the world to develop the men and the methods for doing a good job of it.

Turning Point Number 5 (Part II)

It would have been a sorry moment in American history if so few North Vietnamese troops could have panicked Washington into making such a far-reaching change of course. The truth was bad enough, but not that bad. The Mansfield report came much closer by putting the emphasis where it belonged—on South Vietnamese weakness rather than North Vietnamese strength. "In short," the report stated grimly, "a total collapse of the Saigon government's authority appeared imminent in the early months of 1965." And it linked the need for large-scale American combat forces to this threatened collapse, which it did not attribute to the infiltration of a few hundred North Vietnamese regulars. Later, Secretary McNamara revealed how menacing the outlook had been in the first half of 1965. The United States, he said, had put over 100,000 men into the South in about 120 days to prevent a "disaster" to the South Vietnamese armed forces. The latter, according to him, were being overpowered and destroyed by the Vietcong and Northern Army infiltrators in the summer of 1965. The United States intervened in force, he declared, because the enemy had been "approaching possible victory." [29]

The decision to bomb North Vietnamese military targets was made in February 1965. The decision to commit American combat troops on a large scale was also made in 1965, though different periods of the year have been given by different officials. At the end of 1964, the American combat forces in Vietnam numbered 23,000.[30] The first wave of the vastly enlarged force landed on March 6, 1965. By May 1965, according to the Mansfield report, the number had increased to 34,000 but it was still "basically an advisory organization." The report added that the logistic system to support the vastly expanded United States effort had started "almost from scratch in May of 1965." By July, the United States forces had jumped to 75,000, and on July 28 President Johnson announced that they would go up to 125,000 "almost immediately." [31] By November 20, 1965, the figure was 165,000.[32]

General William Westmoreland, the United States Commander in Vietnam, later revealed: "Early in 1965 we knew that the enemy hoped to deliver the *coup de grâce* by launching a major summer offensive to cut the Republic of Vietnam in two with a drive across the central highlands to the sea. I had to make a decision, and did. I chose a rapid build-up of combat forces, in the full knowledge that we should not have a fully developed logistic base to support those forces." [33] When the former American Ambassador, General Maxwell D. Taylor, was asked when the commitment was made for active American participation in the military operations, he replied: "We, insofar as the use of our combat forces are concerned, that took place, of course, only in the spring of 1965. In the air, we had been participating more actively over two or three years." [34] Ambassador Lodge once dated the "turning point" as July 28, 1965, when the President formally announced the decision to commit American troops on a large scale.[35] According to another source, President Johnson sent Secretary McNamara to Saigon on July 14, 1965, to determine exactly what manpower General Westmoreland needed. McNamara, it is said, returned with the recommendation that the American forces should be quadrupled within a year from the 70,000 troops already there, with another 50,000 sent as soon as possible. Mr. Johnson started the last week of intensive studies leading to his "grave decision" on July 21, and made it public a week later.[36] From this version one gathers that a considerable build-up took place between March and July 1965, but that the "open-ended" decision was actually made between July 21 and 28.*

This background shows that incidents such as the Tonkin Gulf and Pleiku could not possibly account for the decisions in early 1965 to bomb North Vietnam and to introduce thousands more American combat forces into South Vietnam. They were occasioned by a far more endemic and fundamental factor—the progressive deterioration toward the end of 1964 of General Nguyen Khanh's South Vietnamese regime and the subsequent near-breakdown of the South Vietnamese armed forces. South Vietnamese regimes could, by their very weakness, exert an influence akin to political blackmail on American policy. If one of them threatened to disintegrate, and demanded some American action to prevent it from committing suicide, that action was likely to be forthcoming sooner or later, even if the President and Secretary of State were just then protesting that they had no intention of doing any such thing. The American decisions in early 1965 were basically intended to bolster the morale of

* General Earle G. Wheeler also specified the summer of 1965 as the time of decision. "By the late spring of that year, due to a combination of causes, the Viet Cong/North Vietnamese Army was threatening to overwhelm the armed forces of South Vietnam. That summer, at the request of the South Vietnamese, the United States made a decision to commit major forces to halt aggression" (*Department of State Bulletin*, February 6, 1967, p. 187).

the South Vietnam government and to seek some way out
of the military cul-de-sac in the South by extending the war
to North Vietnam. The Gulf of Tonkin and Pleiku incidents
were no more than extenuating circumstances enabling the
President to obscure the real significance and ease the shock
for the benefit of American public opinion.

The crisis in 1965 in South Vietnam was far more inti-
mately related to South Vietnamese disintegration than to
North Vietnamese infiltration. General Khanh, whom Secretary McNamara had praised so highly in March 1964, turned
out to be another illusion. At the Senate Committee hearings,
General Taylor, the American Ambassador in Saigon from
June 1964 to July 1965, the very period leading to the vast
American build-up, was asked whether the present regime of
Air Vice Marshal Nguyen Cao Ky was more stable than its
predecessors had been. Taylor replied: "Almost anything
would be an improvement over what I saw while I was Ambassador." [37] John Mecklin explained the South Vietnamese
"malaise" of 1965 in these terms: "The nation was desperately weary of war, its people verging on such despair that
they would soon accept anything to get it over with." [38]
Bernard B. Fall attributed the trouble to the fact that Diem's
successors evolved a policy which he called "Diemism without Diem." [39] Premier Nguyen Cao Ky described his predecessors in these terms: "Every Prime Minister or even Minister
said: 'I'm here for two months, so money, money, and if
necessary I'll go abroad.' " [40] He explained his own accession
to power in June 1965 as the result of the shortcomings of
the South Vietnamese "politicians," who, he said, "were unable to find appropriate measures to solve their differences." [41]

In effect, the South Vietnamese crisis of 1965 was essentially a reprise of the 1963 crisis, not a totally new phenom-
enon as argued by the State Department. The qualitative
change came *after* the American decision to bomb North
Vietnam and pour troops into South Vietnam. The American
combat forces increased from 23,000 at the end of 1964 to

165,700 on November 20, 1965.[42] According to the Mansfield report, the best available estimates in December 1965 placed the total Vietcong strength in South Vietnam at 230,000 men, of which the North Vietnamese regulars allegedly numbered only 14,000.[43] As in the case of the Dominican Republic, where the State Department tried to play the numbers game with its lists of Dominican Communists, the numbers game of North Vietnamese Army regulars also backfired, thanks mainly to Secretary McNamara and Senator Mansfield, who may or may not have intended to bring about this result.

Again it may be well to note that the decisions of 1965 to bomb North Vietnam and to send thousands of American troops to South Vietnam are not merely or mainly of historical interest. They overshadowed the entire future course of the war and the problem of bringing it to an end. The bombing was intended to reduce the flow of men and materials from the North or to make it more costly and difficult for the North Vietnamese to send them southward. It appears to have been far less successful in the first respect than in the second.

But another question arises: Would it have been so necessary to reduce the flow of men and material to the south if the United States had not made such fateful decisions two years earlier? The figures given by official American sources themselves raise this question. In the summer of 1964, Secretary of State Rusk gave the total enemy force as consisting of 30,000 "hard-core" Vietcong and 60,000 "sort of part-time help or casual help." [44] The Vietcong was doing very well at the time with this limited force. The State Department's White Paper of February 1965 estimated that the "so-called hard-core forces" of the Vietcong numbered 35,000, with another 60,000 to 80,000 of "local forces." [45] This was not a striking increase in over six months. At that point, the bombing started. The Northern troops began to come down, and the more we bombed, the more they came. On August 25, 1966, Secretary McNamara claimed that about 40,000 Northern troops had infiltrated southward during the first eight months of 1966, twice the rate of 1965.[46] In February 1967, General Earle G. Wheeler estimated the enemy force as consisting of about 235,000 Vietcong, both in main-force and guerrilla units, and somewhere between 45,000 and 48,000 North Vietnamese regulars.[47] One wonders how much more the enemy forces would have increased if we had bombed even more to reduce them.

V

"Civil War" or
"Foreign Aggression"

For our purposes, it is less important to determine whether
North Vietnam provoked the United States to intervene in
force or vice versa than to find out what the enlarged American military role in 1965 signified in terms of the problem
we are examining—the supersession of political by military
instrumentalities in the conduct of American foreign policy.

The alleged North Vietnamese Army incursion at the
end of 1964 provided the President and the State Department
with a rationalization for proclaiming a fundamental change
in the character of the war. Until 1965, the official American
line had still considered it a predominantly "civil war." In
that year, according to the policymakers in Washington, it
became a "foreign aggression." The "foreigners" in this case
were the North Vietnamese, who were apparently invading
a "foreign" country, South Vietnam.

Indeed, American officials began to reinterpret the entire
course of the Vietnamese war and to rewrite its history in order to make it a "foreign aggression" from the very outset. As
we have seen, John Foster Dulles tried to do something of
the sort as far back as 1953. But Dulles was ahead of his
time in this respect, and as late as 1964 Secretary of Defense
McNamara still emphasized the "largely indigenous support"
the Vietcong was receiving. The new line made its first ma-

jor appearance in the State Department's White Paper of February 1965. Four years earlier, however, the State Department had issued another White Paper, which had explicitly stated: "The basic pattern of Vietcong activity is not new, of course. It operated with minor variations in China, and Mao Tse-tung's theories on the conduct of guerrilla warfare are known to every Vietcong agent and cadre. Most of the same methods were used in Malaya, in Greece, in the Philippines, in Cuba, and in Laos." [1] But the authors of the 1965 White Paper had apparently forgotten what their predecessors had taught. The 1965 line was just the opposite of the 1961 line: "The war in Vietnam is a new kind of war, a fact as yet poorly understood in most parts of the world." If it was poorly understood, the State Department had only itself to blame for having misled everyone on this point for years. The new version went on: "Vietnam is *not* another Greece, where indigenous guerrilla forces used friendly neighboring territory as a sanctuary. Vietnam is *not* another Malaya, where Communist guerrillas were, for the most part, physically distinguishable from the peaceful majority they sought to control. Vietnam is *not* another Philippines, where Communist guerrillas were physically separated from their moral and physical support." [2] Clearly the State Department could not always have been right in its understanding of this war.

The thesis of the 1965 White Paper was that Hanoi had been responsible for the war from 1954 onward, and that the southern Vietcong and National Liberation Front were nothing but extensions and creatures of the North Vietnamese Communist Party. In the following months American spokesmen restated and elaborated on this theme in various ways.* In August 1965 General Taylor defended the United States air attacks by arguing that they gave the South Vietnamese people the sense of being able to strike back for the first time

* The most extreme version was perhaps put forward by Under Secretary of State George W. Ball in an address on January 30, 1966. The National Liberation Front, he said, "is purely and simply a factitious organization created by Hanoi to reinforce a fiction" (*Department of State Bulletin*, February 14, 1966, p. 243).

against "the source of all their evil, namely, North Vietnam."
He admitted that the southern Vietcong provided the manpower but insisted that "Hanoi is the source of the Vietcong
strength" because its aid was indispensable.[3] By September,
Secretary of Defense McNamara had forgotten that only the
year before he had conceded that the Vietcong received "large
indigenous support" in the South, and now he referred contemptuously to the "small dissident minority in South Vietnam."[4] Early the following year, McNamara was quoted in
the Senate as having said flatly: "The war in Vietnam was
not and is not a civil war. It is a direct and flagrant aggression
by North Vietnam."[5] In January 1966 a high State Department official would allow only that "a number of indigenous Southerners" was included in the Vietcong military
forces.[6]

The post-1965 mystification of the Vietnamese war was
codified, in its most naïve form, in President Johnson's State
of the Union message on January 12, 1966. In it, he told of a
fabled land which had enjoyed peace until its wicked neighbor to the north had decided to molest it. The tale began:

Not too many years ago Vietnam was a peaceful, if
troubled, land. In the north was an independent Communist government. In the south a people struggled to
build a nation with the friendly help of the United States.

But then the villains appeared:

There were some in South Vietnam who wished to force
Communist rule on their own people. But their progress
was slight. Their hope of success was dim. Then, little more
than six years ago, North Vietnam decided on conquest,
and from that day to this, soldiers and supplies have moved
from North to South in a swelling stream that swallowed
the remnants of revolution in aggression.

This little allegory seemed necessary to allay the moral
qualms of American policymakers about massive American
intervention in Vietnam. Under Secretary of State George
W. Ball made the remarkable admission in January 1966

that the United States had no right to inject itself into a civil war. "For if the Vietnam war were merely what the Communists say it is, an indigenous rebellion," he declared, "then the United States has no business taking sides in the conflict and helping one side to defeat the other by force of arms."[7] This inhibition may explain why American officials have gone to such lengths to deny that an essentially "indigenous rebellion" has been raging in Vietnam.

A Special Kind of Civil War

The first thing that strikes one about the post-1965 official American position on the nature of the Vietnam conflict is its cut-off date. Though the rewriting of history has sometimes gone all the way back to 1954, the more responsible statements have maintained, as President Johnson expressed it in his 1966 State of the Union message, that North Vietnam's "invasion" or "aggression" started in 1959 and 1960. At best, then, this theory implies that the pre-1959 conflict was "indigenous" or that there was no pre-1959 conflict at all. It fractures the historical continuity of this struggle which, as every serious historian recognizes, has far deeper roots and began in earnest at least as early as 1946.

One question, bearing on the "indigenous" nature of the struggle in the South, can be answered with some confidence, even on the basis of American sources. It is: Who has been doing most of the fighting, Southern or Northern Vietnamese?

Until the end of 1964, no effort was made to hide the fact that the war in South Vietnam was being conducted by South Vietnamese and even that they could get along almost indefinitely without the North. In an interview published in February 1965, Henry Cabot Lodge was asked whether the bombing of Communist supply lines outside South Vietnam was an "effective measure." Lodge would only say that "there was something in it," but he went on:

But I don't think you can win this struggle entirely by bombing supply lines. I believe that the Communist-led

Viet Cong, certainly south of Saigon, could be self-sustaining for a long, long time. . . . I don't think you could seal the borders—and, if you could, I think the Viet Cong, certainly those south of Saigon, could go on for a long, long time without any external supply.[8]

Senator Stephen M. Young of Ohio visited Southeast Asia from September 28 to October 20, 1965. Later, he reported in the Senate:

It is my considered judgment that South Vietnam is of no strategic importance whatever to the defense of the United States. Furthermore, the fact is that the conflict raging in Vietnam is a civil war. General Westmoreland stated to me that the bulk of the Vietcong fighting in South Vietnam were born and reared in South Vietnam. General [Joseph W.] Stilwell, in Thailand, went further. He stated that 80 per cent of the Vietcong fighting in the Mekong Delta area south of Saigon, were born and reared in that area. They were not infiltrators or Communists from the North.[9]

On January 28, 1966, at the Senate Foreign Relations Committee hearings, Secretary of State Rusk said:

I would suppose that 80 per cent of those who are called Viet Cong are or have been Southerners.[10]

General Wallace M. Greene, Jr., Commandant of the United States Marine Corps, inadvertently, perhaps, cut the ground from under the American position in an interview published in September 1966. General Greene first made the point that, for North Vietnam too, the critical decision rested in the hands of the "people in the South," not in those of its own Northern forces.

I feel that the real key in this war is whether we have success or failure in ripping out the guerrilla infrastructure from these villages and hamlets. I think the North Vietnamese are watching this, because they know that, if they lose the people in the South, they lose the war.

The guerrilla infrastructure in the villages and hamlets,

General Greene said, was made up of what he called "black pajama" guerrillas. Asked who they were, he replied:

> Most are local people, the people who were born in the villages and hamlets of South Vietnam, frequently led by cadres trained in the North and reinfiltrated into the South.[11]

For the overwhelming majority of the Vietcong, therefore, only the material support and training came from the North. But even in these respects the various stages of this war must be kept in mind.

The material support had not always come from the North. On the contrary, the Vietcong had, at least until 1965, lived off the land in the South and, more importantly, its arms had mainly originated *in the United States*.

In March 1963, General Paul D. Harkins discussed this aspect of the war. The Washington *Post* correspondent in Saigon, Ed Meagher, reported his remarks as follows:

> Harkins said the guerrillas obviously are not being reinforced or supplied systematically from North Vietnam, China or any place else. He said they apparently depend for weapons primarily upon whatever they can capture. Many of their weapons, he said, are homemade.[12]

The State Department's forthright Director of Intelligence, Thomas L. Hughes, declared in Panama on June 8, 1964, that "by far the greater part of the Vietcong forces in South Vietnam are South Vietnamese, the preponderance of Vietcong weapons come not from Communist countries but from capture, purchase, and local manufacture." [13] Three months later, Bernard B. Fall stated that "90 per cent of the weapons being used by the Vietcong are captured American weapons." [14] Ironically, then, the Americans had provided both sides of the Vietnamese struggle with arms, one side deliberately, the other unintentionally.

Even the State Department's White Paper of February 1965 was incapable of hiding the fact that most of the Vietcong weapons had come from the South Vietnamese, who had obtained them from the United States. The White Paper set out to provide "incontrovertible evidence of Hanoi's elaborate program to supply its forces in the South with weapons, ammunition, and other supplies." For this purpose, the document's Appendix D presented a list of weapons and other military equipment submitted on January 29, 1964, by the South Vietnamese government to the International Control Commission. This list contained exactly 179 weapons of foreign Communist origin captured in the preceding eighteen months. Of these 179 weapons, 69, or 40 per cent, were Czechoslovak; 65, or 36 per cent, were Soviet; 24, or 13 per cent, were French guns "modified" in North Vietnam; and 18, or 10 per cent, were Chinese.[15] The most striking thing about this list, which was supposed to prove so much, was the paucity of the numbers. An enterprising Washington editor obtained some additional information from the Department of Defense and made some even more revealing calculations. In a 3-year period, from 1962 to 1964, he was told, 15,100 weapons had been captured from the Vietcong guerrillas and 27,400 weapons had been lost to them.[16] If we may assume that about half, or 7550 weapons, had been captured in each eighteen-month period, the 179 weapons allegedly originating in Communist countries constituted 2.5 per cent of the total. Captured American weapons must have made up the other 97.5 per cent or close to it. Once again, it seems the State Department would have been better advised to say as little as possible in order not to produce "incontrovertible evidence" for the other side of the argument.

There remains, then, the factor of indoctrination and training. Until 1965, as we have seen, the State Department's White Paper alleged that a grand total of almost 37,000 officers, soldiers, technicians, and other "infiltrators" had come down from the North in the six-year period from 1959 to 1964. Since the total enemy forces at the beginning of 1965 were estimated by Senator Mansfield at 140,000, the percentage at that time of those sent down from the North must have been quite small. But they may very well have been far more important qualitatively than quantitatively; the Southerners infiltrated from the North may have, toward the end of the six-year period, provided the Vietcong with the core of its leadership and cadre. Nevertheless, in manpower and in weapons, North Vietnam was not, at least until 1965, the main or even a significant provider. It is fair to conclude that until about 1960 the Vietcong was strictly a Southern enterprise, and until 1965 the Northern contribution was mainly limited to training.

Did the training of Southern cadres in the North prevent the struggle in the South from being a "civil war" or "indigenous rebellion"? If so, there have been few internecine struggles in modern times so free of foreign influence and interference that they may be called "civil wars." The classic case was perhaps the Spanish Civil War of 1936 to 1939. No one questions that it was integrally and profoundly a civil war. Yet foreign troops and matériel on a large scale were introduced on both sides, though the Republicans benefited far less than their enemies: General Francisco Franco enjoyed the active support of entire Italian fascist divisions.

A "pure" civil war almost never occurs any longer. It might be said that national civil wars now tend, or at least threaten, to develop into international civil wars. The Spanish Civil War was certainly the outstanding example of this genre. And yet it was undeniably a civil war because its origins and dynamism were deeply embedded in Spanish national antagonisms. Indeed, it may be held that the international forces injected into the struggle enabled the civil war to keep going beyond what its own energies might have permitted. This should be enough to warn us that a "civil war" does not turn overnight into a "foreign aggression" because foreign elements have entered into it. It is necessary to view the struggle as a whole, as a historical entity from beginning to end, to understand the nature of the conflict and to determine whether it is a civil war or foreign aggression. The official American thesis has so muddled the problem that its expo-

nents do not seem to know any longer whether the Vietnamese conflict was ever a civil war or to recognize that a modern civil war may contain a good many foreign elements and
still remain, in essence, a civil war.

The American case made itself all the more dubious by
equating North Vietnam with a "foreign" country in order
to invent a "foreign aggression." Clearly the relationship
of North and South Vietnam was not the same as, for example, that of Germany and Poland in 1939. A conflict between
brothers is not the same as a conflict between strangers. The
Final Declaration of the Geneva Conference of 1954 had
explicitly stated that "the military demarcation line is provisional and should not in any way be interpreted as consti-
tuting a political or territorial boundary." In his State of the
Union message in January 1966, President Johnson committed
the United States to "stand by" the Geneva Agreements.
As a perceptive correspondent, Charles Mohr of *The New
York Times,* pointed out, "the distinction between North
and South Vietnam is not made by Vietnamese in the same
way that it's made by the Department of State in Washington. Even if North Vietnam is committing aggression against
South Vietnam, that in itself is a form of civil war. This is a
partitioned country, but it's one country. Essentially it once
was." [17]

Until 1965, moreover, North Vietnam almost wholly limited itself to training and sending native Southerners to fight
in the South. Roger Hilsman, the former Assistant Secretary
of State for Far Eastern Affairs, quite accurately predicted
what large-scale bombing of the North would do to this
North Vietnamese policy. Hilsman cautioned:

> It would be well for the advocates of bombing and other
> "easy" solutions to such problems to remember that Hanoi's
> policy was not to infiltrate *North* Vietnamese into South
> Vietnam—the infiltrators have almost all been Southerners
> sympathetic to communism who went North in 1954.
> Hanoi has kept to this self-imposed limitation partly to
> maintain the fiction that the origins of the fighting in

South Vietnam were internal, but partly to minimize the risk of retaliation against their precious factories. Once the factories are gone, so is the deterrent.[18]

Professor Hilsman may or may not be right about the reasons he ascribes to the North Vietnamese for their "self-imposed limitation." But he was undoubtedly right about the effect of massive bombing on that limitation. He was able to follow the unfolding of American policy from the inside at close range, and, as he feared, the bombings brought the Northerners in increasing numbers into the war; and the increase of Northerners brought on more bombing.

Again and again, as one studies the record, the official American ideologists of this war seem to have hit on the least persuasive and tenable rationalizations to justify one or another American action. For purely legalistic reasons, in order to avoid violating that diplomatic metaphysics known as "international law," the Department of State considered it necessary to deny that the United States was injecting itself in an "indigenous rebellion" or even had the right to do so. But if it was not an "indigenous rebellion," what was it? The legal pundits had no difficulty coming up with an answer: it was a "foreign" invasion or aggression on the part of North Vietnam. If that did not suffice, they went one step further and made it an aggression on the part of the Chinese Communists, who allegedly used the North Vietnamese Communists as their surrogates. Or it was a combination of both.

One wonders whether anyone would have been any more scandalized if the United States had taken the position that it had a vital self-interest to inject itself in what Charles Mohr called "a special kind of civil war" with international implications and repercussions. Such a position might have been good or bad for the United States, Vietnam, and the world, but at least it would have made more sense.

Voices of Conscience

As long as American policy regarded the struggle as primarily a "civil war," the American line emphasized that the political instrumentality was at least as important as the military. As Secretary McNamara put it in March 1964, "there can be no such thing as a purely 'military' solution to the war in South Vietnam." But, as a corollary of the theory of "foreign aggression," the priorities assigned to the political and military instrumentalities were reversed. Suddenly, almost overnight, American policy shifted into its military phase, and all the blame was heaped on a few hundred or at most a few thousand North Vietnamese Army regulars. American and South Vietnamese officials continued to pay lip service to political and social reforms, but these came to be regarded as the indefinitely postponed by-product rather than the indispensable precondition of military "victory."

By coincidence, of course, all the political and social gimmicks which had been advertised to save South Vietnam from Communist seduction had exhausted themselves by 1965. The "strategic hamlet" program launched in March 1962 had died with Diem in November 1963. In the South, where 2 per cent of the landowners had owned 45 per cent of the land, "land reform" had given the peasants little land and less reform. "Counterinsurgency," "pacification," and all the other well-meaning slogans had bogged down in the South Vietnamese inability or unwillingness to give them meaningful implementation. The House Committee on Armed Services group, under Representative Pike, which made a survey on the spot in June 1965, observed that "rural reconstruction" had been "no great success." The Senate Foreign Relations group, under Senator Mansfield, which investigated the situation at the end of 1965, reported that the so-called pacification or civic-action program had been permitted in large measure to "lapse" after Diem's fall.

The theory of "foreign aggression," therefore, served the purpose of enabling the United States to take flight from the intractable problems of the South and to seek comfort in the illusion that the solution to the whole war was located in the North.

But, to the credit of an important part of the American

press, glimmers of reality persisted in breaking through the official orthodoxy. Just as the decay and downfall of Ngo Dinh Diem's regime in 1963 had caused a crisis of conscience on the part of American correspondents in Saigon, so the political and social failure after 1965 resulted in some equally troubled soul-searching.

In *Newsweek* of September 12, 1966, Everett G. Martin, the bureau chief in Saigon, tried to get at the "crucial error" in our Vietnam policy. The main problem, as he saw it, was nothing less than the failure, at that late date, to make the Vietnamese people feel that it was their war. "And it is indeed true," he wrote, "that although the United States has put heavy emphasis on the need to win the support of peasants living in areas contested by the Vietcong, we have yet to convince even those Vietnamese dwelling in the most secure areas of the country that there is a cause worth fighting for." In the same unrelenting fashion, he added that the Vietnamese in the South "seem to be able to maintain an almost total impassivity," that "most Vietnamese appear to be so many stoic islands, as immune to the war as they are to the monsoon rains," that the American soldier on leave in major Vietnamese cities carried away the overriding impression "of a people abnormally detached from the brutal reality he knows in the battlefield." He noted that Vietnamese soldiers had no incentive to fight aggressively as a result of the "callous unconcern" for their welfare, but that perhaps even more disturbing was "the fact that the greatest indifference to the war effort is found among Vietnam's young people." Relations between the Americans and the South Vietnamese had "degenerated into a kind of ill-defined antagonism," reminiscent of the late Diem period. One American official commented on the growing American cynicism: "You don't find any idealists around any more. They have either given up and gone home, or they are just serving out their time."

For Martin the "root of the problem" appeared to be largely political. He was chiefly impressed by the fact that "while Americans have democratic institutions to defend, the Vietnamese have none." The remedy, he thought, was the encouragement of democracy on a local scale, in the provinces, where the Vietnamese people could learn what it means to make their wishes known through a local council and see them respected by Saigon-appointed officials. Vietnam had once had a local election system which had made the village, in Bernard B. Fall's words, "the real cradle of a Jeffersonian type of representative government in the country." [19] Not even the French had tampered with this traditional village democracy. But in June 1956, Ngo Dinh Diem had arbitrarily abolished this entire system in favor of personal appointees who soon became the targets of Communist terrorists. "Diemism without Diem" had changed nothing in this respect. "We Americans," Martin lamented, "have wasted all the years since the revolution against Diem by not fostering local democracy in areas that were secure. Instead, we have allowed the Vietnamese corps commanders and their subordinates to become further entrenched as local war lords."

A more social analysis of the problem was made by Neil Sheehan in *The New York Times Magazine* of October 9, 1966. Sheehan had served two tours of duty in South Vietnam since 1962, first for the United Press International and more recently for *The New York Times*. He agreed with Martin that Americans came to work in South Vietnam with enthusiasm and good intentions, but extended experience made them leave the country victims of "the cynicism that pervades Vietnamese life." No exception to this rule, he sought to account for the monotonous miscarriage of desperately needed reforms urged by the Americans, such as rent reduction and land distribution. This is what he found:

> All of these measures have been sabotaged because the regimes were and are composed of men who are members of, or who are allied with, mandarin families that held title to properties they have no intention of renouncing. While there are some patriotic and decent individuals among them, most of the men who rule Saigon have, like the Bourbons, learned nothing and forgotten nothing. They

seek to retain what privileges they have and to regain those they have lost.

It was not easy for Americans to read, and it could not have been easy for an American to write—in 1966:

> In Vietnam, only the Communists represent revolution and social change, for better or worse according to a man's politics. The Communist party is the one truly national organization that permeates both North and South Vietnam. The men who lead the party today, Ho Chi Minh and the other members of the Politburo in Hanoi, directed the struggle for independence from France and in the process captured much of the deeply felt nationalism of the Vietnamese people. Perhaps because of this, the Communists, despite their brutality and deceit, remain the only Vietnamese capable of rallying millions of their countrymen to sacrifice and hardship in the name of the nation and the only group not dependent on foreign bayonets for survival.*

Still, even Mr. Sheehan could see no way other than to continue to prosecute the war. But he did not conceal his deepest misgivings:

> We shall, I am afraid, have to put up with our Vietnamese mandarin allies. We shall not be able to reform them and it is unlikely that we shall be able to find any other Vietnamese willing to cooperate with us. . . .
>
> But I simply cannot help worrying that, in the process of waging this war, we are corrupting ourselves. I wonder . . . whether the United States or any nation has the right to inflict this suffering and degradation on another people for its own ends.

Not a few American journalists lived up to the highest ideals of their calling in the Cuban, Dominican, and Viet-

---

* Not too long before, a similar view had been expressed by none other than Premier Nguyen Cao Ky to James Reston, who wrote: "Even Premier Ky told this reporter today that the Communists were closer to the people's yearnings for social justice and an independent national life than his own government" (*The New York Times,* September 1, 1965).

nam crises. But the unflinching honesty and moral passion of Sheehan's article almost put it in a class by itself.* Lest the reader think that I have chosen unduly critical or "liberal" views of the war, I invite his attention to later and equally candid reports in unimpeachably conservative publications. According to Marvin L. Stone in the *U.S. News & World Report* of December 5, 1966, the political situation in South Vietnam at the end of 1966 was worse than ever:

> The political fabric of the country is still shedding. Social progress is held in tight rein. After all these years, the war against the guerrillas in the countryside has not yet really begun.

Stone, who had visited South Vietnam many times since the French had pulled out ten years before, found that "there is less effective presence in the villages now than there was three years ago." Corruption was worse than it had been under the late Ngo Dinh Diem. Domestic output had been going down steadily. The guerrillas' success in the past year "has been almost astonishing." The peasants were suffering more than before at the hands of both Communist extortionists and extortionate landowners. Of the "mandarin families" in South Vietnam, Stone wrote:

> Not only is government security lacking, but Saigon's land-reform program, so vital to the aspirations of peasants, has never really been put in motion. In the secure areas, tenant farmers—that means 70 per cent of all farmers in the Delta —still are forced to pay up to 50 per cent and more of their rice crops to absentee landlords who have no obligation in return. A law on the books since 1955 sets the limit at 25 per cent.
>
> Americans here insist that no progress will be made so long as the men at the top in Saigon are members of mandarin families, or allied with families which have vested

---

* Exception was taken to Mr. Sheehan's "grotesque conclusion that we must continue to prosecute an evil war that cannot be won" by another correspondent with wide experience in Vietnam and elsewhere, David Schoenbrun, in *The Columbia University Forum,* Fall 1966, pp. 4-9.

interests in land that they have no intention of relinquishing.

And another experienced correspondent, Robert Sherrod, summed up his impressions of the war in the pro-war *Life* magazine of January 27, 1967:

After nearly two months in Vietnam I find this the most hateful war we have ever fought. Surely, we never would have got into it if we had known how deep was the well, but we are the victims of one tragic miscalculation after another. We find ourselves supporting a government of mandarins with little basis of popular support, fighting for an army that has little inclination to do its own fighting.

But he too saw no other way than to continue doing what we were doing, hope that "a merciful Providence will show us a way out," and pray. No American official would, of course, have made such a confession, but "Providence and prayer" might not be a bad description of what American policy had been reduced to.

John Mecklin, the former United States Public Affairs Officer, returned to South Vietnam in 1966 and 1967, and his factual report is worth giving in some detail:

On two recent trips to Vietnam, after an absence of two-and-one-half years, my first impressions were uniformly dismaying. Saigon had visibly decayed, much of its charm having been replaced by shabbiness. On a Sunday afternoon on the terrace of the Continental Palace Hotel, once one of the fashionable spots in Asia, a loudspeaker blared a re-broadcast of a baseball game from the Armed Forces Radio Station. At American installations, which are everywhere, young, nervous sentries stood with rifles at the ready, butt on hip, muzzle in the air, finger on the trigger. Everywhere, too, there were barricades and barbwire to frustrate Vietcong terrorists, but having the additional effect of separating the Americans from the people.

Saigon has become a rapacious city. Among the Vietnamese there is a mood of "I'll get mine," and it intensifies each time a political crisis sets office-holders to worrying about losing their jobs. Inflation has become an incalculably dangerous problem. A shoeshine boy with a bright-eyed smile can earn more in an hour with GI customers than his father may bring home in a day; and sad to say, newspaper accounts of the new élite of Saigon prostitutes are all too true. An intelligence officer told me of a report that the Vietcong in the nearby countryside have actually been paying the bus fare to send peasants into Saigon to see for themselves how the Americans are corrupting the city. Another American official told me about a case on the Cambodian frontier where a gang of Vietnamese soldiers had been caught using their Army trucks to smuggle stolen goods across the border.

I also found a subtle but distinct change in the mood among civilian Americans in Saigon. It has never been a happy community; table-hammering anger about the stupidities in Washington or in the embassy down the street has always been a way of life. But now I was struck by a new feeling of discouragement. An official whom I regard as one of the ablest men in the U.S. Mission called the situation "a case of advanced cancer." Another first-rate man, a Special Forces officer, remarked bitterly that "all we're doing here is a bunch of bloody push-ups." The only hopeful thing I can say about the Saigon atmosphere in 1967 is that I was told it was worse a year ago. The significance of this bleak picture, however, is not that the Americans on the scene, or even the Vietnamese, are quitters. Rather it is that a limit exists to human tolerance of ineptitude and endless years at dead center. One of the biggest problems in Vietnam is a dismal absence of effective, imaginative leadership, not only among the Vietnamese but among the Americans, and this complaint applies as much in Washington as it does in Saigon.

Yet, Mecklin concluded that South Vietnam was essential to American security because an American defeat there would "demoralize hundreds of millions of people the world over." He rejected any compromise with the Vietnamese Communists and even considered any negotiation "extraordinarily dangerous." But he also rejected escalation in the form of increased bombing of North Vietnam, or attacking villages in the South. In the end, he thought it most important to "forget about the illusion of some quickie escape from Vietnam," and though this implied a long, clumsy and "needlessly destructive" war, he concluded that it had to continue until "sooner or later the Vietnamese themselves will evolve a healthy, viable government which can survive without foreign help." [20]

One of the saving and most hopeful elements on the American scene throughout the Vietnamese war has been the relative independence and integrity of an important part of the American press. The wonder is not that much of the press was uncritical and covered up for official policy, but that a good part refused to do so. Whatever one may have thought of that policy, the American political system, at least until the spring of 1967, had passed the most severe test a democracy can be subjected to—freedom of the press in wartime.

VI

Escalation: Force and Theory

One peculiarity of American policy in the Vietnamese war has repeated itself again and again. The United States has somehow made a habit of doing what it had protested it would not, could not, do.

In July 1965, only a month after he had taken office, Premier Nguyen Cao Ky presented his own plan for winning the war. He called for more American troops to do more of the fighting in direct contact with the enemy in order to enable the South Vietnamese troops to devote themselves to rearguard "pacification." The television news correspondent Walter Cronkite reiterated: "For the allied troops to go out and hold the perimeter defenses while the Vietnamese can rebuild behind them." Premier Ky replied: "Yes. Right, right."[1]

At that time, this division of labor between the American and South Vietnamese troops seemed utterly repugnant to American policymakers. The United States had only 75,000 troops in Vietnam in July 1965, though ten days after Premier Ky's free advice President Johnson announced an almost immediate increase of 50,000. The American build-up was then designed, however, to prevent a total South Vietnamese collapse, and Premier Ky's plan obviously called for many more tens and even hundreds of thousands.

Premier Ky's plan also brought back unhappy memories

of the French defeat in Vietnam. In effect, the South Vietnamese Premier had proposed that the Americans should take on the major responsibility for the fighting and use the South Vietnamese troops as their "pacification" auxiliaries. At least one outstanding American general, distinguished for his intellectuality, soon warned of imitating the French in this respect.

In August 1965, almost exactly a month after Premier Ky had broached his plan, General Maxwell D. Taylor discussed the difference between the French and American conduct of the war. He pointed out that the French had made the fatal mistake of using their own armed services as the "basic force" to prolong their rule, and had relegated the South Vietnamese to the role of "auxiliaries." As for the Americans, he boasted, "just the reverse is true now." The Americans, he explained, were merely "supplementing" the South Vietnamese, who were still the "main force"—as they had not been in the bad old French days. General Taylor was asked, "Would you say, though, that this was their war, or isn't this getting more and more to be our war?" The general replied confidently, "Not in the slightest. This is their war. We want it to stay that way." In the same interview General Taylor said of the war, "We couldn't take it over and couldn't do it if we tried."[2]

But it refused to stay that way.

Turning Point Number 6 (Fall 1966)

The hard, stark decision reversing the roles of the American and South Vietnamese forces in the war was made at about the time of the Manila Conference of October 1966. The decision was probably made before the conference, but the news was not made public until the following month. It entailed an increase in the number of American troops in Vietnam by approximately 100,000 for a total of nearly 500,000 by the end of 1967. The justification for this enlarged force was a new strategy, which proved to be remarkably sim ilar to the plan that Premier Ky had proposed fifteen months earlier.

As the South Vietnamese Defense Minister tersely described this strategy, "the entire Vietnamese Army will switch to a pacification role in 1967 and leave major fighting to American troops."[3] In effect, the Americans had decided to take over the "aggressive" or "offensive" military operations and leave the rear-guard "pacification" program to the South Vietnamese. Just what the State and Defense Departments' pamphlet had warned against two years earlier had become a reality—virtually "a 'white man's war' against Asians."

Some notion of how top American officials viewed the next stages of the war was vouchsafed by "our mandarin," Ambassador Henry Cabot Lodge.* As of November 1966, he said, we were faced with three different kinds of enemy forces: the North Vietnamese Army regulars ("approximately 50,000," according to the U.S. Commander, General William C. Westmoreland), the Southern-recruited but sometimes Northern-led Vietcong military units (generally estimated at from 50,000 to 75,000), and highly trained "guerrilla terrorist" groups working in the villages (put at "over 150,000" by Lodge). After finding some comfort in such blessings as the absence of an actual famine in the South, Ambassador Lodge went on to admit that five things had changed little or not at all—the mileage of roads open to all kinds of traffic, the percentage of population living under secure conditions, the percentage of population under Vietcong domination, the daily toll of Communist terrorism, and the rate of Vietcong military recruitment.

Lodge's idea of the end was not very clear, but his end was surely not very near. After we had beaten the army of North Vietnam, of which only a small portion had been committed to action, and the organized military units of the Vietcong, then we would first be able to get at what he called "the real

* In 1963, when Lodge was waging his war of nerves with Ngo Dinh Diem, the prize witticism in Saigon's American colony was: "Our mandarin will beat their mandarin."

cancer"—the civilian guerrillas, over 150,000 strong, in the villages. Only the destruction of the latter force, he said, would be regarded as "decisive" by the enemy. Once that was accomplished, he hazarded, the end would probably take the form of a fadeaway. "When it comes to fading away," he declared, "I think there is a good chance that this is what the enemy will do when he makes up his mind that the jig is up."[4] Lodge and others repeated this essential idea several times in the next few months.*

The American line had changed so often, however, that even the Ambassador sometimes seemed to lose track of it. After a terrorist attack in Saigon in December 1966, Lodge commented that the 150,000 terrorists could not be successfully dealt with "until we've rebuilt the whole political, social, and economic structure in this country"—clearly no small order. The Ambassador had apparently forgotten that the line had changed and that social change was now supposed to depend on "security," not vice versa. It may also have come as something of a shock to their mandarins to learn that our mandarin thought it was necessary to reconstruct their entire political, social, and economic system as a precondition for getting an effective "police function."[5]

Some American military men had so little faith in the new strategy that they expressed the belief it would inevitably be followed by the total American military "occupation" of South Vietnam. In the summer of 1966 a "widely respected American commander" told Richard Dudman of the St. Louis *Post-Dispatch*: "We should occupy and rule this country instead of pretending to respect the sovereignty of a government that really is only temporary and illegal and could

* As far as I can tell, this idea was first put forward by General Maxwell D. Taylor on October 25, 1965, in a speech at the Association of the United States Army. General Taylor expressed the belief that the end of the war required no formal surrender or destruction of the Communist regime in Hanoi, but also no negotiation with it. He foresaw the cessation of Vietcong activity and "eventual dissolution" of the guerrilla apparatus by a process of petering out *(The New York Times,* October 28, 1965).

change tomorrow. It would be more efficient and probably the end result would be better if we abandon the idea of assistance and pacification and settled for subjugation, regarding South Vietnam as an enemy country." [6] Five months later, Marvin L. Stone reported in *U.S. News & World Report*: "some ranking military men insist that the 1967 experiment with the Vietnamese forces is going to prove a year of costly waste—and that the United States should face up to reality if it wants to win this war, mobilize reserves and Guardsmen at home, send in an additional 400,000 men and take over the 'other [pacification] war'—the sooner the better." [7] Toward the end of the year, it was made known that American military officers in South Vietnam, backed by "ranking officials" in the Pentagon, had some months earlier tried unsuccessfully to persuade President Johnson to transfer supervision of the "lagging South Vietnamese pacification program" from the American embassy in Saigon to the American military command. [8]

Only time could tell whether this course would be any more successful than the previous ones. But there could be no doubt that the next stage of the war was going to be infinitely more destructive to both South and North Vietnam. The main American military pressure was not going to come from the increased numbers of ground troops. General Westmoreland knew that enemy troops feared most of all "B-52s, tactical air, artillery, and armor, in that order." In the next phase of the war, they were going to get, above all, more B-52s, tactical air, artillery, and armor. In 1963 General Earle G. Wheeler, chairman of the Joint Chiefs of Staff, had called it "a dirty little war." Making it bigger would not make it any cleaner. In April 1966 United Nations Secretary-General U Thant had called it one of the "most barbarous in history." It was not going to become any more civilized.

From the point of view which has been my chief concern, the new phase meant more than anything else the virtual militarization of the struggle. The political and economic instrumentalities, once considered more important than the military, had been practically abandoned until we could force the enemy to "fade away" by the application of overwhelming military power. The drastic decision to remove the South Vietnamese troops from "major fighting" represented official United States recognition that the South Vietnamese common soldier could not any longer be trusted to fight for "mandarin families," which, as Neil Sheehan had put it, "seek to retain what privileges they have and to regain those they have lost." The deeper roots of this political and social "malaise" were touched on in the Martin, Sheehan, and Stone articles, and that is why they had such a close bearing on the 1966 military decisions. The substitution of American for South Vietnamese troops corresponded to the substitution of the American for the Dominican military on April 28, 1965. This pattern, in such different circumstances, had repeated itself clear across the globe.

Escalation of Theory

One could only shudder at what the new strategy was going to do to our "allies"—the people of South Vietnam. But Americans also had more reason to worry about themselves.

One price we have paid has taken the form of a peculiarly noxious virus which has entered our political bloodstream. It has been impossible for the Johnson administration to present all the twists and turns of its policy in a rational and consistent way. Yet, in a democracy such as ours, a President cannot in 1964 disavow the intention of getting tied down in a land war in Asia or of sending American boys to do what Asian boys should be doing, and then in 1965 and 1966 proceed to take these very steps, without making an intellectual effort to justify his actions. The intellects making this effort have produced a squirming mass of contradictions, evasions, half-truths, and worse.

The escalation of force required an escalation of theory. As long as our military intervention was limited, we could make do with aims and objectives that were also quite limited. But half a million men and billions of dollars a year could not be justified on the basis of defending poor little South Vietnam alone. The more we invested in it, the more we had to profit by it. By 1966, we were supposedly defending nothing less than all Southeast Asia and even India in the Vietnamese rice paddies and humble villages. A victory over the Vietnam Communists, we were told, would be a victory over the Communists in half a dozen or more nearby countries, who would not dare to challenge our power if we proved successful in Vietnam. This war was virtually made into that favorite of American wars—the war to end all wars, this time "national liberation" wars.

Another form of the escalation of theory has been the escalation of South Vietnamese war aims, not without American inspiration or encouragement. The more the people of South Vietnam have been made to suffer, the more they have been told to expect from the war. At the Johnson-Ky meeting in Honolulu on February 8, 1966, a declaration which even outbid the Communists was issued. The "Declaration of Honolulu" pledged the Saigon regime to "the eradication of social injustice," to a modern society in which every man has "respect and dignity," to "true democracy" and "a true social revolution." On April 19, 1966, Vice President Hubert Humphrey exuberantly interpreted the Honolulu Declaration as a new "Johnson Doctrine" for Asia. He declared that it pledged the United States "to defeat aggression, to defeat social misery, to build viable, free political institutions, and to achieve peace," all of which he summed up as a "new opening" for realizing "the dream of the Great Society in the great area of Asia, not just here at home." The Communist program, however, made a distinction between North Vietnam, which had allegedly reached the stage of "socialism," and South Vietnam, which was ready for only a "national and democratic" rather than a full-fledged "social" revolution. No one, to be sure, was expected to take the "Declaration of Honolulu" seriously, and a few months later its flights of social fancy were indefinitely postponed in favor of the more pressing need for military victory.

Still, it is noteworthy that war costs and war aims escalated together. This familiar process had the apparent merit of bringing the cost and the return into somewhat better balance, of giving the United States more for its money and its men. But it had little more to commend it.

For, from one point of view, the Vietnamese Communists could not any longer "lose" the war, any more than the United States could "lose" it. In this kind of war, the concept of "victory" is far more elusive than that of "defeat." In fact, neither word may be applicable to the peculiar Vietnam situation. The more realistic approach may be that each side is trying to prevent the other from winning too much and itself from losing too much. The war makes much more sense in negative than in positive terms. For the United States it is important that the Communists should not win power in the South, and for the Communists it is important that their power should not be broken. Both sides are far more perspicacious and adamant about what they cannot surrender than about what they hope to achieve.

In this kind of tug-of-war, the price becomes all-important. The price the Vietnamese Communists had already extorted from the United States, and vice versa, was already a kind of "victory." That "a third-rate nation there now has us pinned down and is heavily draining our resources," as Senator Stennis put it, or that "a little 100th-rated power, North Vietnam, [is] pulling the biggest power in the world around by the nose day after day," as Democratic Representative Jamie L. Whitten of Mississippi complained,[9] represents no small feat. The Vietnamese experience is going to make the United States think twice before getting into another such "quagmire," as David Halberstam has called it, and the Communists of similar countries will think twice before asking their forces to take such punishment in return for an immediate bid for power. But that is about all we can be sure of—that the price will be a partial deterrent on both sides next time.

The idea that the frustration of a Communist bid for power in South Vietnam will be some kind of decisive setback for Communism in Southeast Asia or even in the world is a political fairy tale. It fails to take into account that no Communist bid for power which forces the United States to pay such a high price for "victory" can be said to have been "defeated." If the Communists of other impoverished, diminutive Southeast Asian countries could be sure of making us spend so much blood and treasure on frustrating them, we might well be faced with an epidemic of such wars. In this sense, the Vietnamese war, however it may end, has been more an encouragement than a discouragement to other wars of "national liberation."

Dominoes and Other Games

We have also been told that, since the Vietnamese war is part of a Chinese-Soviet or Chinese or Soviet "world conspiracy," a "victory" in this war is a victory over the whole conspiracy, whichever one it is.

If this premise were true, the inordinate expenditure of men and money on a relatively tiny, marginal outpost of this conspiracy would be strategic lunacy. We can afford the luxury of engaging ourselves so heavily in Vietnam precisely because the Communist world is no longer monolithic and centrally directed. If we need half a million or more men in Vietnam despite the Sino-Soviet conflict, one wonders how many we would need if Soviet Russia, Communist China, and their partisans were pulling together in Vietnam.

Fortunately, the Communists became disillusioned with their own "domino theory" about forty-five years ago. After October 1917, the Bolshevik leaders expected their revolution to set off a falling-dominoes effect in Western Europe. In the next six years or so, they found that national conditions in each country were far more important than their theory of world revolution had led them to expect. In order for a domino theory now to operate in Southeast Asia, it would be necessary to assume that conditions in at least several countries resemble those in Vietnam of the past twenty years. That is, it would be necessary to assume that a number of Communist parties were capable of doing the equivalent of what the Vietnamese Communists had done—inaugurated an armed struggle against French colonial rule in 1946; inflicted a total of 172,000 casualties on the French armed forces in the next eight years; compelled a far larger French army to capitulate in 1954; resumed the struggle in South Vietnam five or six years later; drove the United States to intervene in force to stave off a South Vietnamese defeat in 1965; obliged most of the South Vietnamese forces to withdraw from the front lines in 1966. And it would also be necessary to posit that other Communist Parties face the same kind of weak, corrupt, self-centered, reactionary regimes the Vietnamese Communists have been fortunate enough to find against them. None of this would have been possible if the Vietnamese Communists had not been able to identify themselves with the long-time aspirations of Vietnam nationalism and to convince a large part of the Vietnamese younger generation that they represented their interests better than anyone else.

As far as I know, no other Southeast Asian Communist Party comes near to fulfilling these specifications.* But if many more should happen to do so, the Vietnamese Communists have come so close to victory on so many occasions that their example will embolden the others, not deter them. In any case, I am willing to hazard the view that there is not enough money and manpower in the United States to prevent the South Asian dominoes from falling, whatever happens in Vietnam, if the Vietnamese conditions are so widespread. In the end, the political, social, and economic conditions in

* "No other Communist Party or regime, with the one and partial exception of the Chinese, has been responsible for conducting and guiding revolutionary activities for close to twenty-two years at one stretch" (George Modelski, "The Viet Minh Complex," in *Communism and Revolution,* ed. by Cyril E. Black and Thomas P. Thornton [Princeton: Princeton University Press, 1964], p. 200).

each country will determine the outcome far more than American political, economic, and military power.

The "domino theory" has provided the chief rationale for the unlimited commitment of American power in this war. It has been expounded again and again by American officials and public figures, ever since President Eisenhower first launched it in 1954. In September 1963, President Kennedy subscribed to the "domino theory" without reservations. In an interview, he was asked: "Mr. President, have you had any reason to doubt this so-called 'domino theory,' that if South Vietnam falls, the rest of Southeast Asia will go behind it?" The President replied: "No, I believe it. I believe it. I think that the struggle is close enough. China is so large, looms so high just beyond the frontiers, that if South Vietnam went, it would not only give them an improved geographic position for a guerrilla assault on Malaya but would also give the impression that the wave of the future in Southeast Asia was China and the Communists. So I believe it." [10] In 1965, former Vice President Nixon put the case for the "domino theory" at some length. He maintained that, in the final analysis, the war in Vietnam was not between the South Vietnamese and the Vietcong, nor even between the United States and North Vietnam, but "between the United States and Communist China." He flatly asserted, "A United States defeat in Vietnam means a Chinese Communist victory." Then he added, "What is involved in this war is not just the fate of Vietnam but the fate of all of Southeast Asia." If Vietnam fell, he prophesied, we must write off Laos, Cambodia, Thailand, Burma, and Indonesia ("Indonesia will go the way Sukarno goes"). He even predicted that the United States would have to fight a major war to save the Philippines, that Japan would inevitably be pulled toward neutralism and even toward a pro-Communist position to survive economically, that the Pacific would become a "Red sea," and that the United States would have to face up to Chinese Communist aggression as far as Australia in a matter of only four or five years. With so much at stake, it is no wonder that Nixon held that "we can never negotiate surrender, retreat, neutralization, or partition of Vietnam." The only course acceptable to him was "to end the war by winning it in South Vietnam." [11]

Nixon's views had been rejected and ridiculed by President Johnson in the electoral campaign the year before. But the "domino theory" lived a life of its own. In January 1966 Democratic Senator Russell D. Long of Louisiana demanded support of the President on the ground that if the United States could not "fight to win" against such a small Communist power as North Vietnam, "then, we had better get out of South Vietnam; and not just Vietnam but all of Asia." If the United States could not "stand fast" against "Communist aggression" in Vietnam, he asked, "does anyone think that India is going to stand against Communist China? Does anyone think that Pakistan or Indonesia is going to stand against Communist China?" [12] In July of that year, Brigadier General Joseph W. Stilwell, Jr. (who was lost on a plane trip shortly afterward), told a California audience that the United States had to hold on in South Vietnam "or we're then a third-rate power." [13] And in an interview published in September of the same year, General Wallace M. Greene, Jr., foresaw that a withdrawal from South Vietnam would lead to the same kind of threat all around the world, "either on the Subcontinent, in the Middle East, maybe in Australia and New Zealand, perhaps Thailand, which is already threatened in the northeast corner, and finally, perhaps, even on our own doorstep, in Latin America." [14] And, as President Johnson put it on November 1, 1966, it was better to fight in Vietnam than in Honolulu.

In his book, *Responsibility and Response*, General Taylor discusses the "domino theory" in a way that enables him to have his cake and eat it too. First, he dissociates himself from the theory: "I am not necessarily a convert to this theory. I do not think that, by some inevitable law of nature, the countries in Southeast Asia will fall after South Vietnam in a fixed sequential order. That might be the case, but it might not." Then, however, he goes on to predict just the kind of disaster on the largest scale that the domino theorists have in mind: "But I am certainly deeply convinced that such a disaster would propel a shock wave of dismay which would spread rapidly from the epicenter in South Vietnam, extending around the globe, which would affect every international relation we have and every alliance, including NATO." 15

There is just enough truth in the "domino theory" to make it, for some, a persuasive fallacy. A failure of American policy in Vietnam could not fail to have adverse repercussions on American influence and interests elsewhere, especially in neighboring countries of Southeast Asia. No "final victory," in fact, may be able to compensate for the failures which have already marked American policy in Vietnam. Whatever the outcome, the total effect of America's Vietnam adventure may well be negative. But there is "failure" and "failure," as well as "success" and "success." In this case, the only failure that really matters to the domino theorists is the failure to prevent a Communist takeover of South Vietnam or, for someone like Mr. Nixon, the failure to prevent surrender, retreat, neutralization, or partition. All the other failures will be forgiven and forgotten if only this one can be avoided.

The term used here has been "failure," not "defeat." For the United States obviously cannot be "defeated" in Vietnam in the sense that Hitler's Germany was defeated in 1945. Here, too, there are gradations which, if not carefully heeded, make words like "failure" and "defeat" far more ominous and far-reaching than the circumstances warrant. It can be agreed that no power can make as many mistakes as the United States has made in Vietnam over the years without paying a price for them. In this sense, in my view, the domino effect has already been working for some time. The only question is how high the price will be. In Vietnam, there is not only a price of failure; there is also a price of "victory."

In order to be most intimidating, the "domino theory" is generally presented in an abstract and automatic form. It

assumes that the fate of several different countries is necessarily being settled in Vietnam, and, therefore, makes the
huge investment in Vietnam worth while. This simplicity
and fatalism give the theory its paralyzing popular power.
If one believes that a failure or setback in Vietnam will be
an incalculable disaster, one can believe that it is worth paying an incalculable price to prevent such a disaster.

Fortunately, there is no need to deal with the "domino
theory" wholly as an abstract proposition. Its alleged autom-
atism has already been tested several times in practice, both
in the very area where it is supposed to operate and elsewhere.

In 1954, as we have seen, former Secretary of State Dulles
and Senator John F. Kennedy opposed the partition of Vietnam on the ground that it would start the dominoes falling.
It did nothing of the sort at the time and, but for the fatal
deterioration of Ngo Dinh Diem's regime, might have sta-
bilized the area for a generation. This does not mean that,
from the viewpoint of the Western powers, the loss of North
Vietnam to the Communists was a blessing. On the contrary,
it was an undeniable reverse, brought about by the decadence
and petrification of French domestic and colonial politics.
But it was not a dreadful or even a major catastrophe. It was,
indeed, a better bargain than the West had any right to
expect in the circumstances, and it is just as much a mistake
to exaggerate as to minimize the effect of the Geneva Agreements in 1954.

But Southeast Asia is not the only place in the world
where the "domino theory" is supposed to function. When
it became clear that Fidel Castro was setting up a Communist
state in Cuba in 1960, the same things that have been said
about the Southeast Asian dominoes were said about the
Latin American dominoes. In fact, Ho Chi Minh's regime has
never been so openly and aggressively expansionist as Fidel
Castro's has been. After the Bay of Pigs fiasco in April 1961,
the Cubans were more self-confident, provocative, and mag-
netic than ever. Instead of deciding to use even more force
to save the Latin American dominoes, President Kennedy

accepted the setback with as much grace as possible and permitted Castro to crow over his unprecedented victory at the expense of the United States.

Yet, almost from this very moment, Castro's influence in Latin America began to decline, and no more dominoes fell. The Dominican revolt of 1965 owed nothing to him, and he himself came under attack from some Dominican Communists for failure to help them practically in their hour of need.

The Latin American dominoes did not fall after Castro's victory because the world is far more complex and unpredictable than the theory gives it credit for being. Castro's growing force immediately set in motion counterforces throughout Latin America, not sponsored by the United States alone, which was most ineffective, but in the domestic politics of each Latin American country. If Castro's regime had proved to be an economic as well as a revolutionary success, it might well have set an irresistible example for one or another Latin American country. But Castro's internal policies soon backfired, thanks to no one but himself, and even his admirers in Latin America began to harbor doubts about many of his domestic extravagances. The Cuban experience does not prove that the Latin American dominoes *could* not have fallen; it merely proves that Castro's victory by itself was not enough for them to fall; the revolutionary process in every other Latin American country involves a complex of conditions beyond Castro's—or the United States's—control. Not only was the process not automatically pro-Castro; it could go into reverse and become anti-Castro; and, depending on an ever-changing confluence of social and political conditions, it could go back and forth.

Two Can Play

Thus far we have examined two dominoes—North Vietnam in 1954 and Cuba in 1959 and 1960—that fell without causing any other non-Communist dominoes to fall. But the question can be put in reverse: what happens to the "domino theory" when Communist dominoes fall?

The outstanding case of a falling Communist domino was that of Indonesia in 1965. It also provided a classic test for one of the most dubious and dangerous assumptions on which recent American foreign policy has been built.

Our policymakers and their intellectual factotums have come perilously close to making themselves believe that the only thing that stands in the way of Communist takeovers all over Asia, Africa, and Latin America is American power. From this premise it is a short step to basing our policy on our own forces instead of on the domestic forces at work in each country. In each of the three crises which necessitated some form of military intervention in the past few years, manipulation, or even understanding, of the domestic forces at work in Cuba, the Dominican Republic, and Vietnam was not exactly our strong point. In another famous case, however, we inadvertently permitted the domestic forces in the country to work themselves out more freely. To our astonishment, Communism suffered its greatest defeat in postwar history.

More than six months before the abortive Communist *coup* on October 1, 1965, in Indonesia, the word went out in official and semi-official American circles that Indonesia could not be saved from the Communists. In April of that year, the American outlook in Indonesia was so bleak that one group of American officials argued in favor of cutting off all aid to that country. President Johnson stopped short of following this extreme advice but he reduced the aid mission in Jakarta to a handful. Professor John P. Roche, appointed Special Consultant to the President in 1966, tied up our disentanglement from Indonesia with our entanglement in Vietnam. "I suspect, by the way," he said early in 1966, "that one interesting by-product of the last year has been that the American obsession with Vietnam may have helped in our not getting mixed up in Indonesia. In other words, we were so busy worrying about Vietnam that our cloak-and-dagger men didn't get a chance to monkey around in Indonesia." [16] More probably, however, they "monkeyed around" a great deal until the higher-ups in Washington decided that they had been wasting their time and transferred them to what seemed like more lucrative fields for attention. In a book published in 1965, Guy J. Pauker, head of the Asia Section in the Social Science Department of the RAND Corporation, contributed an analysis of the Indonesian Communists' "road to power." He came to the following conclusion: "The odds are that under these leaders the PKI [Indonesian Communist Party] will come to power in Indonesia." As a final thought, he added: "But, by the same odds, they are not likely either to turn their country into a satellite or to create a carbon copy of previous Communist regimes." [17] Richard N. Goodwin, the former Assistant to Presidents Kennedy and Johnson, went even further: "Our government was fully resigned to the potential domination of Indonesia by a Communist Party close to Peking, since armed invasion seemed the only way to prevent it." [18] In a speech on February 8, 1967, at the University of Chicago, Senator Robert F. Kennedy made the same point: "Yet less than two years ago we were quite prepared to accept the spread of Communism in Indonesia, a nation of 100 million in people, incomparably rich in resources, standing over the critical Straits of Malacca and flanking the Philippines." This "resignation" to a Communist victory in Indonesia is one of the luckiest things that has happened to us in recent years. If we had been foolhardy enough to contemplate armed intervention in Indonesia to frustrate the Communists, we would have injected ourselves into Indonesian domestic politics in such a way that we might have ruined everything. Instead, we decided to cut our losses; we did not know what to do, so we did virtually nothing; we closed down some of our agencies and pulled out many of our agents. The Communists made one misstep, and they are still paying for it. The only credit we could take for our good fortune was that we did nothing to spoil it.*

This should be enough to put to rest the fanciful idea that the Indonesian generals would not have resisted the Communist takeover without the large-scale American intervention in Vietnam. In the first place, the Indonesian Communists took the initiative, and the generals were forced to resist to save their skins. The murder of General Nasution's daughter and colleagues was far more persuasive at that moment than anything the United States was doing in Vietnam. As a matter of fact, the United States was just then beginning to emerge from what had seemed like a desperate situation in Vietnam, and the Indonesian generals were hardly likely to be emboldened by what they had seen happening in Vietnam in 1964 and 1965. In the second place, the Indonesian military could have been inspired by the Vietnamese intervention only if they could count on its being reproduced in Indonesia.† But this is exactly what

* Edward Weintal and Charles Bartlett have written: "Most of the planning for Indonesia was hinged on the assumption that the island nation would go Communist, and elaborate counter-measures were projected to dull the effects of a Communist takeover. When the contrary occurred and the Indonesian Communist Party was dismantled, the State Department was baffled—and delighted. A new U.S. ambassador, Marshall Green, had urgently advocated a hands-off policy—a departure from that of his predecessor, who urged strong U.S. support for Sukarno. The administration complied with Green's advice and the powerful PKI (Indonesian Communist Party) was all but eliminated—without an assist from the U.S." (*Facing the Brink,* op. cit., p. 184).

† Indeed, as George McTurnan Kahin and John W. Lewis point out, the post-Sukarno leaders of Indonesia have not only indicated that they did not want United States intervention in Indonesia but they have also expressed strong opposition to United States intervention in Vietnam. On May 5, 1966, Foreign Minister Adam Malik stated in the Indonesian Parliament: "But the Indonesian Government is still firmly of the opinion that it supports the struggle of the Vietnamese people against U.S. military intervention. The settlement of the Vietnamese problem must be performed on the basis of the freely expressed will of the people of Vietnam, without intervention from any quarter. Indonesia maintains her demand that the U.S. withdraw its military force from Vietnam, and leave the settlement of the Vietnamese problem to the Vietnamese people themselves" (*The United States in Vietnam* [New York: Dial, 1967], pp. 309-10).

all American policy for some months before October 1, 1965, had warned them they could not expect. The important lesson of Indonesia is not that the anti-Communist upheaval was inconceivable without the American intervention in Vietnam, but that the Indonesians, once aroused, did not need American aid in any form to get rid of their own Communists. Those who seek to give the United States credit for the turnabout in Indonesia by linking it to Vietnam are doing no service to the anti-Communist cause; they are taking away some of the rightful self-esteem which the Indonesians should feel for doing the job by themselves without foreign help or inspiration; it would be much healthier and sounder for all concerned if the Indonesian revolt against the Communists were used as an example of what can be done without United States intervention, even at second hand.

This does not mean that the best thing we can do everywhere is to do nothing. It does mean that there is a vast spectrum of policy from nothing to everything, and that nothing is almost always better than the wrong thing. Indonesia is a vastly more important part of Southeast Asia than Vietnam, and yet we were resigned not so long ago to its loss to the Communists. It would be fascinating, incidentally, to find out why we could have resigned ourselves to Communist domination in Indonesia but cannot resign ourselves, under any circumstances, to Communist domination in Vietnam.

Indeed, we might have faced the same prospect in Chile but for the electoral victory of Dr. Eduardo Frei. There was no greater likelihood that we could have saved Chile from Communism through military power than that we could have saved Indonesia. Clearly, even with all the military power at the disposal of the United States, military intervention is simply not feasible in the larger and more important countries of Asia and Latin America, no matter how close they may come to being taken over by the Communists. In countries of even middling status, we must willy-nilly resign ourselves to the working out of their domestic political forces.

The war in Vietnam is therefore not a typical situation: it can at best be reproduced only in certain countries at certain times. It is being made to bear too great a load of significance and meaning in order to justify its cost. In countries which do not lend themselves to military intervention, the political instrumentality will continue to make or break us. In countries which for some reason permit military intervention, the political question must still remain uppermost because military "victory" tends to be built on a foundation of political defeat.

The odd thing is that, when the Communist domino fell in Indonesia, no one considered it to be the beginning of the end of Communist influence in Southeast Asia. The "domino theory" seems to work only one way. This difference in attitude betrays the essential weakness of the theory. When a Communist domino falls, the world Communist movement is clearly weaker than before, but the essentially national character of each Communist party in this period determines what effect the falling domino will have outside its borders. The Communist dominoes do not fall according to some abstract and automatic predestination, and there is no reason why the non-Communist dominoes should fall in this manner.

It should also not escape notice that two can play at the "domino theory," just as two can play with the Munich analogy. If we cannot afford to give up Vietnam because the other anti-Communist dominoes in the region will fall, the Communists can tell themselves the same thing because the pro-Communist dominoes will fall. In 1966, Jean-Paul Sartre's organ, *Les Temps Modernes*, created a stir in the Communist world by demanding that the entire "Socialist camp" should fix "exact limits whose violation will unleash direct reprisals" and should meet American escalation in Vietnam with "counter-escalation." It suggested that Soviet artillerymen could easily hit the air-naval bases and installations of the American Seventh Fleet located on Formosa, on Okinawa, in the Philippines, and in the Gulf of Tonkin. And, among other "parallels" arguing for such action, it gave "the capitulations that preceded and followed the Munich Agreements." [19] These abstract theories and historical analogies are both dubious and double-edged; they will never bring us closer to any kind of peace in Vietnam. The Munich analogy did not even convince the one man in all the world whom it should have impressed the most—Winston Churchill.

And if there were anything to the analogy, the United States should have struck at the source of the trouble. Perhaps the last word on the misuse of the analogy with Germany and Czechoslovakia in 1938 was said by Hannah Arendt, the author of *The Origins of Totalitarianism* and other works. If you think about the parallel with Czechoslovakia, she said, "the absurdity of the whole business can be shown very clearly." She went on:

> It is as if France or England would have tried to stop Hitler, not by making war on him, but by making war on Slovakia as being somehow in collusion with the Nazi government against the Czech government. They would have started bombing Bratislava and intervening in what could only have been a civil war in Czechoslovakia. If anyone in 1938 had thought that this would have helped to stop Hitler, he would not have been very realistic. This is true for all such parallels. Once you really pursue them, they explode. If we say we want to contain China, then we have to take the problem in its own terms; no parallels will help, we have to look at China itself.[20]

It is hardly my intention to argue that we have nothing to learn from the nineteen-thirties or from any other period of history. But if there is any analogy which may be helpful to us in the nineteen-sixties, it is something much closer in time and place—the experience of the French in Vietnam between 1946 and 1954.

VII

China, Russia, and Vietnam

Another oddity of American policy in the Vietnam war is that no one seems sure who the "real enemy" is.

First, North Vietnam was substituted for the Southern-based Vietcong as the "real enemy." Then Communist China was substituted for North Vietnam. It was even held that there was no use asking old Ho Chi Minh to sit down at the table; the only one we could consider negotiating with was old Mao Tse-tung. But since the latter was by that time in the grip of some mania, we were told to wait until we could address ourselves to Mao's successors.[1]

One difficulty with this theory was that North Vietnam's war potential had become increasingly dependent on the Soviet Union and East Europe, not on Communist China. At the Senate Foreign Relations Committee's Vietnam hearings, Secretary of State Dean Rusk tried to get around this awkward circumstance by delivering himself of the view that the "instrument of aggression" is Hanoi but the "doctrine" of aggression "is from Peking."[2] One gathered from his testimony that Soviet Russia was not the real enemy in North Vietnam because it was merely providing most of the heavy matériel, such as MIGs (jet fighters) and SAMs (surface-to-air missiles). Communist China was the true foe because it had made North Vietnam a gift of its "doctrine." If the

Chinese were not so hard to please, they would have shown some gratitude to the Secretary for giving them North Vietnam at bargain rates.

Ho and Mao

Yet few, if any, serious students of Vietnamese-Chinese relations have taken any stock in this view.

Professor P. J. Honey, who has studied the subject more carefully, perhaps, than anyone else, reminds us that two thousand years of Vietnamese-Chinese relations have left the Vietnamese with feelings toward the Chinese "not unlike those of the Irish for the English of Oliver Cromwell's day." Though the Vietnamese have learned to respect and fear the Chinese, they dislike them even more, which is why, Professor Honey explains, "Communist campaigns stressing the 'historical friendship' between the peoples of Vietnam and China had to be abandoned hurriedly when they encountered so much ridicule in North Vietnam." In the years from 1954 to 1956, the Vietnamese Communists slavishly followed the Chinese in their land reform and other policies, but this proved to be the worst mistake ever made by the North Vietnamese and led to disenchantment with the Chinese model. "The end of the North Vietnamese-Chinese honeymoon dates from 1957," Professor Honey writes, "and it is interesting to note that Ho Chi Minh made no attempt to imitate such Chinese policies as the 'Great Leap Forward' and the creation of communes." There has been much speculation that the North Vietnamese leadership has contained pro-Soviet and pro-Chinese factions or at least tendencies, but after a period of trying to avoid taking sides, the dominant wing under Ho, Professor Honey believes, "swung to the Soviet side in early September 1960." Since then, Ho Chi Minh has continued to maneuver between the two great Communist powers, without ever giving up the historic Vietnamese policy which, as Professor Honey puts it, consists of paying "lip service to Chinese pretensions provided they [the

Vietnamese] themselves retained the reins of power in Vietnam."[3]

Some scholars have even inferred that the Chinese Communists put pressure on Ho Chi Minh to settle for half a loaf in 1954 because a latent rivalry for control of the entire region existed between the Chinese and Vietnamese Communists. According to Professor Paul Mus, the former political adviser to the French High Commissioner for Indochina,

> the Chinese were concerned lest the Viet Minh carry out their design to become the successor state of all French Indochina. . . . The Chinese opposed an Indochina under Viet Minh control because it would conflict with a principal Chinese goal in Southeast Asia: hegemony over the Tai-speaking peoples who inhabit southern China, the Shan states of Burma, and northwestern Tonkin, as well as Thailand and Laos.[4]

A qualified American student, Douglas Pike, has written in the same vein:

> Although it cannot be documented from public statements, logic suggests that the Chinese did not particularly welcome the idea of a unified Vietnam, preferring two Vietnams with a Southern regime either pro-Chinese or at least willing to consult with Peking before making any major moves. As the Sino-Soviet dispute deepened, the Chinese of course became prisoners of the doctrine of liberation wars, involving Chinese leadership efforts throughout Asia.[5]

Thus, Pike adds, Communist China was the "best foreign friend" of the National Liberation Front "in its externalization efforts"—a somewhat barbarous term meaning the efforts of the NLF to obtain foreign support and recognition. For some time after the NLF was formed in 1961, the Chinese tried to exploit the Vietnamese struggle to demonstrate that they were the most militant, uncompromising exponents of national wars of liberation. In the early 1960s, Pike thinks, the Soviet Union appeared to the NLF as "a rather remote big brother," though the "Soviet revolutionary experience was regarded as the great model of the NLF, despite the lack of similarities." By 1965, however, the Soviets began to back the NLF unreservedly in South Vietnamese affairs. More questionably, Pike also believes that the Soviets were still primarily interested in any Vietnamese settlement short of a South Vietnamese or American victory.[6]

The relative influence of the Chinese and Soviet Communists in North Vietnam has also been discussed by an outstanding French authority, Jean Lacouture. As of 1964, he believed, the North Vietnamese were more dependent materially on the Chinese than on the Russians.* Therefore, he wrote: "If Ho's heart went out to Moscow because he was a

* According to Lacouture, the aid from China in 1960 and 1961 was "on the order of" $500,000,000 as compared to $200,000,000 in European aid. These figures, he said, remained substantially the same until 1964. As for the South Vietnamese National Liberation Front, however, a well-informed American student has written: "It is impossible to estimate the amount of material assistance that the DRV [North Vietnam], China, and the Soviet Union have furnished the NLFSV in tactical and strategic direction and in cadres and material" (John C. Donnell, "North Vietnam," in *The Communist Revolution in Asia,* edited by Robert A. Scalapino [Englewood Cliffs, N.J.: Prentice-Hall, 1965], pp. 167-68).

Still another study came to the conclusion that economic grants and credits received by North Vietnam from all "socialist countries" came to 2000 millions of old rubles from 1955 to 1960 and to 1330 millions of old rubles from 1961 to 1965. This study summed up: "From the mass of contradictory evidence it would be hazardous to guess the relative contributions of China, the U.S.S.R. and Eastern Europe, but such a guess, based on the relative participation of the Soviet Union in North Vietnam's foreign trade, would estimate that the Soviet Union contributed about half the total amount of aid, and Eastern Europe roughly one-quarter, probably less. The Chinese contribution, mostly labour and experts, is probably exaggerated by enthusiasts of the Chinese model, especially regarding the repair of border-zone bridges, railroads and footpaths, an activity important in the 1955-60 period and again since 1965. The amount of aid in both periods looks quite modest in dollar terms: $380 million in grants (including the questionable $5 million Soviet anti-malaria 'grant') and $452 million in credits, a total of $832 million for the entire decade, compared with about $2 billion in United States support of the South Vietnamese economy from 1955-62. In 1963 alone, U.S. economic aid to South Vietnam amounted to over $200 million. One must consider also that Chinese aid pledges are notoriously over-extended" (Jan S. Prybyla, "Soviet and Chinese Economic Aid to North Vietnam," *The China Quarterly,* July-September 1966, pp. 92-93).

'Khrushchevist,' as did those of his closest companions, the 'belly' of the regime turns to Peking, for Peking furnishes most of the foreign aid and technicians." Despite this material dependence in the pre-1965 period, however, Lacouture was of the opinion that the North Vietnamese regime "continued to turn its eyes toward the Soviet Union." He gave these reasons for the Northern regime's preference: "It distinguished between the technological value·of the Soviet and Chinese experts; it had, moreover, an unlimited respect and admiration for the Soviet Union, that giant world power and head of the socialist camp. And it had no illusions on the true sentiments animating the Chinese with regard to North Vietnam."[7]

The remarkable thing here is that Secretary of State Rusk and other American officials have made the North Vietnamese the doctrinal prisoners of the Chinese, whereas almost all other authorities have agreed that Ho Chi Minh has always been Soviet-oriented. The outstanding North Vietnamese military leader, General Vo Nguyen Giap, has also been reckoned among those most faithful to the pro-Soviet tendency. One American writer has even called him the head of the pro-Soviet faction.[8] A noted speech made in 1963 by Truong Chinh, the putative leader of the pro-Chinese faction, emphasized the uniqueness of the Vietnamese revolution and contrasted it with both the Soviet and Chinese models.[9] Indeed, the Vietnamese Communists have always prided themselves on their individuality within the common Communist tradition.

There is nothing in ancient or recent history that warrants writing off the North Vietnamese Communists as puppets or satellites of the Chinese. The patent on guerrilla warfare is not owned by the Chinese,* and even a common doctrine does

* Why Mao Tse-tung should be given so much credit for his doctrine of "guerrilla warfare" by Secretary Rusk and other State Department officials remains a mystery inasmuch as the former Chairman of the Policy Planning Council in the State Department, W. W. Rostow, had already given them a much more sensible historical view of the matter: "It is now fashionable to read the learned works of Mao Tse-tung and

not necessarily make North Vietnam subject to Chinese control, any more than a common doctrinal heritage has prevented the Sino-Soviet imbroglio. The mistake seems to stem from a continued reluctance to come to terms with the centrifugal forces in the Communist world. Not so long ago, Fidel Castro was also classified as a Maoist disciple because on some points—revolutionary violence and guerrilla warfare— the Cuban and Chinese doctrines coincided. But this did not prevent Castro from assailing the Chinese leadership in terms more abusive than any the Soviets had ever employed.* The present Communist world is full of intersecting lines of tactics and doctrine that can be correlated in different ways, depending on which lines one chooses to correlate. The idea that Ho Chi Minh had to get his "doctrine of aggression" from Mao Tse-tung flatters Dean Rusk as little as it does Ho Chi Minh.

The chief theorist of Vietnamese revolutionary tactics has been Vo Nguyen Giap. George K. Tanham has made the most careful study of the debt owed to Mao Tse-tung by Gen-

---

Che Guevara on guerrilla warfare. This is, indeed, proper. One should delve with care and without passion into the minds of one's enemies. But it is historically inaccurate and psychologically dangerous to think that these men created the strategy and tactics of guerrilla war to which we are now responding. Guerrilla warfare is not a form of military and psychological magic created by the Communists. There is no rule or parable in the Communist texts which was not known at an earlier time in history. The operations of Marion's men in relation to the Battle of Cowpens in the American Revolution was, for example, governed by rules which Mao merely echoes; Che Guevara knows nothing of this business that T. E. Lawrence did not know or that was not practiced, for example, in the Peninsular Campaign during the Napoleonic Wars, a century earlier. The orchestration of professional troops, militia, and guerrilla fighters is an old game whose rules can be studied and learned" (*View from the Seventh Floor* [New York: Harper & Row, 1964], p. 119). Professor Rostow might have been overoptimistic about how well we had learned to combat it, but his main point could still be brought to the attention of the Secretary of State.

* On March 13, 1966, Castro accused the Chinese Communist leaders of being in their "dotage" (*chocheria*) and of having launched a campaign against Cuba "in the imperialist style, in the style of [Nazi Propaganda Minister Joseph] Goebbels, in fascist style."

eral Giap, a former history teacher. According to Tanham, Giap's thinking on the problem of the Vietnamese revolution started out by accepting Mao's concept of the three-phase war—strategic defensive, preparation for the counteroffensive, and strategic counteroffensive leading to the enemy's strategic retreat. But this recipe is so generalized (and hardly original) that any good revolutionary cook must learn how to put in his own national ingredients. As Tanham shows, Giap made a truly creative effort to apply the Maoist formula to Vietnam's special conditions and, in doing so, did not hesitate to go contrary to Mao's ideas whenever he thought the situation called for it.[10]

Most students of Vietnamese communism agree that Ho Chi Minh and Vo Nguyen Giap have never considered themselves to be Mao Tse-tung's political appendages or even junior partners. Why they should be incapable of creating their own doctrine is hard to understand. Ho Chi Minh was a leading Communist before Mao, with far more international responsibilities and experience in the 1920s and 1930s. The Vietnamese Communists have over twenty years of their own armed struggle from which to draw lessons and legends.

Nguyen Ai Quoc, as Ho Chi Minh was then called, was a prominent international Communist long before Communists outside China became conscious of the existence, let alone of the importance, of Mao Tse-tung. In October 1923, Nguyen Ai Quoc was one of the 158 delegates to the First International Peasants' Congress in Moscow. Though he had been living in France and working as the French Communist Party's colonial expert, Nguyen Ai Quoc represented the French colony of Indochina at the Moscow congress. An eleven-member Bureau or Presidium was elected on the last day, October 15, and at the bottom of the list was the name "Ai Quac (Indo-Chine)." [11] This organization was one of the more abortive efforts of the Communist International, or as it was more usually called, the Comintern, and very little more than manifestoes seems to have come from it.[12]

In the summer of 1924, however, Nguyen Ai Quoc was back in Moscow as a delegate to the Fifth Congress of the Comintern. He spoke at length no fewer than three times, always to berate the Western parties for not paying enough attention to the colonial question and to the revolutionary potential of the peasantry. In his first speech, he said, "It seems to me that the comrades have not yet completely taken hold of the idea that the fate of the proletariat of the entire world and especially the proletariat of the colonial countries is closely tied up with the fate of the oppressed colonial peoples." After accusing the Western Communist parties of paying no attention to their own countries' colonies, he cried out, "Why do you neglect the colonies on which capitalism depends to defend itself and to fight against you?"

In his second intervention in the discussion, Nguyen Ai Quoc rallied behind the rising power in the Russian party and in the Comintern, Joseph Stalin, already the Secretary General of the Russian party but not yet the dominant international figure. The Vietnamese delegate, in his mid-thirties, was farsighted enough to praise Stalin's position on the colonial problem. "Comrade Stalin characterizes as anti-revolutionary the conception that the victory of the European proletariat is possible without the closest connection with the colonial liberation movement," he said. "When we judge modes of thought on the basis of deeds, the inactivity of our largest parties, with the exception of the Russian, permits us to conclude that the conception of which Comrade Stalin has spoken dominates in our parties."

Nguyen Ai Quoc's third speech at the congress was perhaps his most important. He devoted it entirely to the misery and exploitation of the colonial peasantry. After pointing out that 95 per cent of the people of the French colonies were peasants, he concluded: "The native peasants are ripe for revolt. Revolts have already taken place repeatedly in several colonies, but they have all been bloodily suppressed. If the peasants have now fallen into a state of passivity, it is because they lack an organization, because they do not have leaders. It is the duty of the International to help them to organize themselves. It is its duty to give them leaders to show them the way to revolution and to liberation." [13]

This Comintern background of Ho Chi Minh should exorcise the idea that he had anything to learn from Mao Tse-tung about the importance of the revolutionary potential of the peasantry for the Communist movement. In 1924, when Ho Chi Minh was instructing the foremost international Communist leaders assembled in Moscow that the peasantry was the key to the revolution in colonial countries, Mao Tse-tung was still a local Chinese Communist functionary without any outstanding achievements or distinguishing ideas to his credit. Mao has claimed that he began to devote himself to the organization of the peasantry in Hunan province the following year, in 1925; his own then heretical view that the Chinese peasantry constituted the leading class force in the revolution seems to have developed between 1925 and 1927. But Mao had an uphill battle for several years thereafter to make his new theory prevail in the Chinese Communist Party. Unlike Ho Chi Minh, who was an exile from his native country for thirty years until 1940 and could only talk about the peasant revolution to Western and other Communists, Mao Tse-tung never left China and could do something about it. Mao Tse-tung was undoubtedly the outstanding practical Asian exponent and organizer of an attitude towards the peasantry that was common to both of them, but one need not be glorified at the expense of the other.

"Certainly," Lacouture writes, "Ho credits his Chinese colleague with a great pre-eminence in matters of strategic invention and doctrinal competence; but he regards him only as one of his peers who has more means at his command rather than more constancy or revolutionary spirit." [14] Giap's "distrust and dislike of the Chinese" have been so open and strong, according to Professor Honey, that some of his political setbacks in the North Vietnamese leadership must be attributed to this attitude.[15] Pike says that the Southern National Liberation Front's technique has been largely based "on a mishmash of piecemeal military maxims and semipolitical aphorisms accumulated over the years chiefly from the writings of Chinese and Vietnamese revolutionaries, foremost of whom have been Mao Tse-tung and Vo Nguyen Giap." Pike acutely observes that "Mao-Giap became to revolutionary guerrilla warfare what Marxism-Leninism is to Communist theory," and also gives Giap credit for reinterpreting or at least revising in practice Mao's "thoughts" to suit the very different Vietnamese conditions.[16] I. Milton Sacks, in a volume edited by Professor Frank N. Trager, writes that the Vietnamese Communists have sometimes rationalized their policies on the basis of Soviet experience, as in early 1946 when they temporarily accepted the return of the French, or have borrowed from the Chinese Communists, as in the Viet Minh's three-phase war strategy against the French. But he never suggests that Vietnamese communism has ever been a carbon copy of Chinese communism or even mentions the Chinese influence in his summing up of the nature of Vietnamese "Marxism-Leninism." [17]

George Modelski has recalled that the early Vietnamese Communist leaders, still in control, were "Moscow trained" and the party's "basic ideological inspiration has been Soviet." Many Vietnamese Communist leaders, including Ho Chi Minh, lived in China for lengthy periods and returned home after 1941 fully familiar with Chinese Communist precepts about building up an independent revolutionary armed force and settling up "land bases" in preparation for a general insurrection. "Acknowledged though this influence is," Modelski observed, "it is not greatly overemphasized, and Hanoi leaders have taken pains to distinguish between Chinese and Vietnamese practice in this important field." In the military sphere, Modelski pointed out, the Chinese Communists defeated for the most part poorly organized local forces, whereas the Vietnamese overcame "the modern, fully trained, and excellently equipped, 'industrial' French Expeditionary Corps." [18]

Communist Leapfrog

Since 1965, all signs have indicated that the Soviets have gained appreciably over the Chinese in Vietnam. By January 1967 an American source had discovered: "Soviet Russia, not Red China, is turning out to be the major enemy of the United States in Vietnam." It estimated that the Soviet Union was then investing close to $1 billion a year in the Vietnamese war, far more than the Chinese had ever done. Soviet military aid to North Vietnam was said to have increased from $35 million annually from 1955 to 1964 to $550 million in 1965, to an estimated $700 million in 1966, and to a promised $800 million in 1967. The Soviets were supplying North Vietnam with surface-to-air missiles, anti-aircraft batteries, jet fighters, coastal ships, light bombers, advanced radar de-fense systems, cargo transports, bridge-building materials, oil, and much else. The Chinese still claimed that they were ahead of the Russians in sheer tonnage, but a Western expert was quoted as saying: "Tonnage from Red China may run higher, but the dollar-per-ton value and the strategic value of Russian aid is much greater." [19]

Another well-informed American source similarly reported that Soviet economic aid to North Vietnam totaled about $350 million in the ten years through 1964. This aid declined somewhat in 1963 and 1964 because Nikita Khrushchev apparently considered North Vietnam to be in China's orbit. But Khrushchev's successors began to compete more actively and successfully with the Chinese. In addition to about $555 million worth of arms, the Soviets sent $74.8 million of ordinary exports to North Vietnam in 1965. In mid-October, it is said, a summit meeting of the Soviet Union and its eight allies agreed to give about $1 billion in military and other assistance to North Vietnam, four-fifths of it from the Soviet Union alone. East Germany is believed to rank next to the

Soviet Union, though far behind, in Soviet-bloc aid to North Vietnam. The Soviets first agreed to send a significant amount of weapons and technicians to North Vietnam in February 1965, but the Chinese held up or damaged much of the matériel. Increasingly, this source reported early in 1967, the Soviet Union was sending its aid and supplies "via the 7500-mile sea lanes from Eastern Europe instead of relying on dubious Chinese cooperation in allowing men and matériel to proceed overland." [20]

In February 1967, a report based on American intelligence information stated:

There's no question that the Soviet Union is the primary supplier of war goods to North Vietnam, even though rival China loudly disputes that fact. U.S. intelligence experts calculate that the Russians have supplied North Vietnam with more than $600 million in military aid, including $500 million in arms alone, since 1953; of that total, 85 per cent has been sent since August 1964, when North Vietnamese ships attacked U.S. destroyers in the Gulf of Tonkin and the Vietnam war began heating up rapidly. Since 1953 the Chinese have given Hanoi only $150 million in military aid, 65 per cent of that since August 1964.

The Soviet arms aid, according to U.S. estimates, has flowed like this: Before 1964, $50 million; in 1964, $25 million; in 1965, $200 million to $225 million; in 1966, about $200 million. Analysts figure Chinese military aid in 1965 was about $35 million and rose to $50 million or $60 million last year, most of it in small arms such as rifles and mortars that play a major role in the war in the south.[21]

These three sources, all probably related in one way or another to official American agencies or intermediaries, tell essentially the same story. Until the end of 1964, North Vietnam was mainly dependent on Chinese aid, which was too meager to permit much more than the kind of guerrilla warfare that the Vietcong had been waging in the south. The Soviet aid to North Vietnam before 1965 was so modest that it betrayed a reluctance to compete with the Chinese in Vietnam or to adopt the North Vietnamese as Soviet protégés in the same manner that the Cubans had been adopted in 1960 and 1961. But something obviously happened in Moscow at the end of 1964 or beginning of 1965 to induce the Soviet leaders to reverse themselves on their previous Vietnam policy. A decision of major import for the conduct of the war by North Vietnam was clearly made in Moscow at this time.

On February 6, 1965, Soviet Premier Aleksei N. Kosygin arrived in Hanoi. On February 7, American planes bombed North Vietnam in retaliation for the Pleiku incident. On February 8, Premier Kosygin announced in the North Vietnamese capital that the Soviets intended to aid North Vietnam if the latter were invaded. Whether or not the Soviets had already made their decision to increase their aid to North Vietnam, the psychological effect of the American bombing on the second day of the Soviet leader's visit to Hanoi could only have served to harden his resolve. If the bombings figured in the Soviet decision to step up aid to North Vietnam, they were among the costliest air force operations in American military history. In any event, there seems to be no doubt that the more the United States bombed, the more the Soviet Union provided military and economic assistance to North Vietnam. This may well have been the chief effect of the equally momentous decision by the United States early in 1965 to bomb North Vietnam massively and to inject large-scale American combat forces into the battle.

An acute student of recent changes in the world Communist movement has rightly observed:

> In the spring of 1965, the most important "concrete question" for world communism was the war in Vietnam. And here one must note that a major factor in the development of inter-party relations after Khrushchev came not from any Communist initiative but from an American move. This was the escalation of the war in Vietnam through the bombing of the North, which took place early in February 1965, while Kosygin was in Hanoi on a fence-mending mis-

sion. One might have expected that this attack on a socialist state would (if anything could) oblige the two Communist giants to settle their differences. Yet it did precisely the opposite. The reasons for this paradoxical situation are too numerous to be explored here, but one basic reason must be noted: the escalation automatically put the Russians in a better position than the Chinese. If the pressure of U.S. airpower was to be endured, let alone repelled, the Vietnamese needed *material* and technical aid that they could get only from the Soviet Union. The Russians might speak softly, by Chinese standards, but they carried a big SAM missile, so to speak. And so, while the bombings continued, the Chinese were driven farther out on the limb of isolation and intransigence; the North Vietnamese were led to greater material dependence on the Soviet Union, without giving up their own neutralist autonomy; and the Russians were encouraged to make "unity of action" in support of Vietnam the touchstone of "proletarian internationalism." [22]

Meanwhile, as we have seen, the official American line insisted endlessly on the Chinese menace in Vietnam and the North Vietnamese subservience to the Chinese Communists. Either Washington did not wake up quickly enough to the fact that the Soviets were replacing the Chinese as the main providers of the North Vietnamese or Washington could not admit that anything untoward was happening in Vietnam because it was just then pursuing a *détente* with Moscow. Another factor may well have been that the Americans were still so overcome with self-congratulation over the Soviet retreat in the Cuban missile crisis of 1962 that they could not bring themselves to believe the Soviets could be doing something of the same sort, this time without missiles that might threaten the American mainland, for another embattled Communist state on the other side of the world.

Whatever the reason, the American reaction to the increasing Soviet sponsorship of North Vietnam was well beyond the permissible limits of self-deception. In April and May 1965, two leading State Department officials, using almost the same words, argued that the United States was in effect fighting in Vietnam to make the Soviet Communist line prevail over the Chinese Communist line. "The 'wars of national liberation' approach has been adopted as an essential element of Communist China's expansionist policy," said Deputy Assistant Secretary for Far Eastern Affairs Leonard Unger in Detroit on April 19. "If this technique adopted by Hanoi should be allowed to succeed in Vietnam, we would be confirming Peiping's contention that militant revolutionary struggle is a more productive Communist path than Moscow's doctrine of peaceful coexistence." [23] On May 13, Assistant Secretary for Far Eastern Affairs William P. Bundy told another audience in Dallas, Texas: "The 'wars of liberation' strategy is at this time an essential element of the expansionist policy of Communist China and her Asian ally, North Vietnam. If we allow it to succeed in Vietnam, we would be confirming Peiping's assertion that armed struggle is a more productive Communist course than Moscow's doctrine of peaceful coexistence." [24] That the prose style of at least one of them was lacking in originality may merely suggest how determined they were to get the very same point across.

Even when the Chinese Communists began to send out broad hints that the North Vietnamese should not be fighting the kind of war the new Soviet weapons were making possible, the highest officials in Washington refused to get the message. On September 3, 1965, the Chinese Minister of National Defense, Lin Piao, published an interminable article in the official organ, *Renmin Ribao* (People's Daily), of Peking. When it arrived in Washington, it was seized on as a veritable confession by the highest Chinese Communist military leader and Mao Tse-tung's heir apparent that the United States had been right all the time about the dreadful designs of the no longer inscrutable Chinese. On October 31, Ambassador at Large W. Averell Harriman, usually one of the less credulous American diplomats, daunted an audience in Tucson, Arizona, with the portentous menace of Lin

Piao's 18,000 words. "It spells out in unmistakable clarity
and detail the Communist Chinese doctrine of world revolution," Mr. Harriman exclaimed. "Its significance is similar
to that of *Mein Kampf*. It states unequivocally what the
intentions of Communist China are, what sort of world it
wants, and how that world is to be created." The Ambassador
took special pains to point out that the "focus" of the
revolutionary movement against the United States was, according to Lin Piao, in Vietnam, and that the Chinese
leader had vowed, "the Chinese people will do everything
in their power to support the Vietnamese people until every
single one of the U.S. aggressors is driven out of Vietnam."
While Mr. Harriman did not give the Soviet leaders a clean
bill of health, he compared them most favorably with their
bloodthirsty, insatiable Chinese rivals.[25]

The Vietnamese Communist leaders, however, were probably most interested in one passage in Lin Piao's dissertation.
After all the revolutionary rhetoric, they read:

> In order to make a revolution and to fight a people's war
> and be victorious, it is imperative to adhere to the policy of
> self-reliance, rely on the strength of the masses in one's
> own country and prepare to carry on the fight independ-
> ently even when all material aid from outside is cut off. If
> one does not operate by one's own efforts, does not inde-
> pendently ponder and solve the problems of the revolution
> in one's own country and does not rely on the strength of
> the masses, *but leans wholly on foreign aid—even though
> this be aid from socialist countries* which persist in revolu-
> tion—no victory can be won, or be consolidated even if it
> is won (my italics, T.D.).[26]

At this very time, according to American intelligence
sources, Soviet arms aid to North Vietnam was increasing
from \$25 million in 1964 to \$200-225 million in 1965, compared with only \$35 million of Chinese arms aid in 1965.
When Lin Piao warned the North Vietnamese Communist
leaders not to make themselves dependent on "foreign aid—
even though this be aid from socialist countries," he did not

need to spell out the countries for the benefit of the North Vietnamese. The surpassing irony of this period is that what Professor John P. Roche has called "bush-league Machiavellianism" on the part of the United States seeking to play off Russia against Communist China only succeeded in substituting a richer Communist state for a poorer one as North Vietnam's main arms supplier. Yet, for another year, the highest American officials persisted in giving Communist China credit which properly belonged to the Soviet Union. One wonders whether the men in the Kremlin were blissfully amused or hopelessly perplexed by this diplomatic sciamachy in Washington.

An authoritative and thoughtful historian of the Sino-Soviet conflict, Professor Donald S. Zagoria, summed up the rivalry for influence in Vietnam in early 1967 in these terms:

I think that Chinese–North Vietnamese relations have been getting worse and worse for the past two years, mainly because Mao has refused united action with the Russians in Vietnam. He is more interested in exposing the Russians as accomplices of the "imperialists" than in taking up Soviet proposals of united action.

For example, Moscow proposed in 1965 that Peking give them an air corridor through China in order to send supplies to Vietnam. They also proposed stationing Soviet planes in airfields in Southern China, all of which was designed to help Hanoi deter American escalation. But Mao turned down this proposal as he has turned down every subsequent proposal for united action, even when it had had the support of the North Vietnamese themselves.

This policy has made it more difficult for the North Vietnamese to get supplies, and it encourages Washington to think that it can escalate the war against a divided Communist world.

Also, contrary to popular opinion, Mao has urged the Viet Cong to go onto the strategic defensive, and the Vietnamese Communists probably believe that the Chinese are doing this for selfish reasons—because Peking fears any escalation of the war might involve China.

For all of these reasons, even the so-called pro-China faction in Hanoi has become increasingly disillusioned with China, and is turning more and more to the Russians. There seems to be a perceptible increase of Soviet influence in Hanoi in the past year.[27]

In any case, there is something hallucinatory about the theory that Communist China is the real enemy in Vietnam or that the Vietnamese war is but the preliminary stage of a showdown with China. If there is any truth in either of these propositions, future historians will surely account our Sisyphean labors in Vietnam as one of the greatest aberrations of modern times. The day a war with China should materialize, Vietnam would become a remote, inconvenient sideshow from which most of our troops would have to be pulled in a hurry. The Mekong Valley is about two thousand miles from the industrial and military heartland of northeast China. The notion that we are weakening, frightening, or deterring China by killing Vietnamese, as if this were a case of mistaken identity, defies all logic and experience. The only thing we are conceivably proving is that if we can bog down in South Vietnam, it should not be too difficult to bog down in the endless expanses of mainland China.

In truth, the proponents of this war have been trying to have it both ways. On one hand, they claim that the "real enemy" in Vietnam is Communist China. On the other hand, they assure us that Communist China has no intention or capability of getting into the Vietnamese war. Why a power which can do so little to decide the issue in Vietnam should be our main foe there remains a mystery. It might be much closer to the truth to say that the only great power in a position to gain much for relatively little from the Vietnamese war may be the Soviet Union, which explains why it has been willing to invest more and more in it.

Mao Tse-tung's "cultural revolution" has convulsed and ruptured the old Chinese Communist movement more effectively than any other force in the world was capable of doing. Mao has cast out and eliminated more Chinese Communists than the United States possibly could, short of using nuclear weapons. And, if the American advocates of a war with China should have their way, nuclear weapons will most likely be used at some stage of the conflict, as Senator John Stennis, the highly influential chairman of the Armed Services Preparedness Subcommittee, has already indicated.*

Yet China is one of the great imponderables in this contest of men, arms, and wills. We may drift, drive, or get dragged into a clash with Communist China. But if this horrible calamity should occur, it would make the present Vietnam war less rather than more meaningful. It is madness or frivolity to justify the present war in terms of an infinitely more dubious and appalling war. There is no greater folly in the theoretical apologetics of our Vietnam policy than the premise that the Vietnam war cannot be settled on the basis of internal Vietnam interests, at least as far as we are concerned, without settling the fate of the entire region, let alone that of Communist China. American diplomacy as well as the American military has a tendency to "overkill." A de-

* On January 27, 1966, in a speech before a joint session of the Mississippi State Legislature, Senator Stennis declared: "For my part I would never put our boys in mortal conflict against the hordes of Red Chinese coolies without being free to use every weapon we have, when and if necessary." Democratic Senator Albert Gore of Tennessee subsequently referred to Senator Stennis's views as follows: "I have had the privilege of discussing his speech with the distinguished Senator from Mississippi. He says that he did not advocate, and I did not understand that he advocated, use of nuclear weapons, but, rather, he expressed the view, in which I have today earlier joined, that a war between the United States and China would make use of nuclear weapons highly likely for the reason, as I have stated—and as I understand the Senator from Mississippi to state—that the American people would not permit their sons to be matched man to man with the masses of Chinese in Asia without using whatever weapons might be at hand." Senator Stennis spoke immediately thereafter to congratulate Senator Gore on his speech and did not take issue with the latter's version of his views on the use of nuclear weapons in a war with China (*Congressional Record,* Senate, February 16, 1966, pp. 3024-25). General Douglas MacArthur's pithy judgment on the wisdom of fighting a ground war in China has been frequently recalled in the Senate: "Anyone in favor of sending American ground troops to fight on Chinese soil should have his head examined."

escalation of theory is needed as urgently as a de-escalation of force.

.

To Win or Not to Win

The relationship of the Southern Vietcong to North Vietnam and that of North Vietnam to Communist China are so important because the United States has made them the critical factors in any peaceful settlement of the Vietnamese war. At the Senate Foreign Relations Committee hearings in February 1966, Secretary of State Rusk declared that "peace would come in almost a matter of hours" if North Vietnam "were prepared to call off the aggression in the South." Then he expressed the belief that "Peking even more than Hanoi has blocked the path toward a conference table." [28] He totally ignored the Soviets, whose influence in Hanoi he had previously dismissed as apparently "limited." [29]

South Vietnam's Premier Ky went further. In the summer of 1966 he urged an invasion of North Vietnam, even at the risk of drawing Communist China into the war. Since war between the Chinese and the "free world" was inevitable anyway, he thought, "it's better to face them right now than in five or ten years." [30]

General Maxwell D. Taylor never seems to have made up his mind what the relationship between North Vietnam and Communist China in this war is. On page 6 of *Responsibility and Response,* he writes: "Although it is sometimes difficult to determine clearly just what the differences are, the purposes of the leadership in Hanoi are not always identical with those of Peking, and hence North Vietnam, even after the end of the current conflict, will need to be given separate attention." On page 34, however, he has Communist China "fighting a war by proxy, fighting to the last North Vietnamese." [31]

This view, whether expressed more cautiously by Secretary Rusk, more flamboyantly by Premier Ky, or more contra-

dictorily by General Taylor, seemed to make any peaceful
moves from the Communist side a very intricate and far-flung
affair. Peking had to stop blocking Hanoi, and Hanoi had
to call off the Southern guerrillas. Or, conversely, the United
States had to invade North Vietnam in full knowledge that
it was risking a war with Communist China. No matter how
much those holding such views protested that they did not
want to escalate the war militarily, their political premises
could not fail to bring about an uncontrolled escalation and
an unlimited commitment.

A somewhat different tack was taken at the Manila Conference in October 1966. The main communiqué seemed to
put the onus exclusively on North Vietnam. The seven participating powers—United States, Philippines, South Vietnam, South Korea, Thailand, Australia, and New Zealand—
promised to withdraw their forces from South Vietnam within six months "as the other side withdraws its forces to the
north, ceases infiltration, and the level of violence thus sub-
sides." Former Vice President Nixon and others soon objected
that the withdrawal of both the North Vietnamese and American regular forces would leave South Vietnam at the mercy
of the native Southern Vietcong, still the main enemy force.
These misgivings soon brought forth the revelation that the
communiqué had been carefully drawn up to provide for
just such a contingency. It was authoritatively explained
that the main-force Southern Vietcong as well as the Northern regulars were embraced in the reference to the "forces"
of the other side, and that even the guerrillas were expected
to contribute to the subsiding "level of violence." [32] In effect,
all the communiqué really said was that the United States
and the other six powers would withdraw their forces within
six months if the "other side," both Northern and Southern,
would "lay down their arms," as Secretary Rusk had put it
almost a year before.[33]

No one has expressed the contradictions in the American
official mind on the relationship of the Southern rebellion to

North Vietnam more unguardedly than General Taylor. On one page, he writes that he called President Kennedy's attention as early as 1961

> to the fact that the real source of the guerrilla strength in South Vietnam was not in South Vietnam but in North Vietnam. It was perfectly clear that the direction, the supplies, the reinforcements, and the leadership came from the North.

On another page, however, he admits:

> I often ask the proponents of this ["get-out"] alternative what would happen if Hanoi were suddenly to disappear. Suppose everything of value in the North were destroyed; we would still have over 200,000 armed guerrillas in South Vietnam who would have to be accounted for in some way. For food they could live off the land without supplies from the North. If they avoided contact with large military forces, they could husband their weapons and ammunition stocks and maintain for a long time a low level of sustained depredations and terrorist activity. If they were determined to carry on the war, if their morale did not collapse at this disaster in the North, they could conceivably remain in action for the next ten years, or the next twenty years, and we might still be tied down by this vast guerrilla force.[34]

These semantic anomalies indicate how difficult it has been for the United States to make up its mind what kind of war this is and, therefore, how to end it. If it is essentially a civil war in South Vietnam, it is one thing; if it is really an "invasion" of South Vietnam by North Vietnam, aided and abetted by Communist China and/or the Soviet Union, it is quite another thing. Our war aims must be made homologous with the nature of the war, and neither of them have ever been thought out with exactitude or consistency.*

* Not so long ago the highest American defense officials expressed the opinion that even the "obliteration" of North Vietnam would not stop the war in the South. On January 26, 1966, the following dialogue took place before the House Appropriations Committee:

REPRESENTATIVE GEORGE H. MAHON (Dem., Texas): If we adopted a-

The United States has never even made up its mind whether its objective in this war is "to win" or to convince the Communists that they cannot win, which is not quite the same thing. In his message of December 31, 1963, to General Duong Van Minh, then the strong man of South Vietnam, President Johnson clearly defined their joint objective as "achieving victory." But on July 28, 1965, the President took the position that our goal was "to convince the Communists that we cannot be defeated by force of arms." Secretary of Defense McNamara was asked the following year, "What is our plan to win?" and he replied that it was to prove to the Vietcong and the North Vietnamese military units "that they cannot win in the South." [35] Curiously, the commander-in-chief of the North Vietnamese Army, General Vo Nguyen Giap, gave almost exactly the same answer to a French correspondent in December 1966. "The day the Americans will see that they cannot win the war," General Giap asserted, "then they will stop." [36]

The difference between winning oneself and convincing the other side that it cannot win has considerable importance for any possible peace settlement. The former implies a military victory which has invariably brought about the collapse of the defeated regime, if not of its social order. The latter merely implies a cessation of hostilities based on the mutual recognition of a stalemate.

But what the United States expects South Vietnam to become, in the event of either a victory or a stalemate, has also

policy, and a program, for the obliteration, for all practical purposes, of North Vietnam, would that end the war?

SECRETARY OF DEFENSE McNAMARA: In my opinion it will not completely stop the North Vietnamese support of the operations in South Vietnam. Most of the arms and ammunition is provided by other Communist countries.

(Discussion off the record). . . .

MR. MAHON: General Wheeler, do you believe that the practical obliteration of North Vietnam would successfully end the war in South Vietnam?

GENERAL WHEELER [Chairman of the Joint Chiefs of Staff]: I doubt it, sir. . . .

been left in doubt. The theory of "foreign aggression" in the South, which the Johnson administration adopted in 1965, implied that North Vietnam was a "foreign" country. In his carefully prepared speech at Johns Hopkins University on April 7, 1965, President Johnson called for "an independent South Vietnam." In his book, General Taylor twice includes the "independence of South Vietnam" in his definition of the American objective in the war.[37] For a time the theory of "foreign aggression" seemed to mean that the Vietnam war might conceivably be settled on the basis of spheres of influence—the South as a client-state of the United States and the North as a client-state of Communist China—and thus it was so important to make North Vietnam a dependency of Communist China.

The advocates of Vietnamese partition point to the German and Korean precedents as arguments in favor of this "solution." The three cases are so different that analogies are again dangerous. One cannot possibly compare a prostrate, defeated Germany with a Vietnam that has struggled for over twenty years to recover its national identity. Moreover, the partition of Germany may well be the single most ominous time-bomb in European politics; the recurrent resort to partition as the easy way out is mainly symptomatic of the endemic disease of American foreign policy—that it tends to pay for the present with the future.

If we were serious about the two Vietnams, the least we could have done was to make sure that South Vietnam had an authentically Southern leadership. But Premier Ky and his immediate entourage happen to be Northerners. Tran Van Dinh, the chargé d'affaires and Acting Ambassador of South Vietnam in the United States in 1964, who later resigned, has pointed out:

> To the increasing resentment of the Southerners, all the key posts in the government of South Vietnam are now held by men from North Vietnam. General Nguyen Cao Ky, the prime minister, is a Northerner; so are the secretary general of the National Leadership Committee which ad-

vises Ky; the minister for National Reconstruction (in charge of pacification); the director general of police and of military security; the ministers for information and for state security; the chief of staff; and the commander of the troops that surround Saigon and protect Ky against a *coup d'état*. Northerners control the Army, the police, the pacification, the propaganda, have all the money, all the power, and thus control 14 million South Vietnamese.[38]

This non-Southern domination of the South Vietnamese government was not new. It was already characteristic of Diem's regime from 1954 to 1963.* Paradoxically, the Vietnamese war has been fought by Northern leaderships on both sides. But Diem at least had never fought for the French. Of the ten generals who made up the junta that put Premier Ky in power, nine either had fought on the side of the French or had been training in French military schools during the Vietnamese war against the French from 1946 to 1954. The chief symbol of the "independent" South Vietnamese state was, therefore, a Northern air-force officer who had trained with the French forces during the anti-colonial phase of the war and who was on record with a somewhat ambiguous remark in praise of Adolf Hitler.

But the "independent South Vietnam" position could not be sustained by the United States because no Vietnamese, in-

* "Another salient feature of the Vietnamese civil service is the minority position of Southerners in its middle and higher levels. President Diem's initial Cabinet apparently contained no Southerners; the first Cabinet created after the declaration of the Republic in October 1955 had seven Southerners matched by four Northerners and three Centralists; and there are presently [1963] six Southerners, four Northerners, and four Centralists. Middle and higher positions below Cabinet rank have been still more heavily saturated with non-Southerners. A rough survey of 186 officials holding administrative posts down to that of service chief reveals 67 Southerners to be greatly outnumbered by the combination of 57 Northerners and 62 civil servants from the Center. Not only have Northerners, practically all of them refugees, pre-empted many of the choice posts in the Diem government, but persons from Central Vietnam, which is only partly included within the territory of the Republic of Vietnam, hold government offices greatly out of proportion to the population of their area" (Robert Scigliano, *South Vietnam: Nation under Stress*, p. 51).

cluding South Vietnam's Premier Ky, could accept it; he and the other Northerners in his regime were, rather, bent on unifying the country in their own fashion. Subsequently the Johnson administration backed away from its concept of "independence" and agreed that the Vietnamese could determine "the question of reunification" by themselves.[39] Without such a concession, moreover, the United States could not have reversed itself on the viability of the 1954 Geneva Agreements. For almost a decade the United States had backed former Premier Ngo Dinh Diem's antipathy for the Geneva settlement. But in 1966 Secretary of State Rusk told the Senate Foreign Relations Committee that what the United States sought in South Vietnam was none other than "a restoration of the conditions contemplated by the Accords of 1954" and of "the integrity of the settlement made between the French government and the Communist forces under Ho Chi Minh." [40] If ever John Foster Dulles's corpse has turned in its grave, it must have been during that session of the Senate Committee's hearings.

VIII

Power and Politics

Why have we permitted ourselves to become enmeshed in these multiple confusions and contradictions? Is it because South Vietnam itself is such a vital American interest that it must be defended at all costs?

In 1954, as we have seen, President Eisenhower decided against an all-out effort and limited himself to an economic aid program which was not given much chance of success. He made this aid so provisional and conditional that he gave himself room to do anything or nothing in the next South Vietnamese crisis. Yet, twelve years later, the same man was willing to entertain the possibility of using nuclear weapons. The change in Eisenhower roughly corresponded to the change in American policy.

The views of Senator Richard B. Russell, second to none in Congressional influence and authority, especially in the military sphere, illustrated an even sharper bifurcation of thought and action. In June 1965, just when President Johnson was moving toward sending the first 100,000 American troops in Vietnam, Senator Russell declared:

I can see why many Americans have difficulty understanding how our national interest is being served by the growing commitment of United States money, munitions and men in Vietnam. I thought, and so stated at the time, that it was a mistake to get involved there in the first place; I have never been able to see any strategic, political, or economic advantage to be gained by our involvement. Most of the military leaders whose knowledge and advice I most respect have warned repeatedly that it would be an incalculable mistake for the United States to engage in a full-scale land war on the Asian mainland.[1]

In August 1965 Senator Russell again unburdened himself on the nature and conduct of the war. "We have made every conceivable blunder," he said. And: "Our greatest mistake there has been in overemphasizing the military and not putting sufficient emphasis on the civilian side." And: "I don't think it [Vietnam] has any value strategically. And if we can depend on our missiles to defend us from here, why we don't have to have South Vietnam to hold back the hordes of communism." [2]

But on neither occasion did Senator Russell conclude that the United States ought to get out of the war. On the contrary, he urged in the earlier speech:

Whether or not the initial decision was a mistake is now moot. The United States does have a commitment in South Vietnam. The flag is there. United States honor and prestige are there. And, most important of all, United States soldiers are there.

In the later statement he put it this way:

I think that as of today that the loss of South Vietnam would very largely—would be a worse blow to our world prestige and to our reputation for keeping our word under all conditions than it would be from either a strategic or a tactical or an economic standpoint.

As late as February 23, 1967, Senator Russell told the Senate:

I did not want this war. I did everything in the world I could to keep America out of it. I had just enough sense to know that we should not have gone in. However, we are there now and I do not know how to get out of it.

Senator Russell, a powerful political figure whom no one

would dream of calling a "radical" or even a "liberal," has long enjoyed the luxury of speaking his mind without fearing the consequences. That he should have been so outspoken in his criticism of the expediency of large-scale American intervention in Vietnam strikingly demonstrates that this war can be questioned from very different political standpoints and motives. Many share Senator Russell's judgment that we must continue to fight a useless and blundering war, simply because we are in it. Indeed, if Senator Russell and those who think like him—perhaps the dominant, and certainly a substantial, body of Congressional opinion*— had come to any other conclusion, American intervention in Vietnam could not have continued unchecked.

The Illegitimate War

This ambivalence toward the Vietnam war in some of the most conservative and influential American political circles has attracted far less attention than the more vehement and passionate opposition of those who, at least in part, may actually sympathize with the Vietcong. The former attitude has been expressed unmistakably from time to time, but mainly on special occasions or put in a way to cause the least political damage or embarrassment. Yet it helps to explain

* Democratic Senator George S. McGovern of South Dakota said in 1966: "I think that perhaps ninety out of one hundred Senators think we made a mistake in ever becoming involved in the first place. There are a good many Senators who will say that privately, but who will then say, 'Here we are, so mistake or no mistake, we have to see it through as best we can.' Certainly, some of those Senators who have been advertised in the press as great hawks are among those who think that it was a disastrous mistake for us to have ever become involved in a combat role in Vietnam" (*Commentary*, May 1966, p. 31). In a National Education Television interview on February 1, 1967, Senator Mike Mansfield described the Democratic Senatorial membership as follows: "I would say all of them are uneasy about it [the Vietnam war]. Many of them are frustrated." Of Republicans and Democrats alike, he estimated that a third would be in favor of "more vigorous action," a third "would like to see an honorable conclusion brought as quickly as possible," and a third "would be in the middle somewhere" (text in *Congressional Record, Senate*, February 3, 1967, p. S1424).

why this war has become something of an illegitimate child which every administration has tried to foist off on its predecessors.

Apologists for the Eisenhower administration have argued that its first intervention in Vietnam in 1954 was no more than a local application of the Truman Doctrine, promulgated in 1947. Members of the Kennedy administration have blamed President Eisenhower and Secretary of State Dulles for having forced it to intervene some more. President Johnson and Secretary of State Rusk have gone to the greatest pains to protest that they have merely carried out the obligatory "commitments" of the two previous administrations.* Every President has somehow tried to make it appear, or others have tried to make it appear for him, that he did not make any key decisions at all, that his predecessors made all the hard decisions, and that he was simply bound by them to get deeper and deeper into the war.†

Once again one is struck by the poverty of intellectual invention to support an official thesis. On examination, the thesis seems to rest mainly on three "commitments": President Eisenhower's letter to Ngo Dinh Diem of October 23, 1954; the SEATO treaty of 1954; and President Kennedy's letter to Diem of December 14, 1961. We have already discussed the first at some length; it amounted to a conditional offer of economic and political aid and made no mention of military assistance whatsoever; it could not by the wildest

* On August 3, 1965, for example, President Johnson declared that his problem was "how to keep an agreement I did not initiate—I inherited it." In a limited sense, he was right; the initiation had taken place before him; but there had been no "agreement" for him to inherit, and in any event, it was not the same "agreement" that he had engaged himself to carry out. But the legend of Mr. Johnson's "inheritance" goes on: "Lyndon Johnson inherited Vietnam from irrevocable decisions made by his predecessors" (Rowland Evans and Robert Novak, *Lyndon B. Johnson: The Exercise of Power*, p. 530).

† A classically minded Senator, Ernest Gruening of Alaska, recalled that the Roman historian Sallust had warned of this danger: "It is always easy to begin a war, but very difficult to stop one, since its beginning and end are not under the control of the same man" (*Congressional Record*, Senate, January 14, 1966, p. 215).

stretch of the diplomatic imagination have "committed" the United States to send half a million troops to Vietnam.

The SEATO treaty was equally noncommittal and permissive; it was typical of former Secretary of State Dulles's now-you-see-it-now-you-don't diplomatic style. In the event of an armed aggression against one of the signatories or any danger to the peace of the area, its operative section merely obligated them to "consult immediately" in order to agree on measures of common defense.* When Secretary Dulles testified before the Senate Foreign Relations Committee in November 1954, he declared: "The treaty does not attempt to get into the difficult question as to precisely how we act." An eminent authority, Professor W. McMahon Ball, commented: "The treaty does not oblige the United States either legally or morally to take any course in southeast Asia than the course it might be expected to take if the treaty did not exist."[3] Secretary of State Rusk has found himself on both sides of the issue. On August 6, 1964, he was asked by Democratic Senator Samuel J. Ervin, Jr., of North Carolina whether the United States had come to the aid of South Vietnam "under an obligation assumed by us under the [SEATO] Treaty." Rusk replied that "we are not acting specifically un-

* The first two sections of Article IV must be read together to savor the escape-hatch technique:

1. Each Party recognizes that aggression by means of armed attack in the treaty area against any of the Parties or against any State or territory which the Parties by unanimous agreement may hereafter designate, would endanger its own peace and safety, and agrees that it will in that event act to meet the common danger in accordance with its constitutional processes. Measures taken under this paragraph shall be immediately reported to the Security Council of the United Nations.

2. If, in the opinion of any of the Parties, the inviolability or the integrity of the territory or the sovereignty or political independence of any Party in the treaty area or of any other State or territory to which the provisions of paragraph 1 of this Article from time to time apply is threatened in any way other than by armed attack or is affected or threatened by any fact or situation which might endanger the peace of the area, the Parties *shall consult immediately* in order to agree on the measures which should be taken for the common defense [my italics, T.D.].

Typically, State Department speeches and documents almost always quote the first paragraph without the second, which is the operative one.

der the SEATO treaty." [4] On January 28, 1966, Senator Fulbright asked him: "Does the Southeast Treaty, Southeast
Asia Treaty Organization commit us to do what we are now
doing in Vietnam?" This time Rusk answered: "Yes, sir, I
have no doubt that it does." But a few minutes later the Secretary of State hedged: "I would not want to get into the
question of whether, if we were not interested in the commitments, policy, and principle under the Southeast Asia Treaty,
we have some legal way in order to avoid those commitments.
I suppose one could frame some argument which would make
that case." [5]

One of the more endearing attributes of former Ambassador
Henry Cabot Lodge was that he often spoke his mind without
the subterfuges and equivocations of lesser mortals. He was
once asked about the legality of the American intervention
in Vietnam, and the following dialogue ensued:

> Q. Recently, questions have been raised in this country
> about the legal aspect of what we are doing in Vietnam.
> What is our justification under international law?
>
> MR. LODGE: To me, the legal aspect of it is the least sig-
> nificant.
>
> Q. Is this an international action in Vietnam?
>
> MR. LODGE: It is a fact that the action we are taking in
> Vietnam is not under the aegis of any international organi-
> zation. It is not under the aegis of the United Nations or the
> Southeast Asia Treaty Organization—SEATO. It is a rela-
> tionship between us—the United States—and the Govern-
> ment of Vietnam. We were invited by the Government. [6]

It may well be that the word "commitment" has caused
some of the trouble. It might be argued that the United States
has been "committed" by the SEATO treaty because it chose
to be committed, whereas other members of the Organization,
such as France, Great Britain, and Pakistan, have not been
committed because they have not chosen to be committed. But
this represents a peculiar use of the term and robs it of the
element of compulsion or obligation, which is necessary to
make the State Department's thesis convincing.

As for President Kennedy's letter to President Diem of December 14, 1961, it merely informed the latter that, in response to his request, the United States intended to "promptly increase our assistance to your defense effort." In terms of American manpower, however, that increase was relatively modest, and nothing was said of any further commitment.* In addition, later statements by President Kennedy insisting that it was "their war," that "they are the ones to win it or lose it," and that we could only send "our men out there as advisers" cannot be ignored in any scrupulous effort to determine the limits of Mr. Kennedy's "commitment."

Under President Johnson, the diplomatic game of unloading all responsibility for the half-million American troops in Vietnam has gone to ludicrous extremes. A legal document issued by the State Department on March 4, 1966, exclusively cited statements by Presidents Eisenhower and Kennedy but none at all by President Johnson. Republican Representative Melvin R. Laird of Wisconsin was able to have some good clean fun with this delightful document:

If some future catastrophe were to destroy every written record of the relations of the United States and Vietnam during the 1950s and 1960s except the State Department's publication "The Legality of United States Participation in the Defense of Vietnam," the historian who tried to reconstruct the facts from this document would write something like this:

"Two Presidents of the United States—Presidents Eisenhower and Kennedy—involved their nation in a war to defend South Vietnam against aggression from North Vietnam. Their pledges of support to South Vietnam led to the sending of military supplies, to the dispatch of 900 military

* One sentence in this letter is noteworthy for the official appearance of the theory that North Vietnam was the cause of all the trouble in South Vietnam: "If the Communist authorities in North Vietnam will stop their campaign to destroy the Republic of Vietnam, the measures we are taking to assist your defense efforts will no longer be necessary." Thus the official line which became predominant in 1965 had been lurking in the background for some years.

advisers, and in 1961 to the commitment of substantial numbers of American troops.

"This conflict may have been going on in Vietnam as late as 1966 under another President of the United States whose name is not recorded. In that year the Department of State issued a document upholding the legality of the actions of Presidents Eisenhower and Kennedy."

Mr. Chairman, this manipulation of history should give us all deep concern. When our Department of State releases a report of this kind, I fear we are closer to 1984 than the calendar indicates. This is the kind of propaganda that makes it difficult for the administration to establish its credibility. This is playing politics with Vietnam.[7]

It is true that the American house Lyndon Johnson built in Vietnam was not erected by him alone. The foundation, so to speak, was constructed by President Eisenhower and the first story by President Kennedy. But President Johnson was the architect of the rest of what has become a many-storied structure. President Eisenhower authorized political support and economic aid, together with a few hundred military "advisers" who deceived themselves into thinking that their advice was making the South Vietnamese army into an effective fighting force. President Kennedy vastly increased the economic assistance program and raised the number of military "advisers" to a few thousand, whose mission was still defined as that of enabling the South Vietnamese to fight their own war. President Johnson decisively changed the course of the war by enlarging it in the air to include North Vietnam and by providing the hundreds of thousands of American troops necessary to take over the main burden of fighting the war from the South Vietnamese. It is one thing to say that President Johnson would not have had to make such far-reaching decisions if his predecessors had not gone part of the way toward them; it is another thing to imply that Presidents Eisenhower and Kennedy had already made those decisions for him.

The question of the American "commitment" has a bearing on the future as well as on the past. For if we have necessarily been committed to the expansion of our force in Vietnam from a few hundred "advisers" to half a million combat troops, the commitment is so elastic that there is no telling where it will end.

Investment in Vietnam

American policy in Vietnam, then, cannot be understood in terms of Vietnam alone. It can more nearly be understood in terms of what we have done in Vietnam. As a result of one miscalculation after another, we have gradually been drawn into making an enormous, disproportionate military and political investment in Vietnam. This investment—not the vital interests of the United States in Vietnam—has cast a spell on us. The same thing would happen if we should decide to put 500,000 troops in Mauretania or even Ruritania. Once American resources and prestige are committed on such a profligate scale, the "commitment" develops a life of its own and, as the saying goes, good money must be thrown after bad.

This, to my mind, is nothing to be scoffed or sneered at. It is serious business for a great power to back into a cockpit so far away and so little understood, fling thousands after thousands of men and billions after billions of dollars into it—and then have second thoughts about the wisdom of having gambled so much for so little. The temptation is almost overpowering to magnify the importance of the game, to try to retrieve one's fortunes with one more raise of the ante, to be prisoners of an ever-changing present because looking back at the past is too painful and peering into the future is too unpromising. Above all, there is need for reassurance that we possess some infallible power to come out right and on top in the end.

That power has become nothing else than—power. From the President down, leading officials have spread the glad tidings that power has given us global responsibilities which seem to be functions not of our infinite wisdom or boundless altruism but mainly of our incomparable power. In his speech at Johns Hopkins in April 1965, for example, President Johnson exhorted that we have the power and now the opportunity, for the first time in centuries, to make nations stop struggling with one another. That is such a large order, the struggle to end all struggles may also be the end of mankind. Not inappropriately, the former Assistant Secretary of State for International Organization Affairs, and present United States Permanent Representative to NATO, published a book in 1966 with the title *The Obligations of Power*. In it he argued that the United States must be "so very much involved, in so many ugly grudge fights, in so many places" simply because it is so large and powerful. He bade us "get accustomed to our own power, and to the implications of its global availability." He berated us for still being "unaccustomed to our power, still doubters of our own prowess." He comforted us with the thought that we do *not* have to be the world's policeman *if* we and other nations can build international peacekeeping machinery. But no such machinery exists, and its future is more than doubtful. Thus this comfort proved to be cold indeed; we were really being told that we must now be, and probably continue to be, the "world's policeman." [8] President Johnson liked the phrase "obligations of power" so much that he put it into one of his own speeches in May 1966.[9] Another form which this line of thought has taken is the theory of the American "shield." As President Johnson put it, the strength of the United States required it to "provide a shield for those on whom the Communists prey." [10] After the "cold war" began, Vice President Humphrey said, "American power was the only shield available to fragile and newly independent nations in non-Communist Asia." [11] Under Secretary of State Ball gave the United States the responsibility of defending *all* boundaries and demarcation lines established by postwar agreements.[12]

The prevailing official orthodoxy that power would pull us through then began to make its way via journalistic channels.

One of the transmission belts for this view put the case this way:

> The central factor in this new picture is power. The cocktail-party philosophers who declare that "there is no military solution" and speak of a struggle "for the hearts and minds of men" cover only a small corner of the truth. The idea of military solutions for political problems went out with the Second World War and no one in Vietnam thinks in these terms. But military success—seizing and exploiting the initiative, harrying and punishing the enemy—is an indispensable condition of political success. With security, everything is possible. Without security, nothing is possible.[13]

Not so long ago, leading American officials spoke very much the same language as the cocktail-party philosophers mentioned above. Secretary of Defense McNamara came close to using their very words. In any case, the notion that military success is an indispensable condition of political success begs the question. For is not political success also the indispensable condition of military success? Less than three years ago, the latter proposition was considered the enlightened assumption of American policy. There was even a time when politics was given precedence over power; then power and politics were linked together, each unproductive without the other; now power has become the precondition of politics, which has been retired to some kind of limbo until we have achieved "military success."

For over a decade, American officials and advisers had been pulling and tugging and hauling to get South Vietnamese regimes to make some meaningful reforms, especially in the sphere of land tenure. The thinking was that it was necessary to win over the peasantry to isolate the guerrillas, and that only serious reforms could win over the peasantry. Then it turned out that all this effort was misdirected because it came before rather than after the "military success." The latest wisdom from the embassy in Saigon unwittingly condemned all the fine projects and programs that used to pass for wisdom.

If "security" were all that mattered, former President Ngo Dinh Diem might have achieved a "political success" because he had tight control of the country for quite a few years. And if their mandarins behind Premier Ky ever get that much "security" again, they are hardly likely to do any more or any better. It is naïve to imagine that a military regime will celebrate its "military success" by making far-reaching political concessions and basic economic reforms. With security, everything may be possible—but only if there is the right political program, pressure, and will. The last thing that will shake the *status quo* in South Vietnam is a feeling of "security" on the part of the powers that be.

We have, in truth, resorted to power because our politics has failed. Since no politician can afford to admit this, we must pretend that we are resorting to power in order to make our politics succeed.

Abuse of Language

The hallmark of the Johnson administration's foreign policy has been its willingness to use and abuse naked military power. In both the Dominican Republic and Vietnam, Mr. Johnson made the critical decisions at about the same time —the first months of 1965. I am quite willing to believe that he sent troops to both lands as a last resort. But the deeper question remains: Why did he have to resort to the last?

As I have indicated, the problem goes far beyond the present administration. The pattern of military intervention to salvage political failure has run through three very different administrations relating to three very different countries. President Kennedy's former aides have differed on the question whether he would have done the same thing as President Johnson has done in Vietnam. I am not altogther persuaded that Kennedy would have acted in quite the same way or gone to the same lengths. He did, after all, draw a line barring the use of American combat troops in the Bay of Pigs adventure, and refused to cross that line despite enormous pressure on him to do so. It is hard to imagine Lyndon Johnson accepting a setback with such restraint and assuming full responsibility for it himself. At least Kennedy would perhaps have spared us the intellectual gimcrackery and pious cant that accompany President Johnson's worst excesses.

I am not, by any means, trying to belittle the importance of power in the conduct of foreign policy. On the contrary, I was one of those who warned against the dangerous implications in the line which began to come out of the Soviet Union in 1960 at the height of Nikita Khrushchev's reign. In brief, the Soviet leadership proclaimed that the world had entered a "new stage" in which the "balance of forces," politically, economically, and militarily, had changed in favor of the Soviet system. When this doctrine became the leitmotiv of Soviet propaganda the following year, I wrote an article for *Commentary* (November 1961) in which I urged that it was necessary for the West to "find a way to demonstrate that the Soviets are wrong about their 'balance of forces.' " I have not changed my mind in the least about the need at that time, and President Kennedy did find a way to prove the Soviets wrong during the "missile crisis" in October 1962.

Now we have gone so far that we are flaunting our power recklessly, ineptly, and unproductively. When the power of politics is so divorced from the politics of power, as it has been in Vietnam and elsewhere, the crisis of American policy has reached the danger point.

This is the crux of the matter. When President Johnson fixed visitors with a steely eye and asked them in effect, "What would *you* do to get the Communists to give us an honorable peace in Vietnam?" he was not posing as crushing a question as he seemed to think. If a patient who has dissipated for years comes to a doctor for an instant cure, the failure to get one may be the fault of the patient, not the doctor. And if the patient also specifies that the cure must be "honorable," any unpleasant diagnosis or course of treatment may not be acceptable to him. In diplomacy, "honor" is hard to negotiate. It is usually waved as a banner to start a war, not to end one by some means short of victory.

It would be one thing if Mr. Johnson had asked his critics for their advice before he got in so deeply. It was quite another thing to put the onus for getting out on those who had had no responsibility for getting in. If the question was so difficult to answer, it was because Mr. Johnson's policies had made it so difficult. After all, no critic of this war was elected President on a platform of not getting tied down in a land war in Asia and not sending American boys nine or ten thousand miles away from home to do what Asian boys should be doing for themselves.

One man's efforts to answer Mr. Johnson's question suggested that it could be a thankless occupation even for the Secretary-General of the United Nations. After the fall of the Diem regime in November 1963, U Thant implicitly suggested to the United States the formation of a coalition government in Saigon to take in non-Communist Vietnamese political exiles who believed in the country's neutralization as the way out of the war. U Thant subsequently made known his view that "there was a very good possibility in 1963 of arriving at a satisfactory *political* solution" (my italics). This advice was not accepted because the generals who succeeded Ngo Dinh Diem, and the new Johnson administration, set their sights on "victory," as President Johnson indicated in his message to General Duong Van Minh on December 31, 1963.

Throughout 1964, American policy was antineutralist and even equated the neutralization of Vietnam with a Communist takeover. In a typical statement of that period, Assistant Secretary for Far Eastern Affairs William P. Bundy said in September 1964: "Neutralization of South Vietnam alone would, therefore, simply be a step toward a Communist takeover, as the Communists themselves know in pushing it as an interim course for South Vietnam." [14] About six months later, in his Johns Hopkins speech on April 7, 1965, President Johnson agreed that South Vietnam should "be tied to no alliance." By January 7, 1966, a State Department press release summed up the United States position on Vietnam in fourteen points, of which number eleven read: "The countries of southeast Asia can be nonaligned or neutral if that be their option." And on March 30, 1966, Under Secretary of State George W. Ball went so far as to maintain that the United States had "never asked anything other than a neutral Vietnam." [15] The war might conceivably be over if President Johnson had taken that advice at the end of 1963.

In September 1964 U Thant made a determined effort to arrange private conversations between the United States and North Vietnam to end the war. The latter agreed, through the Russians, to a meeting. But repeated efforts by U Thant to get an acceptance from the United States failed. Apparently with the encouragement of the late Adlai Stevenson, then United States Ambassador to the United Nations, U Thant went so far as to get the approval of Burma for holding a secret meeting there. The Burmese head of state, Ne Win, replied positively on January 18, 1965; the entire plan was vetoed by Washington ten days later. The official reason for the rejection given to U Thant by Adlai Stevenson evidently made two points: the United States could not enter into discussions with the Hanoi regime without the presence of the Saigon government; and such talks would risk ruining the morale of the Saigon government. Instead of giving U Thant a chance in January, President Johnson decided to expand the war in February.

The first intimation that U Thant had offered some more advice, with equally unhappy results, came from the Secretary-General himself. At a news conference on February 24, 1965, he disclosed that he had presented "concrete ideas and proposals" for a peaceful settlement to "some of the principal parties directly involved in the question of Vietnam," including the United States. That something had gone wrong, and even that he felt a wrong had been perpetrated, was suggested by U Thant in some extraordinarily undiplomatic remarks:

> I am sure that the great American people, if only they know the true facts and the background to the developments in South Vietnam, will agree with me that further bloodshed is unnecessary.
>
> The political and diplomatic method of discussions and negotiations alone can create conditions which will enable the United States to withdraw gracefully from that part of the world. As you know in times of war and of hostilities, the first casualty is truth.[16]

What was the Secretary-General trying to say? What "true facts" were being kept from the great American people? Who had been responsible for making truth one of the war's "casualties"?

Unfortunately, U Thant did not answer these questions, and the great American public remained in ignorance—not without the help of their leaders. George E. Reedy, President Johnson's press secretary, contemptuously referred to the whole affair as "diplomatic chit-chat." [17] Secretary of State Rusk said that the United States was not interested because a "crucial element" was missing, that element being "any indication that Hanoi is prepared to stop doing what it is doing and what it knows it is doing against its neighbor." Without attempting to conceal his annoyance or disdain, he added: "The absence of this crucial element affects the current discussion of something called 'negotiation.' " [18]

In the following weeks, both President Johnson and Secretary Rusk gave the impression that the other side had shown little or no willingness to talk about anything. On March 25, for example, President Johnson protested that the United States sought "no more than a return to the essentials of the agreements of 1954," but that "at present the Communist aggressors have given no sign of any willingness to move in this direction." [19] In an interview on April 2, Secretary Rusk said discouragingly: "Now, again, the point here is: What is there to be negotiated? Who is going to negotiate, and to what end?" He complained that what was missing was "some private contact that indicates that a satisfactory basis of settlement can be found." A British correspondent asked: "You've had silence, completely?" To which Rusk seemed to give an affirmative, if somewhat ambiguous, answer: "No indication that—despite a number of contacts of various sorts—no indication that Hanoi is prepared to leave Laos and South Vietnam alone." [20]

Since the great American public was still unaware of U Thant's efforts to arrange for just such "private contacts," Secretary Rusk's reply went unchallenged. In Congress and outside, however, considerable pressure had been building up to find some way to initiate peace negotiations. On April 7, only five days after Secretary Rusk's brush-off of possible negotiations, President Johnson suddenly inserted in his speech at Johns Hopkins University a passage which put him on record in favor of "unconditional discussions." * The same words were used in the United States reply the following day to an appeal from seventeen nations for negotiations without preconditions. It was not clear whether "discussions" were the same as "negotiations," but the important word seemed to be "unconditional."

Meanwhile, the French tried to so something. In May 1965, Foreign Minister Couve de Murville confidentially told a group of correspondents in Paris that North Vietnam had signified a willingness to talk without conditions, but that he had found Washington unreceptive to the news. At a press conference on August 27, Secretary Rusk was asked about reports that President de Gaulle was waiting for the right moment "to personally negotiate an end to the Vietnam war." The question was raised: "Would we welcome any such efforts by de Gaulle?" After remarking, somewhat acidly,

---

* According to Rowland Evans and Robert Novak, the reference to "unconditional discussions" was "a last-minute concession to the Peace Bloc that amazed those who had seen the earlier version of the speech" (*Lyndon B. Johnson: The Exercise of Power,* op. cit., p. 544).

that neither side had "nominated attorneys in this field," Rusk went on to give some insight into what he considered to be "unconditional discussions." He said that he was waiting for a "key signal," and that his "antennae" had not yet picked it up.[21] Thus, it appeared, the "unconditional discussions" were dependent on the prior condition that Rusk's antennae would pick up a "key signal," the nature of which he failed to reveal. At least something new had been added to the language of diplomacy—the conditional unconditional.

As far as the general public was concerned, however, these references to "discussions," "signals," and "antennae" seemed too abstruse and abstract to rouse much hope or excitement. The issue suddenly became more concrete and urgent as a result of an article by Eric Sevareid, in the November 15, 1965, issue of *Look,* relating his last conversation with the late Ambassador to the United Nations Adlai E. Stevenson. This article for the first time made public the information that the United States had rejected a North Vietnamese proposal in the fall of 1964 for both sides to meet in Rangoon, Burma, to discuss ways of ending the war. The following day, in a talk before a conference of bankers in New Jersey, another correspondent, David Schoenbrun, who had been present at Couve de Murville's off-the-record briefing the previous May, made known—without revealing the nature of the source—that this offer had been made and ignored too.

The Sevareid and Schoenbrun disclosures made it impossible for American officials to go on pretending that no talks of any kind had ever been proposed. The line now changed to the effect that the right kind of talks had not been proposed. The State Department spokesman, Robert J. McCloskey, explained that "on the basis of the total evidence available to us, we did not believe at any time that North Vietnam was prepared for serious talks." He denied that there had been any unwillingness on the part of the United States to "enter into meaningful talks." It all depended on when Secretary Rusk's sensitive "antennae" would recognize "that Hanoi was prepared for peace talks," he said.[22] The State Department also confirmed that the North Vietnamese had approached the French on May 20, 1965, on the subject of possible peace negotiations.[23] Finally, on November 26, 1965, Secretary of State Rusk was asked whether the handling of the U Thant–Stevenson incident did not signify a change in United States policy with respect to "unconditional negotiations." First, Rusk admitted that the Sevareid story had been essentially accurate: "It is true that last autumn Ambassador Stevenson was informed by Secretary-General U Thant that he had been informed indirectly that Hanoi would be willing to have contact with the United States and that the Secretary-General had suggested Rangoon as a suitable site." But, he went on to explain, the United States had at its disposal a great deal of other information which it interpreted as meaning that North Vietnam was not prepared to call off its "aggression against South Vietnam." Asked whether this did not mean that the United States had shifted its position on "unconditional discussions," Secretary Rusk came close to defining what the United States really meant by that term:

There has never been any lack of opportunity to bring this matter to peace—to the conference table—if the other side is prepared to stop trying to impose their will by force on South Vietnam.[24]

There is, of course, no telling what would have happened if the United States had sent someone to Rangoon to discuss peace terms at the end of 1964 or the late spring of 1965. The military position was then so unfavorable—May 1965 was exactly the time the United States expected the enemy to launch an offensive to cut South Vietnam in half —that it could not have failed to prejudice diplomatic negotiations or perhaps to result in a proposal to partition Vietnam again, this time in the South. With the information at hand, it is a futile exercise to speculate what the North Vietnamese had in mind. We may only assume that they must have

stopped short of anything obviously or humiliatingly unacceptable to the United States or it is most unlikely that
U Thant and Couve de Murville would have taken the
proposal so seriously. U Thant, indeed, must have had good
reason for believing that the Rangoon meeting could have
enabled the United States to withdraw "gracefully" from
that part of the world.

But the United States did not want to withdraw, gracefully or not, from that part of the world. It was just then
pouring in thousands of troops to prove that it had the
power to stay and to prevail. The way the U Thant effort was
handled showed that the abuse of power was accompanied
by an abuse of language. The U Thant–Stevenson efforts
to arrange for discussions in Rangoon were managed in
Washington with typical Johnsonian hanky-panky. First, the
impression was created that there was nothing, and no one
with whom, to negotiate. Second, the other side was outbid
with what seemed like a most magnanimous commitment
to engage in "unconditional discussions." Third, the unconditional was gradually conditioned to mean that the
United States had to be previously convinced of the other
side's intention to be "serious" and "meaningful." Fourth,
this in turn depended on Secretary Rusk's "antennae" receiving a "key signal" in advance. Fifth, the "key signal"
was nothing less than the other side's prior undertaking "to
stop trying to impose their will by force on South Vietnam,"
that is, to agree to unilateral renunciation of the armed
struggle.

Even if we do not know enough to judge just what
might have happened in Rangoon if the discussions had
taken place there, we do know enough to recognize that,
if this was an example of "unconditional discussions," words
have lost all meaning. Instead of going to Rangoon to find
a way to get the other side to stop trying to impose its will
by force on South Vietnam, Secretary of State Rusk demanded that it should stop trying before going to Rangoon.
The "crucial element" and the "key signal" that Secretary

Rusk was always waiting for would have made discussions in Rangoon or elsewhere a mere formality of accepting the other side's decision to quit the struggle for power.

After again exploring all avenues toward a possible peace for over a year, U Thant privately communicated the result of his search to the United States late in 1965 and made his recommendations public on March 9, 1966. In brief, U Thant made known, he had reason to believe that peace negotiations could be initiated on the basis of three points: (1) cessation of the bombing of North Vietnam, (2) substantial reduction by all parties of all military activities in South Vietnam, and (3) the participation of the National Liberation Front (Vietcong) in any peaceful settlement. Again the Secretary-General found that Washington was not interested.[25]

In another important statement, on January 10, 1967, Secretary-General U Thant elaborated on his differences with the United States. The points he made indicate what obstacles have stood in the way of a negotiated or other type of peace in Vietnam. Of the bombing of North Vietnam, he said:

First of all, in my view, it is absolutely necessary that the bombing of North Vietnam must stop without conditions. . . . I still feel very strongly that there will be no move towards peace so long as the bombing of North Vietnam is going on.

On the relationship of the National Liberation Front to North Vietnam, he declared:

I do not subscribe to the generally held view that the National Liberation Front in South Vietnam is a "stooge" of Hanoi. I do not agree with this thesis. In my view, the National Liberation Front, although receiving perhaps very substantial help from the North, is an independent entity in the same way as the National Liberation Front of Algeria in the late nineteen-fifties was receiving very substantial help from Tunisia or Morocco or the United Arab Republic.

He then took issue with the "domino theory":

I do not subscribe to the generally held view that if South Vietnam falls, then Country X, then Country Y, then Country Z will follow. I do not agree with this so-called domino theory. In my view the destiny of every country is shaped by its own peculiar circumstances, its national background, own political philosophy. What is true of Country X is not necessarily true of Country Y or Country Z.

Perhaps most significantly, he emphasized the importance of considering Vietnam independent and nonaligned:

I think I know the mood of the leaders in Vietnam. I think that the leaders in Vietnam are very independent. They are obsessed with the principle of nonalignment, which, as you know, is one of the twin objectives of the Geneva Agreements. If Vietnam is independent and militarily nonaligned, as I have been advocating, preferably with the guarantee of the big powers, including the United States, then I do not see how this could pose a threat to international peace or security, or how Vietnam could be strategically vital to the interests of the West. The problem of South Vietnam must be solved primarily by the South Vietnamese people themselves. This is the basic issue. I think it is the basic and fundamental point which everybody should bear in mind.

Was there anything inherently "dishonorable" in U Thant's three points? I do not think so. If there was, Washington should not have urged U Thant to remain as Secretary-General. We could not expect any *quid pro quo* for a cessation of the bombing of North Vietnam, because North Vietnam was not bombing South Vietnam, let alone roads, villages, railroad lines, and oil storage depots in the vicinity of Washington, D.C. The massive bombing of North Vietnam was inaugurated in February 1965, when there were only about 400 North Vietnamese regular soldiers in the South out of an estimated enemy total of 140,000. The second point entailed a military atmosphere conducive to serious negotiations. Both the National Liberation Front and the Hanoi regime had taken exception to it, indicating that U Thant had by no means been representing their point of view. As for the third point, which was controversial mainly for its inclusion of the Vietcong, President Johnson had said that the representation of the Vietcong would not be an "insurmountable problem."

For my part, not only were U Thant's proposals not excessive or unreasonable; they were, in view of all the circumstances, the *minimal* conditions for serious negotiations. They did not involve giving away anything substantive in advance; the fate of South Vietnam, its relationship to the North, and the relationship of both of them to the outside world would still have had to be settled at a conference that might resemble in form the Geneva meeting of 1954. If we seriously wanted peace without victory, we would have snatched at these proposals. The repeated rebuffs to U Thant's efforts in 1965 and 1966 will be counted among the most shortsighted and least defensible imprudences of American policy.

The Scale of Destructiveness

As both sides began to increase their investment in the war after 1965, it became increasingly difficult for them to settle for less than seemed to justify the cost which the war had imposed on them. This was the contradiction which made it more rather than less difficult to arrange for peace discussions, let alone a peaceful settlement, after the American bombings of North Vietnam and massive injection of military manpower began in February of that year. The original purpose of this large-scale American effort was to avoid a South Vietnamese collapse, but soon after this was accomplished by the end of the year, the objective was transformed into a test of American military technology and tactics to combat a new and exotic foe. The American theory was that the more military punishment the Vietnamese Communists received, the less likely they were to carry on the struggle for diminishing returns at astronomically higher costs. But this thinking failed to see that the United States was placing the enemy in the same position in which it had placed itself. The more the southern Vietcong and North Vietnam put into and lost in the enlarging and more destructive war, the less they could back out of it without betraying what was for them two decades of struggle for power and without giving their vastly increased human and material sacrifices the vindication and absolution of ultimate victory.

Both sides were carried along this escalator of military investment and destruction with hesitation and trepidation. Both tried to "win" or at least to avoid losing at different stages by investing and destroying as little as possible. President Kennedy's advisers attest he was always being told that a little more money, a few more men, another economic program would stabilize and strengthen South Vietnam enough to enable it to carry on by itself. But, inevitably, a little more on one side was matched by a little more on the other side. Until the United States began to use its military power on a really massive scale, a stage not reached until 1966, the matching game was not hard for either side. This served to keep down the level of the conflict, but it also made it easier to go from one level to the next. An all-out confrontation between United States power and Vietcong–North Vietnam power was avoidable as long as the South Vietnamese armed forces were expected to carry the main burden of the fighting. The shifting of this burden from the South Vietnamese to the United States forces in the fall of 1966 fundamentally changed the character of the war.

As soon as the American military took over the war, they had to make it over in their own image. The new strategy was exemplified by "Operation Cedar Falls" in January 1967 and the even larger "Operation Junction City" the following month. In order to clear out long-time Vietcong strongholds, they carefully removed civilians from thousands of acres, which were then subjected to systematic devastation from the air and ground. When American forces moved in, they found few enemy troops, but they proceeded to complete the destruction of the homes and villages, to which the native inhabitants could never come back, as well as of the camps and tunnels. These operations were designed to make the areas unusable by the enemy or to destroy whatever usefulness they had had. In the process, however, increasingly large areas of South Vietnam were desolated,* thousands of non-combatants were displaced from their ancestral dwellings, and where there had been for decades and even centuries a human culture, however simple or primitive, there was now a wasteland. In past wars, ground so won was occupied to provide a taking-off place for another forward movement. But this was a different kind of war. The American forces soon moved out; the enemy could, as in other places simi-larly "cleared," return; and if the war went on long enough, the operation might have to be repeated, again and again.

This was the 1967 version of the war in *South* Vietnam. This "strategy of denial" was imposed by both technology and politics. To save men and substitute for politics, it was necessary to exploit the overwhelming American advantage in firepower. It became increasingly difficult, however, to distinguish between friend and foe or between the foe's area and the friend's area well enough to use it most effectively. As long as the American theory of the war (before 1965) was based on training the South Vietnamese army to fight guer-rilla warfare, to meet insurgency with counterinsurgency, the distinction between friend and foe or between the active enemy forces and the passive noncombatants was still capable of being established, in theory if not always in practice. But the shift from the South Vietnamese to the United States type of war, brought about by the former's failure to beat the Vietcong at its own game, increasingly made the new military technology, available in full to the United States alone, the determining factor in the post-1965 stages of the war. The adoption of "open area targets," of "scorched earth" tactics, of the "strategy of denial," was made possible by weapons which increasingly expanded the zone of de-structiveness and, therefore, lent themselves most economi-cally and efficiently to use against land masses rather than

* It has been estimated that 220,000 acres of crop land, and about 340,000 acres of non-crop land, have been destroyed—an area almost equal to that of the state of Delaware (*Congressional Record,* Senate, February 6, 1967, p. S1609).

against human concentrations. There was no way of denying land to one's enemy in South Vietnam without devastating the land of one's friends or at least of those whom one preferred to have as friends rather than as enemies. This indiscriminateness was also true of the widespread use of napalm and the even more horrible white phosphorus.* More and more, the new military technology produces a dehumanized genocide that, even in a friendly country, cannot distinguish between friend and foe.

The moral issue was raised by President Johnson in the following form:

> There are people in our country who denounce air strikes against oil depots in North Vietnam, but they remain strangely silent when the Communists in the South turn their mortars on an American hospital or blow up a busload of farmers or murder the mayor of a Vietnamese town. I just wish they would ask themselves if their standard of judgment is really fair.[26]

The President spoke before it was established and admitted that far more than oil depots and other military targets had been hit in North Vietnam. But the basic issue which he stated in terms of bombers versus mortars contained the essence of the problem. At best, the President put the United States and the Vietcong terrorists on the same moral level;

* The effects of napalm and white phosphorus on Vietnamese children were investigated in the spring of 1966 by William F. Pepper, Director of the Children's Institute for Advanced Study and Research at Mercy College, New York. In an excruciating account of his experiences, he wrote: "For countless thousands of children in Vietnam breathing is quickened by terror and pain, and tiny bodies learn more about death every day. . . . It is omnipresent as the napalm that falls from the skies with the frequency and impartiality of rain in the monsoon season. Napalm, and its more horrible companion, white phosphorus, provide for the children of Vietnam fates more horrible to the civilized conscience than stilling of life. Young flesh is seared, liquidized, and carved into grotesque forms. The finished products are often scarcely human in appearance, and develop after an experience of unimaginable pain and suffering. One cannot be confronted with the monstrous effects of the burning without being totally shaken" (*Columbia University Forum*, Fall 1966, pp. 46-48).

his protest was aimed less at the cruelties on both sides than at the United States' excessive share of the world's indignation. But was there no more to the problem than that two wrongs do not make a right or that one wrong cancels out another? Was there not something deeper that the President failed to consider? A mortar shell lobbed indiscriminately into the center of Saigon is an act of wanton violence. But there is violence and violence; otherwise there would be no difference between a bullet and a hydrogen bomb. The *scale* of destructiveness cannot be ignored in the "standard of judgment." The incineration of 600 or 6000 Jews by the Nazis would have been an infamous crime, but it would not have aroused the horror of the 6,000,000 victims. The "conventional" bombing of Germany and England in World War II was disastrous enough, but the world reacted to the atomic bombing of Hiroshima as an evil of a different order. The scale of destructiveness does decidedly make a difference in the "standard of judgment." If this principle is not recognized, these inhuman enormities could happen again. What has already taken place in Vietnam on a relatively small scale can be repeated on a larger and larger scale. And those with the greatest capabilities of destructiveness face the greatest temptations and bear the greatest responsibilities.

IX

The Politics of Miscalculation

The next stage of the war was preceded by diplomatic maneuvers of unusual complexity, deceptiveness, and promise. Both sides seemed to be coming closer to a basis for negotiation before the American decision was made in February 1967 to intensify and broaden the scale of the attack on North Vietnam.

The form of these maneuvers resulted largely from the "negotiating positions" which both sides had previously taken.

On the North Vietnamese side, the basic position went back to the four-point program enunciated by Premier Pham Van Dong on April 8, 1965. This had called, in substance, for withdrawal of all United States military forces from South Vietnam, neutralization of both South and North Vietnam, settlement of South Vietnam's internal affairs "in accordance with the program" of the National Liberation Front, and peaceful reunification. Pham Van Dong had offered it as "the basis for the soundest political settlement of the Vietnam problem." If this basis were "recognized," he said, "favorable conditions" for the peaceful settlement of the problem would be created and an international conference "along the pattern of" the Geneva conference of 1954 could be convened.[1]

On the surface, none of these four points appeared to be an insuperable obstacle to some form of peaceful negotiations. In his testimony before the Senate Foreign Relations Committee on February 18, 1966, Secretary of State Rusk said that the United States could accept three of the four points, the first, second, and fourth. The only exception he took was to the third, which he called "the core of the Communist position." In order to make it totally unacceptable, however, Secretary Rusk had to engage in one of his most tortuous intellectual exercises.

Instead of being content for diplomatic purposes to view the disputed third point as meaning no more and no less than what it said, he chose to reinterpret it in terms of the original NLF program of December 1960, issued in the heyday of Ngo Dinh Diem's regime. By this means Secretary Rusk sought to convince the committee that Pham Van Dong's third point implied prior recognition of the National Liberation Front as "the sole spokesman for the people of South Vietnam," which "hence should control them." Yet the earlier document had merely called for the overthrow of Diem's regime and its replacement by a broad "coalition government." Mr. Rusk leaped from the 1965 point to the 1960 program to arrive at the utterly gratuitous conclusion that Hanoi had really demanded the acceptance in advance of the NLF "as the sole bargaining representative of the South Vietnamese people." [2] In reality, the December 1960 program was such a lengthy, diffuse, and essentially moderate political mosaic, carefully contrived to appeal to the greatest number and variety of anti-Diem elements, that it could have been used as a basis of negotiations without committing anyone to anything very much in advance.* Unfortunately,

* The December 20, 1960, "action program" of the NLF called for "a broad, national, and democratic coalition government composed of representatives of every sector of the population, various nationalities, political parties, religious communities, and patriotic personalities." It wanted to "abolish the present constitution of the Ngo Dinh Diem dictatorial government and with universal suffrage elect a new National Assembly. Freedom of expression, press, assembly, association, travel, religion, and other democratic liberties will be promulgated. Religious, political, and

no one on the committee seemed to know the documents intimately enough to challenge the Secretary's fanciful exegesis.

In its own propaganda, the NLF had styled itself "the only genuine and legal representative of the South Vietnam people." [3] It based its claim to "legality," however, wholly on the "fraternal support accorded to it by the entire Vietnamese people," and the entire case was little more than a propaganda effort. But Pham Van Dong had made the NLF's nebulous "program," designed to be all things to all men, the issue, rather than its organizational status. Only after the bombing of North Vietnam had gone on for almost a year did Ho Chi Minh demand that the United States "must recognize the NLFSV as the sole genuine representative of the people of South Vietnam and engage in negotiations with it." [4] Whatever significance this hardening of the North Vietnamese position may have had in 1966, it was not at issue in 1965 except to the extent that American diplomacy chose to give the most extreme interpretation to Pham Van Dong's third point, the only one that ostensibly stood in the way of accepting all four as a basis of negotiations. And even for that purpose, it would have been necessary for Secretary Rusk to reinterpret the third point in terms of later rather than earlier Communist statements.

It may be suspected that the real reason for straining at this point was less semantic than military. In April 1965, the United States feared the total collapse of the South Vietnamese military front. Experience had shown that diplomatic

---

patriotic organizations will be permitted freedom of activity regardless of beliefs and tendencies," etc. The entire document may be found in Pike, op. cit., pp. 344-47, who devotes an entire chapter to tracing the various changes in the NLF's programmatic efforts (pp. 344-71). There is a somewhat different but similar translation in Fall, *The Two Viet-Nams*, op. cit., pp. 449-53. It may be argued that the NLF program was democratic window-dressing to lure the greatest number of anti-Diem opponents; it cannot be argued that it was an outright bid for sole Communist control. Secretary Rusk refers to the NLF program as announced from Hanoi on January 29, 1961, instead of using the more usual date, December 20, 1960, when it was first issued.

negotiations, whatever their "basis" may be, tend to reflect the relative positions of power. This was, in my view, reason enough to explain American reluctance to engage in negotiations at that time. The American ability to bring its own overwhelming military power quickly into the balance, however, might easily have given the Communist side pause and forced it to settle for much less than the existing balance of forces within South Vietnam seemed to indicate. In any case, negotiations in the first half of 1965—the last time they might have taken place in a relatively restrained atmosphere —would have demanded that both sides be content with something short of "victory." Instead, the impression was created of irreconcilable positions that were virtually mirror images of each other—of a National Liberation Front that claimed to "represent" all the people of South Vietnam, and of a National Liberation Front that represented virtually no one in South Vietnam.

On the American side, as we have seen, the position changed from no negotiations with the Communist devil in 1964 to "unconditional discussions" in 1965, modified by the condition that Secretary Rusk's antennae should receive in advance an undivulged "key signal." In 1966, however, the problem increasingly turned on the first of Secretary-General U Thant's three points—the cessation of American bombing of North Vietnam. The more destructive the bombing became, the more determined the North Vietnamese were to stop it before entering into anything resembling negotiations.

Thenceforth, the American negotiating position hinged on the concept of "reciprocity." All through 1966, American spokesmen tried to define this accordion-like term. Secretary Rusk tended to stretch it the most. He usually demanded that the "other side" had to give up their "aggression" or "abandon their attempt to take South Vietnam over by force" in return for a cessation of the bombing.[5] In the summer of 1966, President Johnson seemed to demand a more concrete price. He said that the United States had offered to stop the bombing immediately "if they will stop sending troops into South Vietnam." This seemed to imply that North Vietnam did not have to withdraw troops, but the President went on to observe that the South Vietnamese could not decide the kind of government and country they wanted "while armed troops from North Vietnam are waging war against their people and against their villages," which suggested that he expected far more than a cessation of North Vietnamese reinforcements in exchange for a cessation of the bombing.[6]

The various formulas employed in this period were sufficiently vague to give North Vietnam considerable leeway how it might make known its decision to satisfy the American demand, but the essence of that demand was never left in doubt—the abandonment by North Vietnam of the struggle for power in the South. If, as the United States claimed, the North was responsible for that struggle, the withdrawal of the North was equivalent to its total abandonment. While much ink and breath were wasted over such questions as which side had to make the first move, whether the North demanded permanent as well as unconditional cessation of the bombing, and how the North could convince the United States of its "serious" intentions, the "key signal" had not changed and was well understood by both sides—Communist abdication in the struggle for power in South Vietnam. The United States was deliberately vague because it was less interested in the form than in the substance, and because it preferred to treat the struggle for political power as if it were merely a foreign military aggression.

How Not to Negotiate

Toward the end of 1966, another effort was made to break through the diplomatic impasse. According to the first report of this episode, on December 2 and 3 United States Ambassador Henry Cabot Lodge met with the Polish representative on the International Control Commission, Ambassador

Janusz Lewandowski, at the home of the Italian ambassador in Saigon, Giovanni d'Orlandi. Lodge reputedly asked Lewandowski to set up "contacts" with Hanoi. On or about December 4, Polish Foreign Minister Adam Rapacki sent back word that Hanoi had agreed to unconditional talks on the ambassadorial level in Warsaw, and Washington was asked to send a special representative for this purpose.[7] A later semiofficial account gave a fuller American version of what had happened. Lewandowski, it stated, had informed Lodge that North Vietnam was prepared to engage in "secret exploratory discussions" with the United States; the Polish diplomat did not bring up the cessation of bombing as a prior condition. But he offered ten points for discussion, one of which allegedly provided that the United States would not require North Vietnam to make a public acknowledgment of its forces in the South. After accepting the ten points as a basis for discussion, Washington decided that the above point should be "clarified" to mean that the North Vietnamese forces should be withdrawn from the South. Inasmuch as Washington also claimed that the Northern troops were crucial to the enemy in the South, this "clarification" demanded what Washington itself considered to be the decisive element. Whatever the motive for presenting this stumbling block, and before this difference could be resolved, the American bombing offensive was suddenly stepped up.[8] On December 13 and 14, a railway yard and trucking depot close to or within Hanoi were heavily attacked—the first time that President Johnson had permitted the bombing of targets so close to or within the city limits of the North Vietnamese capital. For the next two weeks, a debate raged whether these attacks had caused widespread damage to civilian areas.* Far more significant perhaps, but still unknown to the general public,

---

* It took almost two weeks for American officials to admit officially that the bombings had caused civilian casualties as well as widespread damage to civilian areas, and then only after *The New York Times* of December 27, 1966, had published an eyewitness report from Hanoi by Harrison E. Salisbury of such damage. At this time, American officials still stressed

was the fact that the bombings had abruptly cut short a seemingly promising peace approach. Oddly, almost the same thing had occurred in somewhat similar circumstances exactly a year before.*

---

that the bombs were aimed at "military targets" only, but that civilian casualties were incidental, unavoidable, and, above all, not "deliberate." On December 30, 1966, the military correspondent of *The New York Times*, Hanson W. Baldwin, disclosed that "United States ordnance is being expended in North and South Vietnam at an annual rate of about 500,000 tons, somewhat more than the Army Air Forces expended against Japan in the Pacific during World War II." At this rate, which soon rose sharply, the problem arises whether the inevitability of the consequences are not more important than the deliberateness of the motivation. One who fires a machine gun into a crowd in order to kill a single person can hardly protest that he did not mean to injure anyone else "deliberately"—especially if he misses his intended victim, as sometimes happens in the bombing of military targets. The indirect but unavoidable by-products of a course of action cannot be exempted morally. The same problem is raised by Vietcong terrorists, but the moral equation here is, to my mind, complicated by two questions: (1) whether the terror and counter-terror of Vietnamese against Vietnamese should be put on the same level as the violence and counter-violence of a foreign power against Vietnamese, and (2) whether the scale of destructiveness of a mortar shell balances that of a 1000-pound bomb.
* On November 11, 1965, two well-known Italian visitors to Hanoi, one of them the former Mayor of Florence, Giorgio La Pira, were received by Ho Chi Minh and Pham Van Dong. They came away with what they regarded as a statement of two conditions considered necessary by the North Vietnamese for peace negotiations: (a) a total cease-fire in North and South Vietnam, without the prior evacuation of any United States troops, and (b) acceptance as the basis for negotiations of the 1954 Geneva Agreements, which the Vietnamese chose to regard as embodied in Pham Van Dong's four points of April 8, 1965. The latter lent itself to the interpretation that the North Vietnamese wanted to reduce the four points, only one of which was disputed by the United States, to the Geneva Agreements, the return to which the United States had already accepted. On November 20, the Italian message was communicated to President Johnson by Italian Foreign Minister Amintore Fanfani. Instead of seizing the opportunity to see whether a cease-fire and a reapplication of the Geneva Agreements could bring the two sides together, the United States took two weeks to reply. On December 4, Secretary of State Rusk sent Fanfani a letter raising questions about the Italian version of the Hanoi offer, including disagreement with the contention that the four points constituted an "authentic interpretation" of the Geneva Agreements, and asked Fanfani to get further clarification from Hanoi. On December 13, Fanfani informed Rusk that such a communication had started on its way to Hanoi five days earlier. On December 15, before any reply could be received, United States planes

This many-sided incident was handled in a most peculiar way. At a news conference on February 2, 1967, President Johnson gave the impression that the "other side" had shown little or no interest in any steps toward peace. At one point he said that he was not "aware of any serious effort"; at another that there were no "serious indications"; and at still another that they had "not taken any [step] yet." On February 4, the day after the President's interview was published, interested sources enabled Robert H. Estabrook to divulge the story of the December overtures in the Washington *Post.* That same day, confirmation that something unusual had been going on came from Walt W. Rostow, the President's Special Assistant. Professor Rostow refused to comment directly on the Washington *Post*'s version on the ground that "this is an extremely interesting and delicate phase in what is or might turn out to be a negotiating process." But then he, too, made "serious" the key word in the American attitude to such situations: "Nothing has yet happened that would justify us as saying we have a serious offer to negotiate." [9] One would be justified in interpreting these words to mean that some kind of "pre-negotiating" moves had been going on, and some sort of "offer," serious or not, had been made. Finally, on February 7, Prime Minister Harold Wilson told the House of Commons that he knew all about "events in December" relating to what he referred to as "Polish discussions," whose failure he attributed to "a very considerable two-way misunderstanding," the nature of which he did not specify.[10] Italian Premier Amintore Fanfani confirmed in Parliament on March 7 that Ambassador d'Orlandi had acted on his written instructions.[11] From the Communist side, Wilfred G. Burchett later disclosed that "first contacts for talks" had been "foiled" by the bombings of December

---

for the first time bombed and destroyed a major North Vietnamese industrial target, a thermal power plant fourteen miles from the key port of Haiphong. And that was the end of that interesting and delicate phase of what was or might have turned out to be a negotiating process, to use Professor Rostow's later words. (The Fanfani correspondence may be found in the *Department of State Bulletin,* January 3, 1966, pp. 11-13).

13-14.[12] If, as Prime Minister Wilson claimed, the break-
down had been caused by a "misunderstanding," the question
still remained why, with so much at stake, it could not have
been rectified and the "Polish discussions" somehow rein-
stated.

For a time, indeed, it seemed that such an effort was being
made. Until the end of 1966, the main obstacle seemed to be
Hanoi's four points, despite the incongruity that three of
them were acceptable to the United States and the only
objectionable one had to be given the most extreme and
arbitrary interpretation to make it unacceptable. Early in
January 1967, however, the Hanoi leaders apparently made
an attempt to remove the four points as the main source of
confusion and disagreement. In an interview with Harrison
E. Salisbury on January 3, Premier Pham Van Dong referred
to them as matters for "discussion" rather than as "conditions" prior to negotiations.[13] At the same time, Secretary-
General U Thant made known his view, after two weeks of
behind-the-scenes probing, that the only thing which stood
in the way of peace talks was the question of unconditional
cessation of the United States bombing of North Vietnam.
The reduction of the problem to this one point seemed to
bring both sides closer than ever before to some kind of ac-
commodation. In his press conference on February 2, as we
have seen, President Johnson was asked, "Are you prepared
at all to tell us what kind of other steps the other side should
take for this suspension of bombing?" The President replied,
"Just almost any step." Though he had previously stressed
the word "serious" rather than "any"—another accordion-
like use of terms—the latter received much publicity and
seemed to narrow the gap to a merely formal gesture. In any
event, a reply soon came from North Vietnamese Foreign
Minister Nguyen Duy Trinh. Through the Australian Communist journalist, Wilfred G. Burchett, who had not antici-
pated such a concession,* the North Vietnamese made known

* In a letter dated October 29, 1966, Burchett had expressed extreme
pessimism with respect to a possible basis for negotiations. Previously,

on January 28 that only the bombing of North Vietnam stood in the way of negotiations. "If the United States really wants talks, it must first halt unconditionally the bombing raids and all other acts of war against the Democratic Republic of Vietnam," Trinh told Burchett in a much publicized interview. "It is only after the unconditional cessation of U.S. bombing and all other acts of war against the Democratic Republic of Vietnam that there could be talks between the Democratic Republic of Vietnam and the United States." [14] Burchett also cited Trinh to the effect that "if the bombings cease completely, good and favorable conditions will be created for the talks." That this was intended as a response to the President was shown by the following remark: "President Johnson said he was only awaiting a sign. Well, he's had the sign."[15]

Pressure steadily mounted, during the first two weeks of February, for the United States to respond to this "sign." Senator Robert F. Kennedy, who had been silent on the subject for several months, returned from Paris on February 4, amid reports that he had brought back with him a new North Vietnamese "peace plan." The story was later traced to a "leak" in the State Department, and the "peace plan" turned out to be a second-hand version by a French Foreign Ministry official. Nevertheless, Senator Kennedy made known that he was critical of the official United States negotiating policy, as a result of which a heated, if not sulfurous, meeting took place between him and President Johnson on February 6.[16]

The following day, on the eve of an agreed-on four-day Tet (lunar new year) truce, Pope Paul VI sent messages to President Johnson, President Ho Chi Minh, and South Vietnamese Chief of State Nguyen Van Thieu, urging them to find ways to end the war. The responses from the first two

---

he said, the North Vietnamese leaders had not demanded prior withdrawal of any American forces as a condition of negotiations, but the continued build-up had convinced them that some "concrete acts" of withdrawal would be necessary (*War/Peace Report*, November 1966, p. 5).

were not too encouraging. On February 8, President Johnson stressed that the United States could not be expected "to reduce military action unless the other side is willing to do likewise" and consider a "balanced reduction in military activity." Ho Chi Minh insisted in an answer made public on February 13 that "real peace" could be restored in Vietnam only if the United States "put an end to their aggression in Vietnam, end unconditionally and definitely the bombing and all other acts of war against the Democratic Republic of [North] Vietnam, withdraw from South Vietnam all American and satellite troops, recognize the South Vietnam National Front for Liberation and let the Vietnamese people settle themselves their own affairs." [17] Though there was nothing new in either of these public postures, the Pope's intervention at this moment was not without significance.

On February 8, as the military truce in Vietnam went into effect, Soviet Premier Kosygin arrived in London for talks with Prime Minister Harold Wilson. On that same day, Kosygin pointedly referred to Nguyen Duy Trinh's offer to negotiate in return for a cessation of bombing and gave it his blessings. He saw fit to offer the same advice the following day. Since the Soviet leaders had previously refrained from injecting themselves publicly into the North Vietnam-United States negotiating problem, this deliberate repetition represented a new policy. There is reason to believe that the Soviet leaders decided to back the new, one-point North Vietnam negotiating position publicly because they had had something to do with bringing it about. According to Burchett, it was "open knowledge that a number of Socialist-bloc countries were urging such a move over a year ago," but the North Vietnamese leaders had resisted on the ground that it would have been regarded as a sign of weakness by the United States and would have invited an intensification of the bombing.[18]

Above all, a letter from President Johnson to President Ho Chi Minh dated February 2 was delivered to a North Vietnamese representative in Moscow on February 8. The letter was not made public until March 21 and, therefore, it could not at the time be directly related by outsiders to anything said publicly for the next six weeks. Yet its contents enable us to reconstruct more clearly the kind of thinking that went into the making of American policy before February 8.*

By that date, it had become perfectly clear that the North Vietnamese negotiating position had been reduced to its irreducible minimum. There was no doubt in President Johnson's mind what it was because he explicitly stated it in his letter—"direct bilateral talks with representatives of the United States Government provided that we ceased 'unconditionally' and permanently our bombing operations against your country and all military actions against it." He noted that this position had been confirmed in the last day by "serious and responsible parties"—one of them, no doubt, Premier Kosygin.

The next point of particular interest in President Johnson's letter is why this proposal could not be accepted. It gave two reasons: a halt in the bombing would tell the world that discussions were going on and impair their "privacy and secrecy"; and North Vietnam would use the halt to "improve its military position." The American counterproposal was then put forward to get around these seemingly dire eventualities.

> I am prepared to order a cessation of bombing against your country and the stopping of further augmentation of U.S. forces in South Vietnam as soon as I am assured that infiltration into South Vietnam by land and by sea has stopped. These acts of restraint on both sides would, I believe, make it possible for us to conduct serious and private discussions leading toward an early peace.

The question, which will be long debated, is whether this counterproposal was justified in terms of the two reasons

* These dates may cause some confusion in reference to this letter. I have chosen to identify it with February 8 because it became operative on that date.

given for making it necessary. If an unconditional cessation of the bombing would have given away the projected discussions and impaired their privacy and secrecy, would not a cessation of the bombing plus demonstrated North Vietnamese cessation of infiltration have resulted in exactly the same thing? Would anyone have been deceived any more by North Vietnamese acceptance of the United States terms than United States acceptance of North Vietnam's terms? The first "difficulty," then, could hardly be taken seriously.

The second objection raised by President Johnson was more troublesome—but only if one side used it exclusively against the other. Both sides were capable of improving their military positions in South Vietnam, if they so desired, with or without bombing of North Vietnam. Moreover, the transport facilities of the United States forces were vastly greater than those of North Vietnam. Indeed, the Tet truce was actually used by both sides to bring in new equipment and troops. United States officials charged that North Vietnam made an unprecedented effort to move arms and supplies into the South.* But United States Air Force officials in

* This may have been one of the greatest hoaxes of the war, and one of the greatest derelictions of the American press. *I. F. Stone's Weekly* excepted, I have seen no serious questioning of the propaganda handed out by the Department of Defense to justify the resumption of the bombing. As reported in *U.S. News & World Report,* March 27, 1967, a lavish briefing at the Pentagon on March 17 was said to demonstrate: "While U.S. bombers were grounded from February 8 through February 11, the Communists made hay in the North, moving a staggering volume of arms, equipment, food and supplies toward infiltration routes into South Vietnam for use against American and Allied forces." The tonnage moved from North to South was first given as 35,000 and then reduced to 23,000, all based on "photographic and visual sightings" from the air. As I. F. Stone pointed out (March 27, 1967), the reporting was incredibly sloppy; the Pentagon spokesman did not go further than to claim a knowledge of "resupply activities within North Vietnam," and there was no evidence that any of the trucks sighted had moved out of the North; there was no way to identify whether the trucks carried military supplies or not; and it was even admitted that some of the supplies were nonmilitary and "not all bound for South Vietnam." Inasmuch as the scare stories about the North Vietnamese "resupply efforts" were crucial to the resumption of the bombing, which was crucial to all the subsequent events, a thorough examination of this dubious justification for breaking the truce was more than called for.

Saigon reported that United States cargo planes had carried a one-day record of 2762 tons of equipment to United States troops on February 8, the first day of the truce and the very day President Johnson's letter was handed over in Moscow. The total for February 8-10 was 7042 tons of equipment and more than 17,000 troops delivered by the Air Force alone.[19]

One wonders what the United States would have done and how its citizens would have felt if the positions had been reversed and they had read the following report from the official French news agency in *Le Monde* of February 12-13, 1967:

> While American agencies call attention to a considerable intensification of road, railroad, river, and sea traffic in North Vietnam, press correspondents could affirm on Friday [February 10] on the Saigon-Tay-Ninh road that the American commissariat also took advantage of the Tet truce to increase troop resupply in combat rations as well as arms.
>
> Long rows of trucks belonging to military transport companies were lined up on the North-West road. They were protected by tanks and helicopters flying at tree level. In the area of Tay-Ninh, enormous trucks or towing tractors brought shells for 105 mm. and 155 mm. guns to the American units stationed on the periphery of the Vietcong's Zone C.

Thus, at worst, the United States was quite capable of holding its own, if the issue was improvement of North Vietnam's relative military position. It might even have made more sense for North Vietnam to worry about what the United States could do in this respect in the event of negotiations based wholly on a halt of bombing in the North than vice versa. American officials believed that only the United States was capable of mounting large-scale offensives on the ground in the South. On February 22, more than 25,000 United States and South Vietnamese troops were able to launch a major offensive, "Operation Junction City," in "War Zone C," northwest of Saigon near the Cambodian border, no doubt with some of the matériel brought in during the Tet truce. By this time, whatever their resupply efforts were, the

North Vietnam-Vietcong forces were supposedly incapable of mounting a comparable military effort.* On March 15, President Johnson himself bore witness to the fact that the enemy's tactics had been adapted to "a war of infiltration, of subversion, of ambush; pitched battles are very rare and even more rarely are they decisive." It was almost certainly true that North Vietnam would try by all means to improve its military position during the truce and thus endanger more American lives; it was most questionable whether North Vietnam could improve its position so much or so unilaterally as to change the balance of military power in South Vietnam; and it was extremely doubtful whether fewer American lives would be lost by risking an improvement in the North Vietnam's military position to get negotiations than by risking negotiations to prevent an indefinite extension of the struggle.

President Johnson's letter of February 8 did not reach Ho Chi Minh in Hanoi until February 10. While Washington was waiting for an answer, other voices made themselves heard. On February 10, Secretary-General U Thant urged an "indefinite and unconditional extension" of the truce and renewed his three-point plan, "starting with an unconditional end to the bombing of North Vietnam," which, he said, could "bring about a favorable climate for peaceful talks between the parties." Before the four-day truce ended, Premier Kosygin and Prime Minister Wilson asked for an extension of two days, which was granted. Presumably they

* On January 17, 1967, in an address at Washington, D.C., General Earle G. Wheeler, Chairman, Joint Chiefs of Staff, declared: "Where regimental attacks were once common, and division attacks clearly pended [in 1965], we now find ourselves fighting mostly companies and battalions. We estimate that their battalions are now averaging only one day's fighting per month. And where once the enemy could sustain combat for a month at a time, as in the Ia Drang, he now hits and runs to avoid disaster" (*Department of State Bulletin*, February 6, 1967, pp. 190-91). If this was the state of the enemy's forces in mid-January, it is hard to imagine that three or four days of resupply efforts, which the United States could more than match, would have made all that difference only three weeks later.

would not have asked for it if they had given up all hope.
On February 12, the last day of the now six-day truce, Republican Senator Jacob K. Javits of New York, a serious and thoughtful legislator, came out in support of "unconditional cessation" of the United States bombing of the North. On that Sunday, a *New York Times* correspondent noted, "diplomatic activity appeared to be intense" and senior United States officials in the White House and State Department spent the afternoon in their offices.[20]

February 12 was apparently the day of decision. For on February 13, President Johnson announced the resumption of "full-scale hostilities," including the renewed bombing of North Vietnam. He blamed the decision on the Hanoi government, which, he said, had used the truce for "major resupply efforts of their troops in South Vietnam."

Thus, it appears, only three days elapsed between the time Ho Chi Minh received President Johnson's letter in Hanoi and the President's decision to resume the fighting and bombing. Ho Chi Minh's reply to the letter had nothing to do with the decision because it was not sent until two days later, February 15. Indeed, Ho Chi Minh's reply might have been influenced by the President's decision, not vice versa. The "resupply" of North Vietnamese troops was admittedly not a violation of the truce, which had merely called for a temporary halt to the fighting. Both sides, as we have seen, were using the cease-fire to bring in men, arms, and supplies, as they were legally entitled to do.

Ho Chi Minh's reply of February 15 was obviously intended to influence world opinion more than to persuade President Johnson. Most of the reply charged the United States with aggression and war crimes. Toward the end, however, one section was devoted to conditions for restoring peace and another to a basis for direct talks, the two apparently treated in different terms. To restore peace, Ho demanded that the United States should "definitively and unconditionally" stop the bombing of North Vietnam and all other acts of war against North Vietnam; withdraw all

United States and "satellite" troops from South Vietnam; recognize the South Vietnam National Liberation Front; and permit the Vietnamese people to settle their own affairs. To initiate direct talks between the United States and North Vietnam, he repeated only the first demand.

Other questions, which will be long debated, are whether three days were long enough to wait for Ho Chi Minh's reply, whether North Vietnam's "resupply efforts" were a good enough reason to resume hostilities, and whether they should have been resumed without warning Ho Chi Minh how long the United States was willing to wait. The manner in which the entire exchange was handled suggests that both sides were responding more to outside pressures than to their own inner convictions. It had taken North Vietnam's allies more than a year to get it to agree to a one-point negotiating position, namely, cessation of the bombing. The United States was constrained to make some gesture at the start of the Tet truce and the Wilson-Kosygin meeting in London.* The tenuousness of the President's reasoning for rejecting cessa-

* One of the more curious aspects of this period has been the ignoble spectacle of a Labour Prime Minister running interference for Lyndon Johnson's foreign policy. After assiduously playing the role of middleman, Prime Minister Wilson declared on February 14: "It is true that one gesture by North Vietnam, which could have cost them nothing in terms of security or even face, could have set in motion events which could have led to peace." Was this "gesture" something other than what President Johnson demanded of Ho Chi Minh in his letter of February 8, namely, the halt of North Vietnamese "infiltration" into South Vietnam? If it was more or less the same thing, could it be described as costing North Vietnam nothing, not even a loss of face? And if it was much less, why did the February 8 letter ask for more? Moreover, Wilson went to the trouble to justify intensified American suspicions on the ground that "there were massive military movements by North Vietnam aimed at securing a military advantage" during the Tet truce, but he did not find it necessary to say anything about massive American military movements. *The Times* (London) of February 15, 1967, said that only Wilson and Foreign Secretary George Brown know the "secret" of what Wilson was talking about in his mysterious allusions to the required North Vietnamese "gesture" and other references. If Wilson was right, incidentally, it would seem to have been fitting for him to ask, not only why North Vietnam did not make this "gesture," but also why the peace of the world should be jeopardized for a gesture that would not even have caused North Vietnam to lose face.

tion of the bombing, the precipitancy of his decision to resume hostilities, and the almost immediately enlarged scale of those hostilities did not give the impression of a man who had had his heart in carrying through successful peace negotiations. It was rather that of a man for whom the letter of February 8 was a gauntlet flung before an opponent to make him accept terms which he had already declined to accept and which would have put him at a disadvantage. The Johnson-Ho Chi Minh letters of February 1967 were designed to stake out positions rather than to come to terms with a reality that neither party was yet prepared to accept. They were not the first or the last moves of their kind, and they can be understood only in terms of what had gone on before as well as what would come after them.

Turning Point Number 7 (February 1967)

Suddenly, after all the meetings and letters and go-betweens, the war broke loose again, and on a more destructive scale than ever before.

The resumption of hostilities was not only on a full but also a new scale. On February 22, United States artillery for the first time fired across the demilitarized zone into North Vietnamese territory. On February 26, United States warships for the first time shelled supply routes in North Vietnam on a continuing basis without restrictions. On February 27, United States planes for the first time began to mine North Vietnam rivers. On March 10, United States bombers for the first time attacked a major industrial plant in North Vietnam, the iron and steel combine at Thainguyen, 38 miles north of Hanoi. Inasmuch as unfavorable weather conditions and technical preparations had delayed this operation for about three weeks, it belonged to the military decisions made in mid-February. Subsequent attacks on this and other industrial installations made clear the basic character of the seventh turning point—to destroy the economic foundation or "infrastructure" of North Vietnam's military capability.

The thinking behind this "escalation"—a forbidden word for a familiar fact—began to emerge in statements that were probably less guarded because they were made before the Johnson-Ho Chi Minh correspondence came out publicly. On February 27, President Johnson described, with somewhat uncharacteristic understatement, the three new military actions of the preceding five days as a "step up" and "more far-reaching." He restated the logic of every turning point in these terms: "Our principal objective is to provide the maximum deterrent to people who believe aggression pays with a minimum cost to us and to them." As always, the "maximum deterrent" and "minimum cost" had been forced up to higher and higher levels.

Though he had not concealed his misgivings, Senator Robert F. Kennedy waited until March 2, after the peace efforts had failed and the new United States military policy had gone into effect, to make known his views in some detail. He first associated himself with "nearly all Americans" who, he said, were determined to remain in Vietnam "until we have fulfilled our commitments." He saw the United States "at a critical turning point," instead of having just passed one, and he offered a three-point program, which might have had greater relevance a few weeks earlier. He proposed that the United States should offer to halt the bombings and give North Vietnam a week to start negotiations; to negotiate for a limited period, while the military forces on both sides remained substantially the same; and to seek a final settlement which would permit "all the major political elements," including the National Liberation Front, to participate in choosing a new national leadership and future course in South Vietnam. It was obviously a compromise plan that, according to Senator Kennedy, had to be accepted as a whole; it did not satisfy the North Vietnamese demand for "unconditional" cessation of the bombing; it provided against an indefinite prolongation of negotiations; it merely tried to put to the test the previous intimations by the Northern

Foreign Minister Nguyen Duy Trinh and Soviet Premier Kosygin that the way to break the deadlock was to exchange some form of a bombing halt for some form of negotiations. Nevertheless, Senator Kennedy s proposals were officially knocked down as fast as he set them up, and he himself came under attack as if he were serving the Communist cause or attempting to overthrow the American system.*

* A column by Kenneth Crawford in Newsweek, March 20, 1967, was entitled "Henry A. Kennedy?" It sought to give the impression that Senator Kennedy's role in 1967 was similar to that of former Vice President Henry A. Wallace, who had permitted the Communists to become "his managers, manipulators and all-out partisans" in his unsuccessful bid for the presidency in 1948. Mr. Crawford argued that, despite some apparent differences in the criticism of the official policy by the two men, "in domestic political terms it amounts to the same thing." To identify Kennedy with the Communists, Crawford had to mislead himself or his readers into believing that "Kennedy attracts the New Left," which had actually been trying to expose the Senator as a political opportunist and false liberal, more dangerous even than the outright reactionaries. Crawford's column was not the most extreme example of the genre but it showed that, by March 1967, even the most cautious and circumscribed proposal to settle the war by negotiation was beginning to bring out the worst in American politics and journalism even in relatively respectable quarters. If anything, Senator Kennedy had opened himself to the charge that his proposals were both too little and too late.

In *The Reporter,* March 23, 1967, the editor chose to interpret the Kennedy speech as if it were the signal for an incipient civil war between, as he put it, "The Two USAs." The editorial accused the Kennedy "family" of plotting to impose on the United States "its own Bonapartism that aims at permanent power" and to induce the United States to give "itself and its power of decision to the enemy it is facing in Vietnam." Even an overheated imagination might find it difficult to consider the Kennedys powerful enough to hand over the United States to Ho Chi Minh. But the war had brought on such an unhealthy political climate in the United States that treason, defeatism, dictatorship, and a new stab-in-the-back legend could be read into this speech, so carefully modulated and so long delayed that it was almost defused politically in advance. To make Senator Kennedy feel better, perhaps, the editorialist put Secretary-General U Thant, whom he scorned rather than pitied, and Pope Paul VI, whom he pitied rather than scorned, in the same camp. The moral would seem to be that, if this could happen to Robert F. Kennedy, it could happen to anyone—all in the name of "freedom" and "that America which has its leader in Lyndon Johnson." This editorial constituted the most extreme effort thus far to whip up a

More significant perhaps than anything said by Senator Kennedy were the official reactions to his words.

One line was taken by Secretary of State Rusk. He tried to blunt the effect of the Kennedy speech by declaring that the United States had already made "substantially similar" proposals without result.[21] If this had been the case, Senator Kennedy could hardly have been attacked for making his proposals; the only things apparently wrong with them were lack of originality and Ho Chi Minh's disapproval; Secretary Rusk could, in effect, enter a plea of innocence only by pleading guilty to the Senator's alleged sins. The first impulse of the State Department was evidently to embrace the Senator's proposals to death.

When the Johnson-Ho Chi Minh correspondence became known, Secretary Rusk's line of defense seemed to have been based on the assumption that the truth would never—or only after a long delay—come out. President Johnson's proposal of February 8 and Senator Kennedy's plan of March 2 were not "substantially similar"; they differed essentially in the President's insistence on a military condition for halting the bombing and the Senator's insistence on halting the bombing without military conditions. Even before the facts were known, the Senator protested that Secretary Rusk had distorted both positions by endowing them with a fictitious similarity. But then the Senator himself went too far by implying that he had been willing to accept the North Vietnam-Kosygin offer; in actuality, he had, for better or worse, substituted three points for their one; the Kennedy position might have been mathematically calibrated to stand somewhere between Nguyen Duy Trinh's approach of January 28 and President Johnson's proposal of February 8.

The differences were soon spelled out more sharply. On

war-time hysteria. Significantly, it did not come from a right-wing organ, possibly because the Republicans were somewhat inhibited from making such an effort by the temptation to cash in on a peace move in the presidential election of 1968 as Eisenhower had succeeded in doing for them in 1952.

the day of Senator Kennedy's speech, Democratic Senator Henry M. Jackson of Washington, who had become a chief Administration spokesman on the war, was able to produce a letter from the President demanding an "equivalent action" from the other side as the price to end the bombing.[22] On March 9, President Johnson was asked what the "military quid pro quo and reciprocal action" might be, and his reply compressed in a few sentences the accordion-like ambiguities and contradictions of his peculiar diplomacy:

> Just almost any reciprocal action on their part. We have said that we would be glad to stop our invasion of North Vietnam if they would stop their invasion of South Vietnam. That we would be glad to halt our bombing if they would halt their aggression and their infiltration.

In one sentence, he seemed to be demanding almost nothing in return. In the very next sentence, he seemed to be asking for almost everything. Perhaps inadvertently, he told more than he intended by referring to the new phase of American policy as an "invasion" of North Vietnam equivalent in kind to the North Vietnamese "invasion" of South Vietnam. At another point in the same press conference, he spoke as if stopping the bombing were the same as stopping "half the war," by which he meant the American half.

Further insight into the new policy came in a major address by President Johnson in Nashville, Tennessee, on March 15. In it he reincarnated the "domino theory" in one of its many manifestations by maintaining that "the defense of Vietnam held the key to the political and economic future of free Asia." * He again demanded "reciprocal concessions" and made reciprocity "the fundamental principle of any reduction in hostilities." He hotly accused his critics of "moral double bookkeeping" because they did not equate Vietcong

* By 1967, the "domino theory" was in such disrepute that even Secretary of State Rusk felt called on to disavow it by saying that "there's no need for something called the domino theory" (*Department of State Bulletin,* January 30, 1967, p. 169). But evidently there was still a need for various and changing paraphrases of the theory.

terrorism* with United States bombing. He referred contemptuously to what he called the recent "flurry of rumors
of 'peace feelers,'" as if there had not been any reality to
them at all.

But perhaps the most curious section of the speech had a
bearing on both President Johnson's letter to Ho Chi Minh
of February 8—which had not yet been released—and the
dispute with Senator Kennedy. The President stated the
question that the Senator had been asking: "Why don't we
stop bombing to make it easier to begin negotiations?" The
answer, he said, was "a simple one." To show how simple it
was, he recapitulated the three times that the United States
had stopped its bombing—five days and twenty hours in
May 1965, thirty-six days and fifteen hours in December 1965
and January 1966, and five days and eighteen hours in February 1967. After this recital, he summed up triumphantly:
"They have three times rejected a bombing pause as a means
to open the way to ending the war and going to the negotiating table."

From this, one might have gathered that the President
would have been delighted with the apparent North Vietnamese change of heart at the end of January 1967 and the
Foreign Minister's open bid for negotiations in exchange for
a cessation of the bombing. It would have seemed, as Senator
Kennedy pointed out, that this had been the United States'
position during the first two bombing pauses but not the
third one. President Johnson, however, plainly implied

* Mr. Johnson said: "Tens of thousands of innocent Vietnamese civilians
have been killed and tortured and kidnapped by the Vietcong." Four
days later, a report from Saigon stated: "New U.S. official figures show
that Vietcong terrorists have killed 11,967 civilians and kidnapped 40,988
in the last nine years" (Washington *Post,* March 19, 1967). Presumably
only the killed did not survive their ordeal. In nine years, the annual
average was 1330 and some may not have been so "innocent." This figure
would have to be equated with United States bombing in North and
South Vietnam heavier than the bombing of enemy territory in Europe
in World War II at its peak. And it would be necessary to take into
consideration that political "terrorism" does not have the same cultural
roots or moral stigma in all countries.

that it had still been the United States' position the third time during the Tet truce from February 8 to 13. But five days later, it became known that this was precisely the position the United States had explicitly rejected in President Johnson's letter of February 8 to Ho Chi Minh. In it he had gone to the trouble of giving two reasons, good or bad, why the United States could not accept the formula of "stop bombing" for "begin negotiations." Instead, he assured his Nashville audience that "Hanoi has just simply refused to consider coming to a peace table." Even Ho Chi Minh's letter of February 15 did not justify such an excessive distortion of Hanoi's position; Hanoi had certainly *considered* coming to a peace table—on its own terms, perhaps, but that was no less true of Washington.

Meanwhile, however, the United States' uncompromising rejection of prior cessation of the bombing of North Vietnam unexpectedly paid off in an unexpected quarter. On March 14, 1967, Secretary-General U Thant submitted a new three-point plan which clearly reflected concessions to the American position. For more than two years, he had steadfastly maintained that only unconditional cessation of the bombing could lead the way to a settlement; now he was merely content to mention it in passing as a "vital need," but to leave it out entirely as a practical consideration. His old point one —cessation of the bombing of North Vietnam—was replaced by a new point one: "a general standstill truce" without supervision. Old point two—substantial reduction of all military activities in South Vietnam—was replaced by new point two: "preliminary talks" between the United States and North Vietnam. Old point three—participation of the National Liberation Front or Vietcong in any peaceful settlement—was replaced by new point three: "reconvening of the Geneva conference." A favorable reply was received from the United States on March 18, though it deviated from the Secretary-General's proposal in two ways which might, in any case, have proved troublesome. One reservation implied that it was not enough for both sides to agree to a cease-fire,

and instead demanded preliminary discussions to decide how
it would be carried out; the other required that the South
Vietnamese government, but not the National Liberation
Front, would have to be "appropriately involved throughout
this entire process." A North Vietnamese spokesman unequivocally rejected the new plan on March 27.

Secretary-General Thant's new plan was only a distant
relative of his old one, despite his claim that it was merely
an "adaptation." The latter had implied that the Vietnamese
struggle was essentially a civil war which could be settled by
primarily concentrating on South rather than on North
Vietnam. This was the essential meaning of the first and
third points in the former formula. The new plan, in effect,
shifted the emphasis from the South to the North and pitted
North Vietnam against the United States in the crucial first
steps toward a settlement; it provided a vague role for the
South Vietnamese on both sides only in "a future formal
conference"; it thus inferentially endorsed the American
thesis that the key to the war and peace was in the North.*
Even the South's Premier Nguyen Cao Ky did not like the

* The shift in U Thant's position is one of the more perplexing phenom-
ena of this period. In the first days of March 1967, Mr. Thant conferred
with two North Vietnamese government officials in Rangoon; he later
revealed that he had orally presented them with the new three-point plan
which he had apparently improvised. On March 5, Mr. Thant returned
to the United States. As of March 7, Raymond Daniell, *The New York
Times*'s United Nations correspondent, wrote that Mr. Thant had "returned from his talks in Burma 'more convinced than ever' that cessation
of the raids 'is an absolute prerequisite' to bringing Hanoi to the conference table" *(The New York Times*, March 8, 1967). In his press
conference on March 28, at which he made public his *aide-mémoire* of
March 14, Mr. Thant still expressed this view in his introductory remarks.
At one point he said that "I have never ceased to consider that the
bombing of North Vietnam constitutes an insurmountable obstacle to
discussions." In reply to a question, he reiterated that "I still maintain
that a cessation of the bombing of North Vietnam is an imperative necessity to create conditions for peaceful talks." In the *aide-mémoire* itself,
however, the "absolute prerequisite," "insurmountable obstacle," and
"imperative necessity" were watered down to a "vital need," and, in
any case, left out of the new three points. The question is how Mr. Thant
could bring himself to bypass the cessation of the bombing in the points
themselves if it was an "absolute prerequisite," an "insurmountable

way the United States had taken over the peace as well as the war strategy. "We hear too much about President Johnson's talking to Ho Chi Minh," he said on March 28, "but what about the South?" [23]

In any event, Thant's new plan was doomed because it was based on seemingly formal equality between unequal forces, resulting in unequal consequences. Without a prior cessation of the bombing, North Vietnam was still placed in the position of agreeing to terms with a gun at the temple. The relatively compact, traditionally organized American military forces could easily be regrouped and supplied during a cease-fire; their morale was likely to rise in the absence of combat. The Vietcong guerrillas were by their very nature difficult to coordinate, especially if North Vietnam did not control them as much as the United States wanted to believe; their morale was bound to fall in the absence of combat. The North's regular troops in the South ran the risk of becoming hostages, cut off hundreds of miles from their home bases, scattered in jungles and forests. The only conceivable *modus vivendi* for an effective cease-fire in the peculiar South Vietnamese circumstances would have required a physical separation of the two sides, amounting to *de facto* division of South Vietnam into regrouping zones—a form of provisional partition which the United States had many times ruled out. The very nature of guerrilla warfare made an old-fashioned cease-fire, based on some fixed line, incongruous. The Vietcong guerrillas and even the North Vietnamese regulars cooperating closely with the guerrillas could not be made to "stand still," suddenly and indefinitely, without risking their disintegration as a fighting force, a danger not faced by the United States troops. Inasmuch as U Thant's new plan was

---

obstacle," or an "imperative necessity" to get to the conference table. One gets the impression that at his press conference on March 28, Mr. Thant tried to have his cake and eat it, too; he may not have changed his mind about the need for a cessation of the bombing but, for some reason, he saw fit to change his practical proposals, which received most of the publicity and earned him the gratitude of those who had formerly execrated him most. Thant subsequently withdrew the new plan.

introduced at a very late date, after the diplomatic break-
down of the preceding two months and the exacerbation of
the bombing against key North Vietnamese economic cen-
ters, already largely or partially destroyed, the time was not
very propitious for another effort which on its face posed
almost insuperable practical problems and represented a
sharp political shift in favor of the United States' position.
In the end, this initiative did no good and merely compro-
mised the Secretary-General.

At the United States-South Vietnam conference at Guam
on March 20-21, Premier Ky may have blurted out, as he had
done before on other matters, what "negotiations" and an
"honorable peace" were really supposed to mean. On the first
day of the meeting, he exhorted the Americans to intensify
and enlarge the war against North Vietnam even more, and
then proceeded to explain:

> We must convince Hanoi that its cause is hopeless. Only
> then will Hanoi be ready to negotiate. Then, when we do
> negotiate, we must, Mr. President, work for an honorable
> peace.

A power which has been bludgeoned into hopelessness is,
of course, in no position to "negotiate." It can only come to
the "peace table" to beg for crumbs from the victor—if it
chooses to beg. A one-way "honorable peace" is merely a
gentle circumlocution for one side's victory. Premier Ky was
not the only one to misuse these terms, but he did it somewhat more crudely and clearly than others. In any meaningful negotiation, both sides must be able to bargain from a
position of some strength, though they may be strong in different ways, as in the case of private corporations and trade
unions. The Japanese came to a "peace table" aboard the
USS *Missouri* in September 1945, but they were in no sense
capable of negotiating. A "peaceful settlement" may be a
total surrender as well as a mutual compromise which by its
very nature cannot be totally satisfactory to either side—
or totally unsatisfactory, either. The issue was not whether

Premier Ky had the "right" to demand that the United States should batter North Vietnam into virtual surrender for him; it was rather that these words—"negotiation" and "peace" and "honor"—were misused so much that they portended the opposite of what they seemed to convey. The chief victims of this systematic abuse of language were not the leaders in Hanoi, who knew just what would happen to them if they tried to "negotiate" with a hopeless cause; the main effect, if not the purpose, was to pollute the political stream in the United States with a virus of words that said one thing and meant another.

The Reciprocity of Unequals

At the core of the American case, making meaningful negotiations difficult, if not impossible, was the concept of "reciprocity." It became the leitmotiv of official American policy in 1966-67, though it was another word that lent itself to different interpretations. When President Johnson asked almost plaintively on March 9 for "just almost any reciprocal action on their part," it seemed to mean any kind of North Vietnamese response, even of a purely symbolic character. Yet when he went on, almost in the same breath, to demand that North Vietnam should stop its "aggression and infiltration," he implied that he expected a more or less equivalent or analogous response. On March 16, he made reciprocity "the fundamental principle of any reduction in hostilities," and again seemed to be using the concept in the second, more inclusive and far-reaching sense. When his February 8 letter to Ho Chi Minh was made public on March 21, the latter interpretation could no longer be questioned. The letter concretely defined reciprocity as: for the United States to halt the bombing of North Vietnam and stop further augmentation of its forces in South Vietnam, and for North Vietnam to provide assurance that its infiltration forces into South Vietnam by land and sea had ceased. Clearly, when President

Johnson called on February 2 for "just almost any [step]," and on March 9 for "just almost any reciprocal action," he had not intended these words to be taken literally.

But—and this was the critical question—what could "reciprocity" mean between a strong, rich power like the United States and a weak, poor power like North Vietnam?

In February 1967, for example, the United States and allied foreign forces in South Vietnam numbered: United States, more than 400,000; South Korea, 45,000; Australia, 4500, New Zealand, 360—for a total of more than 450,000. The North Vietnamese forces in the South were estimated at about 50,000. President Johnson's proposal of February 8 amounted, in effect, to freezing the forces on both sides in the South in return for a cessation of United States bombing in the North but not in the South. By stopping all movement to the South, which was undoubtedly what would have been required, North Vietnam could not even have maintained the forces which it already had in the South because it could not provision them by plane and ship, as the United States was able to do. Just as the United States felt that it could not accept any offer which might discourage or demoralize its South Vietnamese wards, so the North Vietnamese leaders doubtless felt the same way about their own troops and protégés in the South.

President Johnson, it should be noted, did not offer a military truce or cease-fire in the South in exchange for halting the bombing of the North. In the event of a total cessation of the fighting in both North and South, the freezing of the numbers in the South would not have mattered so much. But if the war in the South went on unabated, with the North Vietnamese troops cut off from their sources at home and the United States committed only to a limitation of men but not matériel, the latter factor would have become increasingly decisive in the further conduct of the war. On the American side particularly, firepower rather than manpower counted. Thus, morally, numerically, and materially, the proposal of February 8 was palpably unequal because the sides were so unequal.

The United States was, in effect, doing what General James M. Gavin (ret.) warned against in his testimony before the Senate Foreign Relations Committee on February 21—using the bombing of the North as a bargaining instrument. The bombing, as we have seen, had been initiated in February 1965 primarily to bolster the South Vietnamese government's faltering morale, when, as we have seen, North Vietnam's regular troops in the South had numbered only about 400, and the bombing could not have been justified on the ground that it was necessary to interdict their lines of communication with the North. First came the bombing, and then came an escalation of the war on both sides, which provided the major justification for the bombing. In February 1965, the bombing of the North represented a desperate United States effort to save the South Vietnamese forces from defeat; in February 1967, it represented an offensive effort to bring about North Vietnam's defeat. After two years of bombing, which had unilaterally changed the pre-1965 rules of the war, the North Vietnamese and United States conceptions of "reciprocity" were understandably different. North Vietnam could not stop bombing the United States in exchange for a similar courtesy on the part of the United States in North Vietnam. The price the United States demanded was in South Vietnam, where the advantages and disadvantages on both sides were so different that the concept of "reciprocity" was far from the simple numerical arrangement that President Johnson proposed on February 8.

A cessation of the bombing of North Vietnam was vital to the latter precisely because it had nothing to exchange for it in the North or in the United States and could pay for it only by reciprocating unequally in the South. The bombing was so important to the United States' bargaining position that President Johnson had, perhaps excessively, referred to it on March 9 as if it were the United States' entire "half the war" or as if its half depended on it. For the United States, the bombing was an infinitely extensible threat. In January 1967, Secretary McNamara told two Senate committees: "I don't believe that bombing up to the present has significantly reduced, nor any bombing that I could contemplate in the future would significantly reduce the actual flow of men and material to the south." [24] When this was established, the United States stepped up its bombing the following month to reduce North Vietnam's industrial base to a mass of rubble. At best North Vietnam could retaliate only against South Vietnam, which it considered part of its own country, not against the United States, which it considered its main enemy. Germany's indiscriminate bombing of Britain in late 1940 was answered with equally indiscriminate and even more punishing bombing of Germany later in the war. But the positions of the United States and North Vietnam were so different that nothing comparable could take place.

The United States' escalation of February 1967 invited North Vietnam to step up and enlarge those tactical operations for which it and its South Vietnamese partners were best suited, such as terrorism. For anything more, North Vietnam was dependent on China and Russia, especially the latter. As soon as United States bombing raids were resumed on North Vietnam that month, Soviet President Nikolai V. Podgorny pledged the Soviet Union to continue to provide North Vietnam and "the South Vietnamese patriots" with the necessary assistance.[25] Later Soviet statements promised to meet United States escalation with escalating Soviet aid. The seventh turning point, then, was almost as much a form of pressure on the Soviet Union as on North Vietnam. For some time, indeed, United States policymakers had been watching the increasing Soviet aid to North Vietnam with mixed feelings: it gave North Vietnam more and more effective arms for fighting American troops, but it also gave the Soviet Union a larger place in North Vietnam's military planning and capability. Secretary Rusk's unusual solicitude for Soviet sensibilities was not without is pragmatic calculations. In January 1967, before the truce and resumption of the bombings on a larger scale, he had commented favorably on the "prudence" of the present Soviet generation and had commended it to the Chinese.[26] Two months later, he inferentially exculpated the Soviet leaders from responsibility for North Vietnam's obduracy. "They cannot tell Hanoi what to do," he said. "The problem of peace out there is with Hanoi."* He even seemed to associate the United States and the Soviet Union in order to emphasize the "great gulf which exists between all of us and Hanoi." [27] Considering the enormous importance which Soviet-bloc aid to North Vietnam had assumed, these were singularly amiable intimations of how he regarded, at least for public consumption, the Soviet role in the war.

But if the Soviets could not tell Hanoi what to do, they still had to tell themselves what to do. By giving North Vietnam so much aid since 1965, they had committed themselves more and more deeply to preventing the North from collapsing just as the United States had committed itself to the South. The United States' favorable appreciation of the Soviet role had been based on the well-founded assumption that the Soviet leaders were not happy about expending so much of their country's substance in North Vietnam and risking another confrontation with the United States. Moscow had clearly influenced Ho Chi Minh and his confrères to come down from their four points and to rest their negotiating case wholly on a cessation of the bombing. When this had proved unsatisfactory from Washington's point of view, the next step was to hope that the Russians might put even more pressure on North Vietnam to accept something resembling President Johnson's February 8 version of "reciprocity" or to get the Soviets to induce North Vietnam to back down in some other way. As some influential political figures in Washington saw it, the Soviet Union was caught

* Consistency has never been Secretary Rusk's hobgoblin. In 1965, he insisted that Hanoi owed so much to Peking that it was virtually the latter's prisoner or puppet. In 1967, Hanoi owed even more to Moscow but could not be told "what to do."

in a most disagreeable dilemma in its relations with the United States, North Vietnam, and Communist China. This thinking was openly expressed by the Johnson Administration's spokesman, Senator Jackson, in the Senate on February 24, soon after United States artillery for the first time shelled North Vietnam across the demilitarized zone:

There are some reasons for thinking that the Soviet leaders would prefer a settlement. The bombing of the North, for example, is probably a source of embarrassment, for it demonstrates that the Soviet Union cannot prevent the United States from bombing a brother Communist state. One can surmise that the Russians are having to do a lot of explaining in other Communist capitals. For Moscow's situation in Vietnam puts in doubt what she could do to protect the interests of other Communist states if they sometime found themselves in similar jeopardy. In this sense, the bombing of North Vietnam has political significance—control over it is one of the few political assets and bargaining levers we have in encouraging the Russians to pressure Hanoi to de-escalate militarily and to negotiate.

It must also be a source of some worry to the Soviet rulers that their aid to Vietnam, particularly in connection with their antiaircraft defense system, is steadily mounting.

At the same time, however, without Russian aid and support Hanoi would probably be unable to sustain its efforts, and the Russians are therefore partly responsible for the prolongation of the war.[28]

We have here a strange combination of giving the Soviets credit for wanting a settlement, of gloating over them for not being able to do anything about the bombing of North Vietnam, and of holding them partially responsible for our predicament. It typifies the temptations into which the United States had been led by the disproportionate investment in the Vietnamese war. In a peculiar way, the United States seemed to be faced with nothing but frustrations in South Vietnam at the same time that it was able to do almost as it pleased to North Vietnam. So long as the American leaders considered the bombing to be one of their few assets and bargaining levers, they were bound to try to extort as high a price as possible for it in the guise of "reciprocity." Senator Jackson was quite right to suggest that the bombing of North Vietnam was the United States' trump card—and that is why the game had become so dangerous. The bombing was the thing that could be most easily and destructively intensified and enlarged to increase the pressure on North Vietnam and enhance the embarrassment of its allies. The power at the disposal of the United States was so great and so unprecedented that the only questions were how much power it was willing to use and how much punishment North Vietnam was willing to take. Inescapably, the more punishment North Vietnam was willing to take, the more power the United States was willing to use. The more power the United States used, the less difference it made how much more power it would use, for beyond a certain point, degrees of destructiveness begin to lose their meaning.

This was the vicious circle which had been set in motion by transferring the main arena of the war from South to North Vietnam and by deciding to use bombing to impose the will of the United States on North Vietnam. The only way to break the circle was to halt the bombing and reconsider the problem of South Vietnam on the basis of genuine reciprocity—among the Vietnamese. Once the United States threw its weight into the balance, there could be no meaningful reciprocity, unless a great Communist power reciprocated on behalf of North Vietnam. Instead of bringing peace nearer, this concept was more likely to bring about a Vietnamese edition of the 1962 "missile crisis" in circumstances far less favorable to the United States. In 1962, the United States could claim to be directly threatened by offensive missiles only 90 miles from its shores; in 1967, the United States was not directly threatened and could not appeal to world opinion on that ground; and it was inviting two or more to play at its own game.

The escalation of the war *in* Vietnam thus threatened to bring about an escalation of a war *over* Vietnam. Those who wished to taunt or goad the Soviets, if not the Chinese, to put up or shut up were living in a fantasy world if they thought that the Cuban precedent would necessarily be followed in Vietnam. On the contrary, there had been and continued to be a stubborn underestimation of how far the Communists could go to escalate their side of the war.* A report in mid-April 1967 that the Soviets and the Chinese had managed to reach an agreement to facilitate aid to North Vietnam was generally credited. Once again, the United States was faced with the price to be paid for the "politics of miscalculation" rather than what has been called the "politics of inadvertence."

The Phantom of Vietnam

Why had these miscalculations become so chronic? Because we were still chasing the phantom of military "victory" in Vietnam. It was a phantom because this was not a war that either side could "win" any more in the conventional sense. The South Vietnamese army had already lost it, in all but name, at least twice. It had become a war, which we never intended to fight, of American boys doing what Asian boys should have been doing for themselves. It was a war to prove that we could not be beaten by the North Vietnamese militarily, which did not need to be proved of a power which possessed the hydrogen bomb. It was a war which could result in no meaningful "victory" precisely because it had become primarily military. It was a war in which the cost and the return had become hopelessly out of balance and had to become more so with every month. It was a war based on the mistaken premise that power could substitute

* In an interview with a French editor, Emmanuel d'Astier de la Vigerie, Ho Chi Minh did not exclude the possibility of accepting "volunteers" from Communist countries. "Hundreds of thousands of volunteers from the socialist countries and other countries have declared their readiness to fight the U.S. imperialists by our side," he said. "We warmly thank them for their militant solidarity with us. When necessary, we will appeal to them" (*Solidarity With Vietnam,* Hanoi, December 1966, p. 1).

for politics, with the result that we used more and more power and less and less politics. It was a war in which, in order to "deny" ground to the enemy, we had to devastate the land of our friends. It was a war which we had to continue to delude ourselves into "winning," but which the Vietnamese people could no longer win. It was a war to make guerrillas fade away, as if this were the same thing as doing away with them or removing the political and social conditions which bred and nourished them. It was a war that was isolating us, distorting our economy, and corrupting our intellectual and political life. The more we stressed the strictly military side of the prospective "victory," the more we encouraged pressure in the United States to save lives and money by using more and more extreme military measures, from the invasion of North Vietnam to the employment of nuclear weapons. If the pessimists should again be right, the next stage of this war could bring us to the brink of scorched-earth frightfulness and tear the conscience of this country apart.

Some of the most prescient words on the problem of ending the war have been written by David Schoenbrun, an American correspondent with long experience in Vietnam and the surrounding region:

I would suggest first of all that we stop using such loaded words as withdraw or retreat. Our problem is rather to *extricate* ourselves from a difficult position, not to fight our way out or to turn tail and run. To extricate ourselves would require a lot of truthtelling. Yet very few Americans even try to examine what others think is the truth.

More concretely, Schoenbrun went on:

I have never believed that America's vital interests were at stake in the Vietnamese civil war. I have never accepted the correlation between Munich and a settlement in Vietnam. Mao Tse-tung is not a Hitler, nor is Ho Chi Minh his servant. North Vietnam is not a powerful imperialist nation like Germany. If Ho is comparable to any European, he is the Tito of Asia. That is, a national Communist, at the head of a small state, trying to keep independent of an enormous Communist neighbor—in the case of Tito, Russia; in the case of Ho, China. If we can live with Tito to the tune of one billion dollars of aid, why is it so unthinkable to live in a world with Ho? Why do we fight for the South Vietnamese when we did not go to war for the Freedom Fighters of Hungary or for the East Germans? By what logic do we now offer more trade and closer relations with Russia and all of Eastern Europe but feel we must make war in Vietnam?

The crux of the matter is this: should not the Vietnamese have been permitted to determine their own fate in the first place? And is it now too late to reverse that error? Can we not return to the basic principle of the Geneva Accords: the creation of a military cease-fire and the beginnings of a negotiation among the Vietnamese themselves by themselves, between the NLF and Saigon in the South and also between South and North? It seems to me to be possible and certainly desirable for the United States to change its role from belligerent to interested party, one among many who have an important stake in peace in Asia. Japan, India, and Pakistan surely should be associated with efforts to end the war and encourage negotiations among the Vietnamese. The only way such negotiations could succeed and produce an enduring peace would be to quarantine Vietnam off from the world power competition, that is, to neutralize it.[29]

It may be argued there is no reason for the United States to seek to put an Asian Tito in power and that, as Communists go, the Titos are merely a "lesser evil." But American policy has preferred another line of argument that has made a Chinese "Ulbricht" out of Ho Chi Minh. That Ho Chi Minh may, in fact, be more like an Asian Tito than an Ulbricht does not by itself mean that the former alternative necessarily represents the best of all possible eventualities for the United States or for the West. But it does mean that the policy would at least be based on a more realistic and less scaremongering appraisal of Ho Chi Minh's potential role in the Asian balance of power. It would mean that the choice is not between such extremes as a Southern military usurper, who could stay in power without American support even less than Ngo Dinh Diem could, and a Northern puppet or henchman of Mao Tse-tung. The art of politics, as has been said many times, is the art of the possible, and by making Ho Chi Minh into a Chinese appendage, American policymakers have sought to make him impossible. Another poor, weak little Communist state in Southeast Asia would frighten American voters much less than the prospect of the glacial advance of Chinese expansionism.

I, for one, would far prefer to see an Asian democratic reformer or even an honest civilian, rather than the most "independent" Communist, in power in South and North Vietnam. But the best the United States has been able to come up with is a self-imposed military junta, composed almost wholly of Northerners, without a shred of legitimacy and social conscience. If the NLF cannot be dealt with because it does not represent the people of South Vietnam, it is a mockery to pretend that Premier Nguyen Cao Ky represents anything more than a military junta kept in power by the United States. As long as the United States does not have a regime in South Vietnam which can remain in power through its own resources and popular support, the United States will never be able to pull out of South Vietnam, whatever the North Vietnam regime may do. As long as the United States also refused to recognize that the key to its long-time involvement in Vietnam was located in the South, not in the North, and that military "victory" based on constantly eroding political sands could not be meaningful, the "fading away" of this war was only one more illusion, the political equivalent of a mirage in the desert. The alternative of a Vietnamese Tito could not be ignored, precisely because the United States, which had made and unmade South Vietnamese governments, had not offered anything better. The new constitution of 1967, which in many ways strikingly resembled the Ngo Dinh Diem constitution of 1956, was more likely to produce a constitutional cover for the junta's rule than a genuine civilian successor.

If the most responsible American leaders would only re-
member why they said the French were defeated, they would
also know why the United States had not been victorious, and
why meaningful "victory" would continue to elude it whatever military pressure might be brought to bear on North
Vietnam. It was not fortuitous that former Ambassador Lodge
should have been so fond of reciting the wisdom of General
Walter Bedell Smith—it is worth repeating: "Any second-
rate general should be able to win in Indochina if there were
a proper political atmosphere"—before the turning point of
February 1965 but never afterward. In essence, a "proper
political atmosphere" would long ago have identified the
South Vietnamese government with nationalism, unification,
democratic liberties, and basic social change. American
spokesmen had, to be sure, embraced all these causes at one
time or another, but they had been far more successful in
convincing Americans than in converting Vietnamese. The
very gigantism of the American build-up in a poor, little
country had violated South Vietnamese nationalistic self-
respect. As late as March 1967, a correspondent for the
normally prowar organ *U.S. News & World Report*, reported: "It is easy to see there is far more friction between
Americans and Vietnamese at every level now than before.
Some of the friction is the result of resentment by the Vietnamese at what they consider to be infringements on their
sovereignty." [30] All the destruction of North Vietnam would
not create the "proper political atmosphere" in the south
which would enable us to end the war in the only way that
it could be ended meaningfully—to give it back to the Vietnamese. By mid-1967, events seemed to have demonstrated
that outsiders were not capable of ending the war in South
Vietnam. Their own interests and need to save face had
infinitely complicated the indigenous difficulties. The best
chances for peace were probably dependent on the Vietnamese themselves. The more patriotic or nationalistic among
them, on both sides, would not forever tolerate an orgy of
destruction which had started in order to save them and

which would end by leaving little or nothing to save. It was not yet perceptible, but the decisive impulse for peace might have to come from the Vietnamese themselves.

The American crisis is bad enough when we consider how hard it is to get out of this inopportune and thankless war. But, whatever one may think about getting out, there is still the larger and deeper crisis of how we got into it, and how we got into the Cuban and Dominican military interventions. It is tempting to turn our eyes away from the history of these past twenty years, which has brought us to this pass, but we will then learn nothing from it and fatally go on making the same errors and blunders. We cannot continue to live wholly in the moment, holding on to every *status quo,* however rotten and unstable, to maintain the line against Communism at whatever cost. In the new worship of power, we are squandering our power by using too much too frequently and too maladroitly. All great powers which have overestimated, overindulged, and overextended their power have come to grief. Whatever one may think about the present military imperatives, we cannot go on failing politically and "succeeding" militarily without ultimately inviting disaster beyond anything yet known to mankind. President Johnson and his closest associates might do well to keep in mind what was said of another military victory by Pyrrhus, King of Epirus, in 279 B.C.

Reference Notes

I. The Pattern of Intervention

1. Philip W. Bonsal, "Cuba, Castro and the United States," *Foreign Affairs,* January 1967, pp. 272-73.
2. *El Tiempo* (New York), July 10, 1966.
3. John Bartlow Martin, *Overtaken by Events* (New York: Doubleday, 1966), pp. 204, 613, 675, 696.

II. From Roosevelt to Eisenhower

1. *Public Papers of the Presidents of the United States: Dwight D. Eisenhower, 1954* (Washington, D.C.: Government Printing Office, 1960), pp. 250, 253; *U.S. News & World Report,* November 7, 1966, p. 42.
2. *U.S. News & World Report,* February 15, 1965, pp. 70-71.
3. Philippe Devillers, *Histoire du Viet-Nam* (Paris: Editions du Seuil, 1952), p. 105. There is a different and much vaguer story in Hoang Van Chi, *From Colonialism to Communism* (London: Pall Mall Press, 1964), p. 59. One would like to believe Devillers. The name Ho Chi Minh was adopted in 1944, according to Jean Sainteny, *Histoire d'une Paix Manquée* (Paris: Amiot-Dumont, 1953), p. 164. An American student says the Viet Minh was formed "largely through Chinese Nationalist efforts," but that Ho Chi Minh "ousted the pro-Chinese elements from his personal entourage in the summer of 1946" to align himself with the French (Melvin Gurov, *The First Vietnam Crisis* [New York: Columbia University Press, 1967], p. 3).

4. Devillers says that the OSS sought to replace its shrunken French sources and made contact with the Viet Minh to compensate for these losses (ibid., p. 133). An American writer claims that the Viet Minh established contact with the OSS and "received a small amount of support" (I. Milton Sacks, "Marxism in Viet Nam," *Marxism in Southeast Asia,* ed. by Frank N. Trager [Stanford: Stanford University Press, 1959], p. 149). Hoang Van Chi says that the Americans provided the Viet Minh guerrillas "with portable radio-equipment and hundreds of light machine-guns" (op. cit., p. 60).

5. Ellen J. Hammer, *The Struggle for Indochina 1940-1955* (Stanford: Stanford University Press, 1966), p. 101.

6. Ibid., p. 115.

7. Joseph R. Starobin, *Eyewitness in Indo-China* (New York: Cameron & Kahn, 1954), p. 50.

8. Devillers, op. cit., 207-208.

9. Hammer, op. cit., pp. 188-89.

10. Devillers, op. cit., p. 359.

11. W. W. Rostow, *The Two Major Communist Offensives* (Washington, D.C.: Department of State, 1964), pp. 2-3. This is the text of an address given on November 20, 1963. Professor Rostow was then Counselor of the Department and Chairman of the Policy Planning Council. He was still of the same mind and used almost the same words in his *View from the Seventh Floor* (New York: Harper & Row, 1964), p. 149.

12. Sainteny, op. cit., p. 167.

13. Devillers, op. cit., p. 232.

14. Raymond Barbé, *Cahiers du Communisme* (Paris), October 10, 1946 (cited in I. Milton Sacks, op. cit., pp. 326-27).

15. Harry S. Truman, *Memoirs,* Vol. II *(Years of Trial and Hope),* (New York: Doubleday, 1956), pp. 399, 519.

16. *Department of State Bulletin,* April 5, 1954, p. 513; June 28, 1954, p. 972.

17. *Congressional Record,* Senate, February 21, 1966, p. 3410.

18. Ibid., April 6, 1954, p. 4672. I have quoted from another portion of Secretary Dulles' speech *(Department of State Bulletin,* April 5, 1954, p. 512).

19. *Department of State Bulletin,* November 9, 1953, p. 631.

20. Dwight D. Eisenhower, *Mandate for Change* (New York: Doubleday, 1963), p. 372.

21. Ibid., p. 360.
22. Henry Cabot Lodge, Speech in Miami, Fla., January 16, 1965 (*Congressional Record,* Senate, January 19, 1965, p. 913). Lodge was so fond of General Smith's aphorism that he repeated it the following month with even more enthusiasm in an interview in *U.S. News & World Report,* February 15, 1965, p. 66. This time he called it "the best thing that I think any American has said about Vietnam."
23. Anthony Eden, *Full Circle* (Boston: Houghton Mifflin, 1960), p. 106.
24. Ibid. Yet, it should be noted, Eisenhower wrote in *Mandate for Change* that "the three service chiefs—Army, Navy, Air Force—had recommended against" United States intervention by an air strike in Indochina (p. 354).
25. General Matthew B. Ridgway, *Soldier* (New York: Harper, 1956), pp. 275-76.
26. *Congressional Record,* Senate, February 16, 1966, p. 3007.
27. Senator John Stennis, on CBS television program, January 30, 1966 (text in *Congressional Record,* Senate, January 31, 1966, pp. 1504-12, especially p. 1507).
28. Eisenhower, *Mandate for Change,* op. cit., p. 343.
29. Eden, op. cit., p. 117.
30. Testimony of Lt. Gen. James M. Gavin in *The Vietnam Hearings* (New York: Vintage Books, 1966), pp. 67-69. Also see Ridgway, op. cit., p. 276. The report issued by the House Republican Committee on Planning and Research, "Vietnam: Some Neglected Aspects of the Historical Record," says General Ridgway estimated that five to ten U.S. combat divisions would have been required at the outset to win such a war (*Congressional Record,* House, August 25, 1965, p. 21032).
31. *Congressional Record,* Senate, January 31, 1966, p. 1498.
32. *Department of State Bulletin,* May 24, 1954, p. 782.
33. Ibid., June 28, 1954, p. 972. On other occasions, Secretary Dulles propounded only three conditions.
34. Eisenhower, *Mandate for Change,* op. cit., p. 375.
35. *Life,* January 16, 1956. Emmet John Hughes says that Dulles told him: "We have a clean base there now without a taint of colonialism. Dien Bien Phu was a blessing in disguise" (Emmet John Hughes, *The Ordeal of Power* [New York: Dell, 1964], p. 182).

36. *Congressional Record,* Senate, March 9, 1954, p. 2904.

37. Ibid., April 6, 1954, pp. 4672-74.

38. Ibid., pp. 4674 and 4679.

39. Eisenhower, *Mandate for Change,* op. cit., p. 372.

40. *Congressional Record,* Senate, August 6, 1965, p. 18942.

III. From Eisenhower to Kennedy

1. Bernard B. Fall, *Viet-Nam Witness* (New York: Praeger, 1966), p. 124. Hoang Van Chi says that the revolt took place in Quynh-Luu district of Nghe An province (op. cit., pp. 227-28). P. J. Honey states that "revolts flared up locally and had to be forcibly suppressed" (*Communism in North Vietnam* [Cambridge, Mass.: The M.I.T. Press, 1963], p. 13). Philippe Devillers refers to "the small peasant revolt of Nghe An" (*The China Quarterly,* January–March 1962, p. 10). General Vo Nguyen Giap, the North Vietnamese Commander-in-Chief, who acted as the party spokesman at the Tenth Congress of the Lao Dong (Communist) Party in 1956, admitted: "We have made too many deviations and executed too many honest people. We attacked on too large a front and, seeing enemies everywhere, resorted to terror, which became far too widespread. . . . Worse still, torture came to be regarded as a normal practice during party reorganizations" (Hoang Van Chi, op. cit., p. 210).

2. Wilfred G. Burchett, *Vietnam: Inside Story of the Guerilla War,* (New York: International Publishers, 1965), pp. 112-15.

3. *"Les Américains au Vietnam,"* Les Temps Modernes (Paris), January 1966. This article was published in German in *Das Argument* (Berlin), February 1966, where it was signed by Georg W. Alsheimer. An English translation appeared in *Alternatives* (La Jolla, California), Fall 1966.

4. Robert Shaplen, *The Lost Revolution* (New York: Harper Colophon edition, 1966), p. 141. In *Asia,* No. 4 (Winter 1966, p. 93), however, Shaplen says that the "real turning point" in Diem's fortunes came in 1956. Carver states that Diem "reached his political highwater mark some time around mid-1957" (George A. Carver, Jr., "The Faceless Viet Cong," *Foreign Affairs,* April 1966, p. 358).

5. Dean Rusk, Statement before the House Foreign Affairs Committee, August 3, 1965 (*Congressional Record,* House, September 1, 1965, p. 21702).

6. Douglas Pike, *Viet Cong* (Cambridge, Mass.: The M.I.T. Press, 1966), pp. 77-78. Pike served for six years in Saigon as an official of the United States Information Agency.

7. Dean Rusk, Statement before the House Foreign Affairs Committee, August 3, 1965 (op. cit., p. 21702).

8. Philippe Devillers, "The Struggle for the Unification of Vietnam," *The China Quarterly* (London), January-March 1962, p. 15.

9. Jean Lacouture, *Vietnam: Between Two Truces* (New York: Random House, Vintage Books, 1966), pp. 53-55.

10. John Mecklin, *Mission in Torment* (New York: Doubleday, 1965), p. 17.

11. Arthur M. Schlesinger, Jr., *A Thousand Days* (Boston: Houghton Mifflin, 1965), p. 322.

12. Theodore C. Sorensen, *Kennedy* (New York: Harper & Row, 1965), p. 654.

13. Trager, op. cit., pp. 111-15.

14. *Saigon Times,* May 11-14, 1961 (cited by the House Republican report, "Vietnam: Some Neglected Aspects of the Historical Record," *Congressional Record,* House, August 25, 1965, p. 21035).

15. Schlesinger, op. cit., pp. 544-47.

16. *The Vietnam Hearings,* op. cit., p. 171.

17. Sorensen, op. cit., p. 653.

18. Schlesinger, op. cit., p. 547.

19. Mecklin, op. cit., pp. 13-14.

20. Schlesinger, op. cit., p. 538.

21. Sorensen, op. cit., p. 651.

22. I am inclined to believe that the historical verdict on the Kennedy administration will be much closer to the more skeptical view in Henry Pachter's essay, "JFK as an Equestrian Statue: On Myth and Mythmakers," in *Salmagundi,* Spring 1966, pp. 3-26.

23. Mecklin, op. cit., pp. 48 and 204-205. The "second step in the American commitment to Diem" is vividly described in David Halberstam, *The Making of a Quagmire* (New York: Random House, 1964), pp. 65-74. Halberstam ascribes the decision to back Diem with everything but large-scale combat forces to the advice of General Maxwell Taylor (p. 67).

24. Shaplen, op. cit., p. 189.

25. Trager, op. cit., p. 178.
26. Nguyen Cao Ky, speech of October 1, 1965 (text in *Congressional Record*, Senate, October 22, 1965, pp. 27367-70).
27. Schlesinger, op. cit., p. 997.
28. Letter of Frederick E. Nolting, Jr., *The New York Times*, October 29, 1966,
29. Shaplen, op. cit., p. 211.
30. Mecklin, op. cit., p. 278.
31. Sorensen, op. cit., p. 659.
32. *U.S. News & World Report*, February 15, 1965, p. 66.
33. Richard M. Nixon, speech of March 15, 1965, in New York City (text in *Congressional Record*, Senate, September 2, 1965, pp. 21928-30).
34. Schlesinger, op. cit., p. 997.
35. Mecklin, op. cit., p. 186.
36. Robert S. McNamara, speech of March 26, 1964.
37. *Aggression from the North: The Record of North Viet-Nam's Campaign to Conquer South Viet-Nam* (Washington, D.C.: Department of State Publication 7839, Far Eastern Series 130 [February], 1965), p. 27.
38. Denis Warner, *The Last Confucian* (Baltimore: Penguin Books, 1964), p. 236.

IV. From Kennedy to Johnson

1. *Viet Nam: The Struggle for Freedom* (Washington, D.C.: Government Printing Office, 1964), p. 21.
2. *Saigon Post*, July 23, 1964 (cited in full in *I. F. Stone's Weekly*, September 12, 1966, p. 3).
3. *Congressional Record*, Senate, August 6, 1964, pp. 18423-25.
4. Tom Wicker, "Lyndon Johnson vs. the Ghost of Jack Kennedy," *Esquire*, November 1965, p. 152.
5. Seymour Topping, "Khanh, Warned of Plots, Seeks to Bolster Regime," *The New York Times*, August 5, 1964.
6. *The New York Times*, May 20, 1966.
7. *Department of State Bulletin*, September 7, 1964, p. 336.
8. Ibid., October 19, 1964, p. 538.
9. Charles Roberts, *L.B.J.'s Inner Circle* (New York: Delacorte Press, 1965), pp. 20-21.
10. *Department of State Bulletin*, December 21, 1954, p. 869.
11. *The New York Times*, April 3, 1966.

12. Richard N. Goodwin, *Triumph or Tragedy: Reflections on Vietnam* (New York: Random House, Vintage Books, 1966), p. 31.

13. Philip L. Geyelin, *Lyndon B. Johnson and the World* (New York: Praeger, 1966), p. 216.

14. General Maxwell D. Taylor, *Responsibility and Response* (New York: Harper & Rowe, 1967), pp. 25-26.

15. Ibid., p. 25.

16. *Aggression from the North: The Record of North Viet-Nam's Campaign to Conquer South Viet-Nam,* op. cit., p. 3.

17. *Department of State Bulletin,* May 17, 1965, pp. 750 and 753.

18. *Report of Special Subcommittee to South Vietnam* of the Committee on Armed Services, House of Representatives, June 10-21, 1965, committee reprint, p. 3248.

19. CBS television Special Report, August 16, 1965 (text in *Congressional Record,* Senate, August 24, 1965, p. 20653).

20. Bernard B. Fall, "Vietnam Blitz," in *The New Republic,* October 9, 1965, p. 17.

21. "The Vietnam Conflict: The Substance and the Shadow," Report of Senators Mike Mansfield (Dem., Montana), Edmund S. Muskie (Dem., Maine), Daniel K. Inouye (Dem., Hawaii), George D. Aiken (Rep., Vermont), and J. Caleb Boggs (Rep., Delaware) in the *Congressional Record,* Senate, January 24, 1966, p. 908.

22. *Department of State Bulletin,* November 29, 1965, p. 855.

23. Ibid., May 16, 1966, p. 773.

24. Ibid., June 6, 1966, p. 886.

25. Mike Mansfield, address at Yeshiva University, June 16, 1966 (text in *Congressional Record,* Senate, June 16, 1966, pp. 12856-58).

26. Ted Knap in Washington *Daily News,* June 23, 1966, and other Scripps-Howard papers.

27. Both *The New York Times* and the Washington *Post* of June 17, 1966, reported the speech but omitted mention of this passage. A letter in *The New York Times* of November 15, 1966, by William L. Standard and Joseph Crown of the Lawyers Committee on American Policy Towards Vietnam quoted the relevant sentence.

28. *Department of State Bulletin,* September 19, 1966, p. 423.

29. Robert S. McNamara, News Conference, Johnson City, Texas,

November 5, 1966 (*The New York Times,* November 6, 1966).

30. *Congressional Record,* Senate, October 10, 1966, p. 24855.

31. Lyndon B. Johnson, speech of July 28, 1965.

32. *Congressional Record,* Senate, October 10, 1966, p. 24855.

33. *U.S. News & World Report,* November 28, 1966, p. 49.

34. General Maxwell D. Taylor, testimony before Senate Foreign Relations Committee, February 17, 1966.

35. *U.S. News & World Report,* November 21, 1966, p. 67.

36. Rowland Evans and Robert Novak, *Lyndon B. Johnson: The Exercise of Power* (New York: New American Library, 1966), p. 548.

37. *The Vietnam Hearings,* op. cit., p. 183.

38. Mecklin, op. cit., p. 290.

39. Bernard B. Fall, "The Year of the Hawks," in *The New York Times Magazine,* December 12, 1965, p. 48.

40. *The New York Times,* December 3, 1966.

41. Nguyen Cao Ky, speech of October 1, 1965 (*Congressional Record,* Senate, October 22, 1965, p. 27368).

42. *Congressional Record,* Senate, October 10, 1966, p. 24855.

43. Ibid., January 13, 1966, p. 141.

44. *Department of State Bulletin,* August 17, 1964, p. 235. The statement was made on July 26, 1964.

45. *Aggression from the North,* op. cit., p. 3.

46. *Department of State Bulletin,* September 19, 1966, p. 418.

47. *U.S. News & World Report,* February 27, 1967, p. 41.

V. "Civil War" or "Foreign Aggression"

1. *A Threat to Peace: North Vietnam's Effort to Conquer South Vietnam* (Washington, D.C.: Department of State Publication No. 7308, Far Eastern Series No. 110 [December], 1961), p. 1. This point has been noted in the compilation *Viet Nam,* edited by Marvin E. Gettleman (Greenwich, Conn.: Fawcett Publications, 1965), p. 284.

2. *Aggression from the North,* op. cit., p. 1.

3. General Maxwell Taylor, CBS television Special Report, August 16, 1965 (text in *Congressional Record,* Senate, August 24, 1965, pp. 20651 and 20654).

4. Robert S. McNamara, Statement before the Defense Subcommittee of the Senate Appropriations Committee, August 4,

1965 (text in *Congressional Record*, House, September 1, 1965, pp. 21704-706, especially p. 21705).

5. Cited by Senator Stephen M. Young of Ohio, *Congressional Record*, Senate, April 25, 1966, p. 8454.

6. George W. Ball, address of January 30, 1966 (text in *Congressional Record*, Senate, January 31, 1966, pp. 1517-20, especially p. 1519).

7. Ibid., p. 1518.

8. *U.S. News & World Report*, February 15, 1965, pp. 62-63.

9. *Congressional Record*, Senate, January 14, 1966, p. 214.

10. *The Vietnam Hearings*, op. cit., p. 24.

11. *U.S. News & World Report*, September 5, 1966, p. 38.

12. Ed Meagher, Washington *Post*, March 6, 1963.

13. *Department of State Bulletin*, July 6, 1964, p. 10.

14. Interview, *U.S. News & World Report*, September 28, 1964, p. 60.

15. *Aggression from the North*, op. cit., pp. 38-42.

16. *I. F. Stone's Weekly* (Washington, D.C.). March 8, 1965, p. 1.

17. National Education Television broadcast, August 1, 1966 (WNDT, New York).

18. Roger Hilsman, "Orchestrating the Instrumentalities: The Case of Southeast Asia," in *Foreign Policy in the Sixties*, edited by Roger Hilsman and Robert C. Good (Baltimore, Md.: The Johns Hopkins Press, 1965), p. 199.

19. *Foreign Affairs*, October 1966, p. 6.

20. John Mecklin, "Should We Negotiate in Vietnam?" *The New Leader*, March 13, 1967, pp. 14-19. This article was adapted from an address to the Institute of Current World Affairs.

VI. Escalation: Force and Theory

1. Nguyen Cao Ky, CBS television interview, July 18, 1965 (text in *Congressional Record*, Senate, July 27, 1965, pp. 17682-83).

2. CBS television Special Report, August 16, 1965 (text in *Congressional Record*, Senate, August 24, 1965, pp. 20650-655).

3. UPI, Los Angeles *Times*, November 18, 1966.

4. *U.S. News & World Report*, November 21, 1966, pp. 66-68.

5. *The New York Times*, December 5, 1966.

6. St. Louis *Post-Dispatch*, July 8, 1966.

7. *U.S. News & World Report*, December 5, 1966.

8. R. W. Apple, Jr., "U.S. Military Sought Control Over Pacification," *The New York Times,* December 21, 1966.

9. John Stennis, speech to the Mississippi Manufacturers Association, November 4, 1966; Jamie L. Whitten, *Congressional Record,* House, March 15, 1966, p. 5561.

10. NBC interview, September 9, 1963.

11. Richard Nixon, speech of March 15, 1965 (text in *Congressional Record,* Senate, September 2, 1965, pp. 21928-30).

12. *Congressional Record,* Senate, January 31, 1966, p. 1500.

13. Joseph W. Stilwell, Jr., speech of July 22, 1966 (text in *Congressional Record,* Appendix, August 3, 1966, pp. A4095-96).

14. *U.S. News & World Report,* September 5, 1966.

15. Taylor, *Responsibility and Response,* op. cit., p. 21.

16. John P. Roche in "Containing China: A Round-Table Discussion," *Commentary,* May 1966, p. 32.

17. Guy J. Pauker, "Indonesia: The PKI's 'Road to Power,'" in *The Communist Revolution in Asia,* edited by Robert A. Scalapino (Englewood Cliffs, N.J.: Prentice-Hall, 1965), p. 285.

18. Richard N. Goodwin, op. cit., p. 15.

19. The discussion aroused in France and Italy by the proposal of *Les Temps Modernes* may be followed in *Atlas,* November 1966, pp. 19-24.

20. Hannah Arendt in "Containing China: A Round-Table Discussion," op. cit., p. 34.

VII. China, Russia, and Vietnam

1. *The Reporter,* November 17, 1966, p. 14.

2. *The Vietnam Hearings,* op. cit., p. 269.

3. P. J. Honey, *Communism in North Vietnam,* op. cit., pp. 1-14, 81.

4. Interview with Professor Paul Mus by John T. McAlister, Jr., "The Possibilities for Diplomacy in Southeast Asia," *World Politics,* January 1967, p. 273.

5. Pike, op. cit., pp. 319-20.

6. Ibid., pp. 332-43.

7. Lacouture, op. cit., pp. 41, 46.

8. John C. Donnell, "North Vietnam," in *The Communist Revolution in Asia,* op. cit., p. 146.

9. Ibid., pp. 158-59.

10 George K. Tanham, *Communist Revolutionary Warfare: The*

Vietminh in Indochina (New York: Praeger, 1961), pp. 15-28. Only Gurtov, op. cit., pp. 15-16, seems to believe that Giap merely followed Mao's prescriptions.

11. *Ire Conférence Internationale Paysanne: Thèses, Messages & Adresses,* October 10-15, 1923 (Paris: Bibliothèque Paysanne [1924/?], p. 110. The spelling of Nguyen Ai Quoc's name differs in all the early Comintern documents, but it is usually unmistakable.

12. Edward Hallett Carr, *The Interregnum 1923-1924* (New York: Macmillan, 1954), pp. 198-200.

13. *Protokoll: Fünfter Kongress der Kommunistischen Internationale* (Berlin: Verlag Carl Hoym Nachf., 1925), Vol. I, p. 237, and Vol. II, pp. 686 and 793. The abridged English version of the Fifth Congress gives very brief versions of these speeches, spells his name "Nguyen-Ai-Quack" and once identifies him with China instead of Indochina (*Fifth Congress of the Communist International* [London: Communist Party of Great Britain] 1925/?). Ho Chi Minh's *Selected Works,* Vol. 1 (Hanoi: Foreign Languages Publishing House, 1963), pp. 74-88, contains a "Report on the National and Colonial Questions at the Fifth Congress of the Communist International." This "Report" is made up of the second and third of Nguyen Ai Quoc's speeches at the congress; for some reason, Ho decided to omit the first one; and they were not delivered as a "Report." I have chosen to translate from the *Protokoll* because German was then the main language at the Comintern, and the English version in the *Selected Works* leaves something to be desired.

14. Lacouture, op. cit., p. 47.

15. Honey, op. cit., p. 31.

16. Pike, op. cit., pp. 33-40.

17. Sacks, op. cit., pp. 159-60, 162, 166-68.

18. George Modelski, "The Viet Minh Complex," *Communism and Revolution,* ed. by Cyril E. Black and Thomas P. Thornton (Princeton: Princeton University Press, 1954), pp. 206-209.

19. *U.S. News & World Report,* January 30, 1967, pp. 27-29.

20. Albert Parry, "Soviet Aid to Vietnam," *The Reporter,* January 12, 1967, pp. 28-33.

21. Frederick Taylor, *The Wall Street Journal,* February 14, 1967.

22. Kevin Devlin, "Which Side Are You On?", *Problems of Communism* (Washington, D.C.), Jan.-Feb. 1967, p. 55.

23. *Department of State Bulletin,* May 10, 1965, p. 713.
24. Ibid., June 7, 1965, p. 895.
25. Ibid., November 29, 1965, pp. 864-65. Other State Department officials took the same line months later. Under Secretary Ball spoke of the Soviet people's "stake in stability" in January 1966 (ibid., February 14, 1966, p. 245); Secretary of State Rusk detected "a certain prudence in Washington and Moscow" in March 1966 (ibid., April 11, 1966, p. 558).
26. Lin Piao, *Long Live the Victory of People's War* (Peking: Foreign Languages Press, 1965), pp. 41-42.
27. *U.S. News & World Report,* January 30, 1967, p. 56.
28. *The Vietnam Hearings,* op. cit., pp. 241, 269.
29. Dean Rusk, Statement before the House Foreign Affairs Committee, August 3, 1965 (*Congressional Record,* House, September 1, 1965, p. 21702).
30. Interview in *U.S. News & World Report,* August 1, 1966, p. 22.
31. Taylor, *Responsibility and Response,* op. cit., pp. 6, 34.
32. Neil Sheehan, "We Hedge Our Offer to Get Out of Vietnam," *The New York Times,* November 13, 1966.
33. Interview with Canadian Broadcasting Company, December 30, 1965.
34. Taylor, *Responsibility and Response,* op. cit., pp. 26, 38.
35. Testimony of Secretary McNamara, text in *Congressional Record,* House, March 15, 1966, p. 5563.
36. Jacques Decornoy in *Le Monde* (Paris), December 8, 1966.
37. Taylor, *Responsibility and Response,* op. cit., pp. 16, 40.
38. Tran Van Dinh, "The Ky Question," *The New Republic,* January 21, 1967, p. 21.
39. *The Vietnam Hearings,* op. cit., p. 242.
40. Ibid., p. 240.

VIII. Power and Politics

1. Richard B. Russell, address to Georgia Association of Broadcasters (text in *Congressional Record,* Senate, June 15, 1965, p. 13193).
2. Interview on CBS television network, August 1, 1965 (text in *Congressional Record,* Senate, August 6, 1965, pp. 18942-44).
3. These quotations and others were cited by Republican Representative Melvin R. Laird of Wisconsin (*Congressional Record,* House, March 15, 1966, pp. 5558-59).

4. *The New York Times,* November 27, 1966, p. 4.
5. *The Vietnam Hearings,* op. cit., pp. 11-12.
6. *U.S. News & World Report,* February 15, 1965, p. 64.
7. *Congressional Record, House,* March 15, 1966, p. 5558. The full text of this legal memorandum, "The Legality of United States Participation in the Defense of Vietnam," may be found in *Department of State Bulletin,* March 28, 1966, pp. 474-89.
8. Harlan Cleveland, *The Obligations of Power* (New York: Harper & Row, 1966), pp. 14-16, 135.
9. Speech at Princeton University, May 11, 1966.
10. Speech at Manchester, N.H., August 20, 1966.
11. Address at West Point, N.Y. June 8, 1966.
12. *Department of State Bulletin,* February 14, 1966. p. 244.
13. Richard C. Hottelet, "Vietnam in Perspective," *The Reporter,* November 3, 1966, p. 20. Virtually the same words were used by Arnaud de Borchgrave in *Newsweek,* December 5, 1966, p. 55.
14. *Department of State Bulletin,* October 19, 1964, p. 537.
15. Ibid., April 18, 1966, p. 613.
16. *The New York Times,* February 25, 1965.
17. Ibid., November 17, 1965.
18. *Department of State Bulletin,* March 15, 1965, p. 636.
19. Ibid., April 12, 1965, p. 527.
20. Ibid., April 19, 1965, p. 570.
21. Ibid., September 20, 1965, p. 484.
22. *The New York Times,* November 16, 1965.
23. Ibid., November 18, 1965.
24. *Department of State Bulletin,* December 13, 1965, pp. 931-33.
25. Mario Rossi in *The New York Review of Books,* November 17, 1966, pp. 8-13; Emmet John Hughes in *Newsweek,* December 12, 1966, pp. 62-63.
26. *Department of State Bulletin,* August 15, 1966, p. 227.

IX. *The Politics of Miscalculation*

1. The full text of the four points first appeared in *The New York Times,* April 14, 1965, and this version may be found in *The Viet-Nam Reader,* op. cit., pp. 342-43. The problem of correctly interpreting or even translating the third point is discussed in George McTurnan Kahin and John W. Lewis, *The United States in Vietnam* (New York: Dial, 1967, p. 210). They

report that the Chinese version would have made the third point completely innocuous. A literal English translation of the text used by the *Jen-min Jih-pao* (People's Daily), the official Peking organ, of April 14, 1965, reads: "According to the program of the Southern National Liberation Front, the affairs of the South must be settled by the Southern people themselves without foreign interference." Of such stuff are diplomatic imbroglios sometimes made, when there is no will to get together.

2. *The Vietnam Hearings,* op. cit., pp. 246-47.

3. *The NFL of South Vietnam* (South Vietnam [?]: Liberation Editions, 1965), pp. 28-30. This is a pamphlet, probably published in Hanoi but attributed on the cover to "South Vietnam."

4. Ho Chi Minh, letter to world Communist leaders, dated Hanoi, January 24, 1966.

5. *Department of State Bulletin,* January 17, 1966, p. 87, and April 11, 1966, p. 569.

6. Ibid., September 12, 1966, p. 369.

7. Robert H. Estabrook, "1966 Hanoi Approval of Talks Reported," Washington *Post,* February 4, 1966.

8. John M. Hightower, Associated Press, *The New York Times,* May 9, 1967. Also, Richard Hudson, "The Nearest to Negotiations Yet," *War/Peace Report,* March 1967, pp. 3-4.

9. Hedrick Smith, *The New York Times,* February 5, 1967.

10. Anthony Lewis, ibid., February 8, 1967.

11. *Il Messagero* (Rome), March 8, 1967 (cited by Hudson, op. cit., p. 4).

12. Wilfred G. Burchett, ibid., Washington *Post,* February 8, 1967.

13. Harrison E. Salisbury, *The New York Times,* January 4, 1967.

14. *Vietnam Courier* (Hanoi), February 6, 1967, p. 6. An editorial in the Hanoi paper, *Nhan Dan,* of January 29, 1967, chose to italicize these two sentences.

15. Burchett, op. cit. Curiously, the otherwise similar version of Burchett's article published in *The New York Times,* February 8, 1967, does not contain the second sentence.

16. *The New York Times,* February 6, 1967; *Newsweek,* February 13, 1967; *The New York Times,* March 13, 1967; *Time,* March 17, 1967.

17. *The New York Times,* February 14, 1967.

18. Burchett, op. cit.

19. *Facts on File* (New York), February 9-15, 1967, p. 41.

20. Neil Sheehan, *The New York Times,* February 13, 1967.

21. *The New York Times,* March 3, 1967, for Kennedy's speech of March 2 and Rusk's statement.

22. Ibid.

23. Ibid., March 29, 1967, for U Thant's statement, the United States reply, the North Vietnamese rejection, and Premier Ky's remark. (See also ibid., March 30, 1967.)

24. Ibid., February 21, 1967.

25. Henry Kamm, *The New York Times,* February 28, 1967.

26. *Department of State Bulletin,* January 30, 1967, p. 169.

27. ABC television program, March 12, 1967 (*The New York Times,* March 13, 1967).

28. *Congressional Record,* Senate, February 24, 1967, p. S2578.

29. David Schoenbrun, "Vietnam: The Case for Extrication," *The Columbia University Forum,* Fall 1966, pp. 4-9.

30. Sol W. Sanders, "The Change in the War as Seen by a Veteran Observer," *U.S. News & World Report,* March 6, 1967, p. 31.

Index